TO MY FATHER

ACKNOWLEDGMENTS FOR THE SECOND EDITION

Once again, on a very tight time deadline, a variety of people assisted splendidly with the preparation of this book. Donna Lovecchio provided skilled research assistance and, as the project coordinator, kept all the pieces in view and well connected throughout the effort. Laurie McDonald contributed, as she did the last time, superb design and production support. Linda Gordon and Jennifer Kandzor effectively attended to a wide variety of production issues. Judy Corley, Marc Elias, Brian Svoboda, Karl Sandstrom, Rebecca Gordon and Ezra Reese helped to develop the approach to specific revisions and offered helpful and critical commentary. As always, I owe much to the support of my partners in the Political Law Group, Judy Corley and Marc Elias. My wife Anita still one more time encouraged the effort and made it, in the end, possible.

Contents

CHAPTER 6

CHAPTER 7

AN INTRODUCTION

The law discussed in this book has been known in the Senate as McCain-Feingold, and in the House as Shays-Meehan, but its official "short title" is the "Bipartisan Campaign Reform Act of 2002."[1] And so it will be cited as the Act or BCRA throughout this book. The law that it amended, the Federal Election Campaign Act, will be termed (with reference to those portions amended by BCRA) "the old law" and existed generally until November 6, 2002.

The Act is intended mainly as an attempt to control "soft money."[2] This is a term with a confused history, but it refers primarily to monies spent by unions and corporations for political purposes, and also to spending by individuals beyond the relatively modest limits set by federal law. It is not a longstanding legal term of art—it did not appear in federal law until the passage of this Act.

To some extent, the term encompasses any political spending believed in some fashion inimical to sound democratic practice. An example is spending by millionaires—or more precisely, by people with a lot of money, whether in the millions or not—to advance their candidacies for federal office. The Act tries to protect candidates who do not have lots of money to spend from opponents who do, and the way in which it proposes to do this is complex. Is spending by the wealthy "soft money?" Probably not—because while the Act attempts to limit their influence, this spending is lawful, protected indeed by the First Amendment as it has been read by the U.S. Supreme Court. By contrast, those strongly favoring the Act have generally viewed "soft money" as a loophole exploited by parties and others to navigate around legal restrictions on union, corporate, and individual spending.

What's in a name?

"Soft money": apparently not good

---

[1] The "long title" appears to be "AN ACT To Amend the Federal Election Campaign Act of 1971 to provide bipartisan campaign reform." Difference between the long and the short: 10 words. Significance: None.

[2] Hence, in the words of a key sponsor in the Senate: "The ban on soft money defines the legislation." 147 Cong. Rec. S2886 (daily ed. Mar. 26, 2001) (statement of Sen. Feingold).

The problem with party "soft money"

Hence the Act aims principally to control soft money spent by political parties, though it treats national parties differently—and more restrictively—than state or local parties. By and large national parties, and those associated with them, may not have anything to do with soft money—may not raise or receive, or have any direct hand in spending, soft money.[3] State and local parties are allowed more leeway, particularly to raise and spend soft money where their purpose is solely to advance the prospects of state and local candidates. Yet the Act assumes that in each election where a federal candidate *appears* on the state ballot, state and local party activity has some federal election effect; and so in that case, the Act sharply restricts the soft money that state and local parties can spend for a variety of general party purposes, such as voter registration and get-out-the-vote (GOTV) activities.

The Act also addresses "soft money" spent in different ways by organizations that spend resources to influence the public's opinions on public policy issues, and also on candidates and officeholders in relation to those issues. For purposes of this book, the term "outside groups" refers to corporations, unions, so-called 527 political committees, or other groups, and it is used to distinguish these entities from parties, and also from political committees controlled by or contributing to candidates. Whether all organizations traveling by that name are "independent" from, say, candidates, is often hotly disputed. At any rate, these organizations also spend "soft money," and, unlike parties, that is all they spend: they raise and spend funds without regard to federal limits, and except in certain limited instances, they do not disclose to the public their resources or how they spend them.

Outside groups' "soft money": the problem with mentioning Congressman Jones

Moreover, these groups will dispute that their ads are even intended to influence elections, insisting that they are merely seeking to express themselves on the issues of the day. Example: "Congressman Jones voted seven times to sell your children into slavery. Call Congressman Jones today, and tell him to drop dead."

---

[3] "The purpose of these provisions is simple: to put the national parties entirely out of the soft money business." 148 Cong. Rec. H408 (daily ed. Feb. 13, 2002) (statement of Rep. Shays).

Now where, these organizations ask, does there appear in this sort of ad any expressed appeal to viewers or listeners to VOTE one way or the other?[4]

But, for several reasons, the Act does not go as far in restricting these outside groups as it does in the case of political parties, and the reasons are several. First, the drafters believed that soft money contributed to parties is contributed, in effect, to their candidates, and presents the greater danger of violating the longstanding prohibition on corporate, union, and unlimited individual contributions to candidates. Second, the drafters imagined that a broad ban on soft money spending by political parties stood a better chance of surviving Supreme Court review than a ban on spending by "outside groups." Third, there are some in the Congress who, believing fervently in the constitutional rights of these kinds of organizations, would not have supported the Act if spending by "outside groups" had been more harshly treated.

The Act, while most aggressive in its treatment of soft money, sought to limit the effects of other political spending thought unhelpful to healthy politics. In addition to its concern with spending by wealthy candidates, the law also addressed other campaign finance issues, such as the making of contributions by minor children, the raising of contributions on federal property, and contributions by foreign nationals.[5] It looked overall to improved enforcement by promulgating new disclosure requirements, and by assessing enhanced penalties—including most notably, new criminal penalties—for certain violations.

The Act also departs from its main theme in one key respect—by raising "hard" money contribution limits. It allows individuals to contribute twice as much to candidates as the previous law permitted, and it raises the

But up with the hard money

---

[4] As one Congressional supporter of reform has stated the case against these ads: "Today corporations, wealthy individuals, and others can spend unlimited amounts of money running political ads as long as they do not ask people to vote for or against a candidate. These phony issue ads...have become the weapon of choice...." 147 Cong. Rec. S2886 (daily ed. Mar. 26, 2001) (statement of Sen. Kennedy).

[5] As noted later, the prohibition on contributions by minor children did not survive constitutional review.

limit for their contributions to state and national political parties. To make room for this additional authority, it also raises the aggregate limit on an individual's contributions to candidates and political committees. In a sense, this is a departure, as stated: the law generally limits giving, and these provisions encourage more of it. But in another sense, the increased individual limits serve the tactical necessity of offering some additional resources to replace the ones, in the form of prohibited soft money, that are lost.

This book will try to lay out all of these restrictions and provisions in reasonable detail, providing where necessary background on the old law so that the new one makes some sense. Past is prologue, it is said, and much of the Act—indeed virtually all of it—is a reaction to a perceived breakdown in the regulatory regime. As noted, "soft money" is believed to be an escape from controls on political money enacted beginning with the first decade of the 20th century, when Congress passed, and Theodore Roosevelt signed, a prohibition on corporate contributions in federal elections.[6] Those provisions of the bill concerned with "issue advertising" paid with soft money, hark back to the advent of this kind of advertising in the 1990s by parties and outside groups, and to the alleged inability of the Federal Election Commission (FEC) to deal with the problem. Other provisions tightening penalties for enforcement are intended to shore up weak regulatory enforcement, and to put the Fear of Government into political actors supposedly grown accustomed to working the fringes of the law.

Then the Courts and the FEC had their say On December 10, 2003, the Supreme Court issued its decision in the constitutional test of McCain-Feingold: the case of *McConnell v. FEC*. The decision, invalidating a few portions of the law but upholding most major provisions, has required some revision of the discussion contained in the first edition of this book. The decision is discussed, both in a Note at the end, but also as

---

[6] "I just point out we are trying to enforce the 1907 law banning the corporate treasury money, the 1947 law banning union dues money, and the 1974 law which bans unlimited sums by one individual in a campaign and to enforce all three laws." 148 Cong. Rec. H345 (daily ed. Feb. 13, 2002) (statement of Rep. Shays).

required in the discussion of affected sections. Significant portions of the decision are reprinted in the Appendix. Still more significant in scope have been the rules enacted, and the Advisory Opinions issued, by the FEC interpreting provisions of the new law. Once again, the discussion in the first edition has been revised to reflect these developments, and the Appendix contains the full text of the key rules.

The development of the law will not end there. The FEC will issue more Advisory Opinions, and over time, new rules. When it enforces alleged violations, it will add additional information to the record about its views of the law. Court challenges are inevitable.

To enable readers to follow changes in the law, a website has been established—www.moresoftmoney-hardlaw.com—on which will be posted legal developments not in place when this second edition was completed. So what appears in the following pages tells a continuing and complex story, and it does not attempt to supply exhaustive detail, or answer every question; but its purpose is to provide a basic understanding of the structure and purpose of the law. It is, after all, only fair that those expected to comply with the law, such as candidates, parties, officeholders, contributors, and volunteers, should have multiple opportunities to understand it. As the political laws of the land become both more voluminous and more complex, the task of understanding becomes also more demanding. Consulting a lawyer can help—but it is expensive, and not always enlightening. Few care to contemplate the pleasures and pains of politics while being billed, sometimes enthusiastically, by the hour.

So this Guide might, for some, who just wish to have an idea how all this works, raise the understanding while lowering the bill. It is meant to be user-friendly—not heavy on citations but liberal with examples. More specific questions about the Act, particularly questions about its application to proposed political activities, may in all prudence require a lawyer's attention. **A second edition still costs less than a consultation**

The use of "legislative history" in this book in exploring the meaning of various provisions of the Act requires some explanation. There was no substantial

Committee report explaining the intended purpose of various provisions, and the floor debates also are bereft of detailed exposition. Of course, there are those commentators, even Justices of the U.S. Supreme Court, who are skeptical about the value or meaning of "legislative history." Nonetheless, the book refers to statements by sponsors of the Act of their "intent" behind certain important provisions. The statements may not be decisive on these points, but surely they have influenced, and will continue to influence, views about the issues they address. The FEC received a significant number of comments from the "Congressional sponsors" on the development of the implementing rules. In some instances, the FEC adopted the views of the sponsors, and in other instances, it did not; and where the differences surfaced, as will be seen below, the sponsors and other critics were not reluctant to file suit against the agency for failing to follow what they held to be their original intention.

A final note on citations: to avoid clutter, they are provided sparingly. Citations to the new law include both the cite to the Public Law, and also to the related provisions of the U.S. Code. The cite to the Public Law (Public Law 107-155) is simply, for example, "BCRA § 201." The related Public Law provisions can be found in the Appendix. The Appendix contains the full Public Law text and selected corresponding FEC regulations.

CHAPTER 1

THE POLITICAL PARTIES

National parties, soft money, and the new law

Each of the major parties operates three national organizations recognized by federal law: the national committee of each party,[7] and the "congressional campaign committees" representing the parties' interests in House and Senate, as well as other elections.[8] The Act imposes different rules on the different kinds of political party committees, and national party committees take the lash more than the others.

What's a national committee of a political party?

Under the Act, these committees are broadly restricted to raising and spending only hard money—that is, monies "subject to the limitations, prohibitions, and reporting requirements of the Act." That means—

—They may <u>not</u> receive corporate or union contributions.

—They <u>may</u> accept contributions from the "multi-candidate" political committees or PACs established by corporations and unions, or other PACs, up to the applicable limits, generally, $15,000 per calendar year.[9]

What they can raise.... and what they cannot

---

[7] In the case of the major parties, these are the Democratic and Republican National Committees.

[8] The National Republican Senatorial Committee and the Democratic Senatorial Campaign Committee, active on the Senate level, and the Democratic Congressional Campaign Committee and National Republican Congressional Committee, active in House campaigns. These committees answer to and are directed in their operations by the incumbent Members of the Senate and House of each party.

[9] As under existing law, there remains a difference under the Act between the contribution limits of "multicandidate" PACs and other non-multicandidate committees. Most corporate and union PACs are "multicandidates," which means that they have been registered with the FEC for at least 6 months, have supported at least 5 federal candidates, and received contributions from more than 50 persons. Under the new law, effective in 2003, a multicandidate PAC may contribute, as under existing law, $15,000 to a national party committee in a calendar year, while a PAC not satisfying multicandidate status may contribute $25,000. Most reasonably active PACs, likely to provide support at the federal level, will be multicandidates and will have to comply with the $15,000 annual limit.

—They _may_ receive contributions from individuals in an amount per individual up to $25,000 per calendar year—and no more. _BUT individuals must contribute to parties within an overall limit in any two-year election cycle on all their contributions to FEC-registered political committees and to federal candidates._[10]

The Act "indexes" some, but not all, of these contribution limits for inflation, and so they will change to numbers calculated and published by the FEC.

Prohibiting national parties from soliciting, receiving, or directing "soft money"

National party committees may solicit and receive these monies—hard monies—but they are prohibited absolutely from soliciting or receiving soft money, or directing it "to another person." Parties do not, of course, do these things—people do—and so the Act makes clear that this prohibition falls 1) on parties' "officers" or "agents" who are "acting on their behalf," 2) federal candidates or officeholders, or 3) any "entity" that parties establish, finance, maintain, or control.[11]

Officers and "agents" of national parties

Now because parties may not spend soft money under the Act, a fair question is why the statute bothers with a prohibition on the solicitation of such monies. Why would anyone solicit funds that cannot be received or used? The answer may lie in the additional restriction—"directing to another person" such monies. The Act has mounted the parapet and is maintaining a watch over the more indirect solicitation of "soft" funds by persons acting on behalf of the national party committee and its purposes.

A national party committee "agent" might otherwise, for example, solicit contributions for another organization able to receive them—such as a tax-exempt organization engaged in voter registration or GOTV activity. It might do so on the express understanding with the donor and the other organization that the monies would be used for these purposes. Or these "agents" could raise the money

---

[10] See below for a discussion of this limit. Also note that the Act does not allow the parties to accept contributions from foreign nationals lacking permanent resident status, an open question after the 1996 presidential election.

[11] BCRA § 101; 2 U.S.C. §§ 441i(a) and 441i(e)(1)(A).

for an "independent group" buying time for "issue ads" on a major public policy issue thought helpful to that party.

May the law successfully prevent someone active with the party from stepping outside that role and raising monies for other political purposes elsewhere, for other organizations? Here the prohibition adjusts its sights somewhat, and prohibits only those fundraising activities by officers and agents "acting on behalf" of the national committee. A Vice Chair of a national party may be involved with voter registration elsewhere, with other organizations that are not political parties. She is able under the Act to raise money for them—if not doing so "on behalf" of the party. It may be clear when the Vice Chair is acting "on behalf" of the party, as for example, when the Chair directs her to do so, explaining in telling detail the importance to the party of the registration efforts. But the Vice Chair also may just know that this activity is important, and from the beginning of her public career, may have separately pursued the goal of encouraging tax-exempt organizations to register voters.

In its post-enactment rulemaking, the FEC turned its attention to the issues presented by the statutory reference to the term "agent." As noted in the first edition, the FEC could have used a general definition of "agent" adopted for other purposes: that definition focuses on "the authority, express or implied, to make or authorize the making of party expenditures." The agency chose a different course, crafting a different approach to "agency" for specific use in determining the scope of the new soft money fundraising restrictions. [12] Under this definition, and in this specific case of national party committees, "agent" means:

More on "agents"

Any person who has actual authority, either express or implied, to engage in any of the following activities on behalf of the specified persons:

(1) In the case of a national committee of a political party:

(i) To solicit, direct, or receive any contribution, donation or transfer of funds; or

(ii) To solicit any funds for, or make or direct any donations to, an organization that is described in 26 U.S.C. 501(c) and exempt

---

[12] 11 C.F.R. § 300.2(b).

from taxation under 26 U.S.C. 501(a)...or an organization described in 26 U.S.C. 527....

Of course, a full understanding of the term "agent" hinges on all the elements of the definition. The terms "solicit" or "direct" are of particular significance in determining the types of activities an "agent" can be authorized to conduct. Yet no individual can perform any of these activities, and hence become an "agent," unless he or she has received "actual authority, express or implied" to act "on behalf of" the national party in doing so.

The question of authority The Congressional sponsors were unhappy with the FEC's focus on "actual authority," and the dispute between them and the agency on this point helps to illuminate the scope of the definition that was eventually selected. The sponsors believed the definition of "agent" to be "critical to prevent evasion," and to this end, they urged the adoption of a standard of "apparent authority." Under a standard of "apparent authority," the rule would examine what a third party might reasonably take to be the authority of the possible agent. If a donor had reason to be believe that someone soliciting a contribution was doing so as agent of the national party, this apparent authority would be enough to create agency.

The FEC rejected "apparent" in favor of "actual" authority, basing its definition on the authority actually conferred by the national party on its agent. Actual authority does not require express instructions from the party: "implied" authority is enough. Even this implied authority must rest on an actual grant of power from the principal to the agent: the principal must have intended the person under instruction to act as an "agent." In this way, the Commission concluded, the definition would avoid imposing liability on national party committees for the actions of a "rogue or misguided volunteer." [13]

This concern with "actual authority" provides some better context for the phrase "acting on behalf," for the agent expressly authorized to act as agent for the principal is in a complete sense acting on the principal's "behalf."

---

[13] 67 Fed. Reg. 49,083 (July 29, 2002).

The FEC built one additional limitation into the definition, one concerned with the types of activities in which an agent for purposes of the soft money fundraising restrictions can engage. The agency created by this rule attaches only to certain activities which, for a national party committee, are: 1) soliciting or directing contributions generally; and 2) soliciting or directing funds for a 501(c) organization or a 527 "political committee." Moreover, the reach of the rule would extend both to these actions, and to other acts incidental to or reasonably necessary to accomplish these actions. In developing its rules, the FEC emphasized that liability would attach only to "the agent's performance of prohibited acts for the principal."[14] Hence, the FEC specifically accepted the notion that political actors could wear "multiple hats"—serving the goals of different political organizations so that in soliciting contributions, they could be "acting on behalf" of one of them, and not the other.

Authority to do what?

Mulroney (Multy) P.L. Hats, an officer of a national party, is also active in local politics, frequently assisting state and local officials with fundraising in his work for a large County Committee. Hats raises soft money for that committee, while remaining prohibited from doing so for the national party. Yet, for legal purposes, there are two Hats—the one working for the national party and the other for the local committee, and if Hats, in raising soft money, is raising it as agent for the local committee and on its behalf, then his association with the national party does not prohibit him from doing so.

This subject of agency will surface again in the discussion of "agency" as it applies to the prohibition on soft money fundraising by federal officeholders and candidates. As will be seen, the FEC has issued an "advisory opinion" applying the "multiple hats" theory to the facts of a particular case.[15] The Supreme Court appears to have endorsed the FEC's reading of the

---

[14] *Id.*

[15] FEC Advisory Opinion 2003-10.

"Soliciting" and "Directing"

statute. The Court found that the prohibition "bars only solicitations of soft money by national party committees and by party officers in their official capacities."[16]

Since the enactment of the statute, the FEC has also tackled the definitions of "soliciting" and "directing" within the prohibitions on the raising of soft money by national parties, federal officeholders and candidates, and their "agents." In the proceedings before the agency, a serious disagreement surfaced over the approach to crafting these definitions. Some commenters, ever concerned with the possibility of evasion, argued for an elastic definition, one that would not allow mere "suggestion" or, in a favorite term, "winks and nods" to escape regulation even if the person suggesting, or winking or nodding, did not exactly say: "I would like you to contribute." An opposing point of view held that the regulation required very precise definition, so that those subject to the statute could be reasonably certain how to avoid violating it.

In the end, the FEC defined "solicit" to mean, simply, "to ask that another person" make a contribution.[17] This is the key, then: "asking." Consider the following hypothetical from the first edition:

> *Smith is the treasurer of a national party committee, and he is anxious about voting turnout in a Congressional race. In the course of a conversation with Turner, a philanthropist affiliated with the same party, he stresses the critical role of resources for turnout. He invites Turner to discuss current plans for turnout with a nonprofit community organization that devotes money and personnel to "getting out the vote."*
>
> *Later a memo surfaces in the press, detailing a) the conversation, b) Turner's subsequent meeting with the community organization; and c) Turner's donation of substantial funds to the community organization to support its turnout efforts. The opposition party demands an investigation, claiming on these facts that Treasurer Smith "solicited" soft money from Turner in violation of the Act. Everybody hurriedly hires lawyers.*

---

[16] *McConnell v. FEC*, No. 02-1674, slip op. at 48 (S.Ct. Dec. 10, 2003).

[17] 11 C.F.R. § 300.2(m).

As stated in the first edition:

"In the preceding example, Treasurer Smith could mount the defense under the Act that even if he did have the stated meeting with Philanthropist Turner, he did not "solicit" him. He merely commented on the need for resources to Turner, never explicitly asking Turner to contribute to the community organization. Turner, in turn, did what he thought it made sense to do. Smith also could deny that he was "acting on behalf of" the party. He did not act on formal instructions from the party: he was merely discussing the Congressional race with Turner, who has known him for years and often discussed with him the political issues of the day."

As it happens, the FEC sanctioned this defense in its formulation of the definition of "solicit." Smith did not "ask" for a contribution. There is still peril in these conversations for the agent of a national party committee. For all the other elements of "agency" appear to be present: Smith is arguably acting on behalf of the national party in worrying about the effects of turnout on the Congressional race. And should he be soliciting a contribution, he would be engaged in one of the acts— raising money for a 501(c) organization—specifically included within the range of acts prohibited to agents of a national party committee. The only question is: did he "ask," and of course, on such questions, recollections can differ. Smith might believe in good faith that he did not ask, while Turner remembers events differently.

Soliciting means asking

Nonetheless, the FEC definition does require that, to solicit, he must "ask"—that he not merely engage in provocative banter about common political objectives, but that he explicitly request that another contribute soft money. It would seem, on these facts, that Smith has avoided a prohibited solicitation as "agent" of a national party committee. The FEC also made clear in its deliberations over the rule that the "asking" for a contribution will not be inferred from a series of conversations that, taken together, could be construed to be a request for contributions. The legal test looks to a specific communication and it rests in the end on a specific fact: whether the "covered person" subject to the solicitation prohibition actually "asked" for a contribution.

Directing is a kind of asking

Then there is the matter of "directing" a contribution, and the FEC offered a definition of this term as well.[18] As the FEC construed the term, the "directing" of a contribution occurs whenever someone expressing an intent to make a contribution is encouraged specifically to do so. In the case of Smith and Turner, an issue of "direction" would arise if Turner had approached Smith with specific questions of whether he, Turner, should contribute to the tax-exempt get-out-the-vote organization. Should Smith act on behalf of the party in affirming that a contribution to that organization would be very helpful, Smith would be engaged as an agent of a national party committee in "directing" a soft money contribution in violation of the law.

What should Smith do, when confronted by Turner with an expressed interest in contributing? Smith would be well advised to deflect the inquiry by specifically stating that, by law, he may not encourage someone who otherwise has the inclination to contribute soft money. May Smith refer Turner to someone else for advice? The law does not prohibit Smith from offering Turner the names of others to consult. No doubt there are facts imaginable that would arouse the regulator's concern—such as where Smith has already arranged for some third party to urge Turner to make the proposed contribution. In that case, that third person would be acting as Smith's agent, and the FEC would likely take the position that Smith cannot arrange to do indirectly what the law prohibits him from doing directly. In the absence of such pre-arrangement, however, Smith could, having deflected the inquiry, refer Turner to someone knowledgeable about the community organization who could answer Turner's questions about the proposed contribution.

Learning about the law is legal

The regulations create, in fact, an allowance of much the same kind for "merely providing information or guidance" about the law. It is neither a solicitation, nor a "direction," for a national party official or agent to advise a potential contributor of which types of organi-

---

[18] 11 C.F.R. § 300.2(n).

zations can accept which types of funds, even to supply the names of groups of interest that could accept different types of money. Smith could, for example, explain the law under which Turner could give soft money to a tax-exempt organization rather than a national party, and such an explanation will not be taken to be an implicit suggestion that a contribution be made to such an organization.

These definitions became a source of much contention as the FEC developed the rules. The agency's final decision did not end the dispute: organizations seeking more elastic definitions, ones that they considered adequate to address their fears of "winks and nods" and other evasions, filed suit alleging that the agency had not followed the intent of Congress.[19]

The statute's drafters anticipated the possibility that national party organizations would vitiate the restriction, by directly or indirectly establishing organizations to raise the now-prohibited money. The law specifically prohibits soft money fundraising by any organization that has been "established, financed, maintained, or controlled" by a national party committee, its officials or employees, or "agents." The prohibition applies to both "direct" and "indirect" establishment, finance, maintenance or control by national parties and their agents of such organizations.

Shadow organizations: organizations "established, financed, maintained, or controlled" by a national party organization

By rule, the FEC established a range of "factors" to be applied in determining when such a control relationship existed between a party and another organization.[20] No one factor is necessarily decisive, though in the specific case, it could be. Instead the FEC will examine the factors in the context of the "overall relationship" in determining whether the presence of any factor or factors is evidence of establishment, finance, maintenance, or control. These are the factors:

- A controlling interest in stock or securities;

Affiliation factors

- Participation by one organization in the governance of the other, "formal or informal";

---

[19] Readers following the progress of the suit may do so on www.moresoftmoneyhardlaw.com.

[20] 11 C.F.R. § 300.2(c).

- One organization's power to hire, appoint, demote or otherwise control officers or other decision-making employees;
- Common overlapping officers or employees;
- Employment by the party committee of former members of the other organization;
- The provision by one organization to the other of "funds or goods in a significant amount on an ongoing basis" (including causing for such goods or funds to be provided by another);
- A party's "active or significant role in the formation of the entity"; and
- Similar patterns of receipts and disbursements.

Severing old ties

More generally, the rules are concerned with a "formal or ongoing relationship" between the national party committee and some other entity. The FEC did make room for the possibility that such a connection might once have existed, say, prior to the statute, but that the connection was then severed. It provided for a party or entity to seek a Commission determination that an organization once connected to the party had severed, at least two years earlier, all "material connections." An additional and disputed limitation was imposed on the time period during which any of the factors could be considered: the rule was applied, with one exception, only to activities after November 6, 2002, the effective date of the statute. The exception concerned any funding provided to an entity prior to that November 6 date, but still unspent by the entity after that date.

An accusation of "affiliation"

The significance of this provision became clear when, only fifteen days after the statute became effective, reform organizations filed a complaint with the FEC, alleging a "control" relationship between certain entities, on the one hand, and Democratic and Republican Party organizations, on the other. The complaint more specifically alleged "multiple schemes...created and implemented by national and state parties." One such organization, the Democratic State Party Organization, was alleged to have been created by the Democratic National Committee. Another, the Leadership Forum, came under attack in the complaint for alleged ties to the National Republican Congressional Campaign

Committee and members of the House Republican leadership. In the case of the Leadership Forum, an additional source of aggravation to the complainants was one million dollars, in so-called "building fund" (soft) money, transferred by the NRCC to the Forum prior to November 6, 2002, and held unspent by the Forum after that date. While the complaints were pending, the Forum returned the funds to the NRCC, and eventually, the DSPO disbanded. The complaints, while later dismissed by the FEC, drew attention to other "entities" of concern to the complainants, making clear that while these other organizations had raised no money, their alleged ties to the national parties would provoke close scrutiny of their actions.

Prohibiting solicitations of certain tax-exempts and 527s

Another provision more specifically bars the national parties—and also state and local committees—from soliciting funds for, or financially supporting, either 1) 501(c) tax-exempt organizations engaged in activities "in connection with" federal elections, such as voter registration or GOTV activities, or 2) so-called "527" organizations.[21]

What is a "527"?

At this point, some explanation is needed for the term "527" organization. These are organizations treated under the tax laws as political committees, which means that they are not required to pay tax on the contributions they raise for their election-related activity. A 527 organization may elect not to contribute monies to, or coordinate its activities with, federal candidates; and so it may not be a "political committee" compelled to register with the FEC and comply with limits on the source and amounts of contributions. In other words, these types of organizations may take "soft money"—indeed any kind of money from anyone in any amount. 527s of this kind register with and report their activities to the Internal Revenue Service only, not the FEC. Their activities might consist of educating voters on issues, or conducting voter registration and GOTV activity.[22]

---

[21] 11 C.F.R. § 300.11.

[22] For a useful and more detailed discussion of "527"s, within the overall context of changes in the world of campaign finance, *see* Frances R. Hill, "Exempt Organizations and Campaign Finance," 91 Tax Notes 477 (2001). *See also,* Richard Kornylak, "Note: Disclosing the Election-Related Activities of Interest Groups Through 527 of the Tax Code," 87 Cornell L. Rev. 230 (2001).

National party committees can help with hard money— not soft

Under the Act, national parties may generally not raise monies for these 527s, nor for other kinds of tax-exempts engaged in election-related activity, like 501(c)(3) charitable organizations or 501(c)(4) "social welfare" organizations, on the theory that these other organizations could serve as vehicles for the parties to avoid their own soft money limits. The FEC rules clarify the obvious: that since all political committees are 527s, the prohibition does not operate to prevent a national party from raising "hard money" for political committees; or for state, local or district party committees; or for the personal campaign committees of state and local candidates. The prohibition as applied does extend to entities established, maintained, financed, or controlled by national party committees, and also to contributions made on behalf of such committees by their "agents." As applied to tax-exempt organizations, it does not matter whether they are nonpartisan or partisan, or whether the national committee, in raising the money, directs how it is spent.

The Supreme Court in the *McConnell* decision read the statute to allow national party committees to donate "hard money" to 501(c) or 527 organizations. The Court seemed to suggest that these party committees could also *raise* hard money for such organizations, but did not make clear how, in practice, this fundraising would work.

The soft money prohibition is absolute: the parties may not assist these organizations with soft money fundraising. There is one qualification: that a party may "respond to a request for information about a tax-exempt group that shares the party's political or philosophical goals." By endorsing those goals upon request, a party is not engaged in prohibited fundraising.

The national committee of a political party is impressed with a tax-exempt organization committed to educating voters on the right to vote, and recruiting "first-time" voters in disadvantaged communities. The national committee has never coordinated its activities with the group, because the group seeks to maintain its reputation as nonpartisan. The Chair of the committee, speaking to a meeting of party activists and donors, notes the organization's work, closing with the remark: "This is important work, and all of us in the party should support it. Give it your time, or give it your money—but please do what you can." The Chair has violated the Act's prohibition on "soliciting" funds for tax-exempts engaged in this kind of work. Later, the Chair directs a contribution from the party's hard money sources to the tax-exempt. The contribution is lawful.

The FEC rules anticipate that parties may not be certain whether, for purposes of the prohibition, a certain tax-exempt organization is receiving or spending funds "in connection with a federal election." The rules provide that parties may seek and rely upon a written certification from the organization that it is not engaged in such activities. The certification must be signed by an officer or an authorized representative of the organization "with knowledge" of the organization's activities, who is able to certify that "within the current election cycle," the organization has not made and does not intend to make federal election-related expenditures. This certification does not allow an organization to escape the restriction for the current cycle, if it is paying election-related debts from a prior cycle. Moreover, in still more evidence of the preoccupation in this field with circumvention, a party cannot rely on a certification of this kind if it possesses "actual knowledge" that it is false.

Figuring out who you're dealing with

The FEC declined in its rulemaking to specify the nature of the activities that would be deemed to be "in connection with a federal election." Rather casually, the Commission noted that time would tell: closed enforcement matters, reflecting action taken by the agency against monies improperly raised for such organizations, would shed some light on the agency's view of which organizations conducted election-related activities. In other words, the law would be clarified by its enforcement—something of a cart rolling along well ahead of the horse. Yet the FEC took this course out of concern that more specificity "might result in an overbroad definition."[23]

---

[23] 67 Fed. Reg. 49,081 (July 29, 2002).

Restrictions on federal candidates and officeholders

Another—and highly significant—restriction on national party fundraising falls on federal candidates and officeholders. These are the individuals who bear the principal burden of raising money for the parties, national, as well as state and local.[24] They are "agents" of their parties for this purpose. The Act does not restrict their activities only under the "agency" rules previously described, but prohibits them as special cases from involvement with "soft money" fundraising. This prohibition states that:

> A candidate, individual holding federal office, agent of a candidate or an individual holding federal office....shall not
> (A) solicit, receive, direct, transfer, or spend funds in connection with an election for federal office, including funds for any Federal election activity, unless the funds are subject to the limitations, prohibitions, and reporting requirements of this Act....[25]

The Chair of the Republican National Committee (RNC) is asked by a state party for assistance in raising "soft money" for GOTV. The Chair, an officer of the RNC, cannot solicit or "direct" soft money to another. So he passes on the request to a Member of Congress from that state. The Member of Congress, however, is separately enjoined under the Act from "soft money" fundraising and cannot act in place of a party officer for this purpose.

The same Member of Congress is approached at a party event by a supporter eager to help the national party who offers to contribute $100,000 to support its activities. The Member notes that the party cannot accept a contribution of that size under the Act—it is "soft money." When the donor suggests that he would like to do more to fulfill his political objectives than the party's contribution limits allow, the

---

[24] The Congressional campaign committees are directed by federal office-holders who join with federal candidates to raise money for the parties' congressional campaigns and other political efforts.

[25] BCRA § 101; 2 U.S.C. § 441i(e)(1)(A).

*Member suggests that he consider donating the money to a
527 organization, Committee for Clean Air, known to be
preparing a nationwide voter education campaign on the
environment. The Member, who was not asked for this assistance by the Committee, nonetheless would be liable under
the Act for "directing" soft money to a 527 organization.*

Federal candidates and officeholders may, however,
raise money in other capacities, and the Act makes
complicated allowance for them. Federal candidates
and officeholders may "attend, speak, or be a featured
guest at a fundraising event for a state, district, or local
committee of a political party."[26] As will be discussed
below, the state and local parties are not prohibited
from raising soft money under the bill, but they are
restricted in how these funds are used. Federal candidates and officeholders may help with this soft money
fundraising as attendees, featured guests, or speakers.

**But candidates
and officeholders
can attend and
speak at state
party events...**

*A federal officeholder is invited to participate as the
featured guest and to speak at a fundraising event for a
county committee of his party. He is asked to exhort those in
attendance to "give what you can" to the county committee
to support its various political programs. Although he is
clearly soliciting "soft money," which the county committee
may accept for various purposes, he may accept the invitation under the exception for attending and speaking at a
state or local party fundraising event.*

*After the event, the officeholder is invited to a private
reception for the county committee's most honored guests,
including its largest contributors. The Chairman of the local
committee requests that he buttonhole some of these donors
and press the case for large contributions. The officeholder
is unsure whether he can agree to the request—the
"fundraising event" at which he spoke has ended, and now
he is being asked to have one-on-one conversations that
could be construed under the Act to be prohibited solicitations. He need not be unsure: he cannot solicit soft money
from individual donors in these circumstances.*

---

[26] BCRA § 101; 2 U.S.C. § 441i(e)(3); 11 C.F.R. § 300.64.

The guest speaker can speak freely

Still an additional issue that arose during consideration of the implementing rules was whether the allowance for "speaking" at an event covered an explicit appeal for funds. Could the invited officeholder go beyond thanking those in attendance, to urging them to support the party with their financial contributions? Proponents of stricter rules urged the Commission to restrict in some manner what the candidates could say—to condition, in effect, the "speaking" allowance with a limit on what could be spoken. The FEC concluded, however, that the right to speak in this context was unrestricted: "Candidates and individuals holding Federal office may speak at such events without restriction or regulation."[27] Does this mean that a federal candidate could say: "Gee, it's nice to be able to speak freely again about wonderful soft money—so give as much as you can to the state party!" While it might be in some states and political circumstances politically imprudent to frame the appeal in precisely this way, it would not be illegal.

May the national party refer federal candidates and officeholders to state parties for these appearances, urging the state and local parties to invite them to attend in these defined ways? The Act does not say. Nor do the FEC rules. There appears little basis for doubting that such referrals are permitted.

The Chair of a party Senatorial campaign committee wishes to assist a state party with the raising of soft money for its various activities for which these funds can be spent. He contacts the state party Chair and offers to help arrange for an appearance at its fundraising event of a prominent U.S. Senator or Congressman. The Senatorial committee Chair is not raising money but arranging for an appearance that the Act allows, though it will result in the raising by the state party of "soft money."

Another chapter of the book, Chapter 4, addresses more generally and in greater detail the provisions of the new law affecting the activities of federal candi-

---

[27] 11 C.F.R. § 300.64(b).

dates and officeholders. There are developments reflected in that Chapter considerable significance to the fundraising restrictions in particular, including recently issued Advisory Opinions addressing candidate fundraising for state and local candidates, and also for state ballot initiatives.

"Building funds"

The old law very directly authorized one other use of soft money by political parties—to purchase or construct an "office facility." The national parties have raised soft money to put up buildings and other related office facilities, and their soft money has paid the costs of the outstanding mortgages and other related expenses payable under the exemption. The Act ended all that, deleting the allowance effective November 6, 2002. State parties are subject to different rules in the operation of building funds, discussed further in the text below.

The state parties and their "Federal election activity"

National parties, it has been stressed, are prohibited under the Act from raising and spending soft money. The question so far has been whether officers and agents of the parties, and the candidates who raise their funds and direct their activities, may raise soft money beneficial to party purposes without impermissibly "acting on behalf" of the party in doing so.

State and local parties are not prohibited from raising soft money in the same way. Their officers and agents are free to raise soft money, though federal candidates and officeholders—prohibited from soliciting soft money for national party committees—also are enjoined (with exceptions noted here and in the chapter on Restrictions on Federal Candidates and Officeholders) from such fundraising for state and local parties as well.

No soft money for "Federal election activity"

The state and local parties may not, however, "expend" or "disburse" soft money for any "Federal election activity." This is the key term of the restriction, and unlike other terms used in the Act, it is specifically defined to include some activities and to exclude others.[28] It is important to note in particular that Federal election activities are not necessarily activities *intended* to influence federal elections in whole or in part. The drafters assumed that some activities conducted by parties have the *effect* of influencing federal elections, and they concluded that the effect alone justified a prohibition on the use in those activities of any monies other than the "hard money" authorized by federal law for federal elections. The restrictions on state and local party committees are equally applicable to associations or similar groups of candidates for state or local office or of individuals holding state or local office. How broadly the FEC will apply the restrictions to groups of state candidates remains to be seen.

Types of Federal election activity
The statutory definition distinguishes between two categories of "Federal election activity." One category consists of voter registration activity, "public communications" (popularly known as "issue advertising"), and those employees on the state or local party payroll engaged in "activities in connection with a federal election." The other category includes "voter identification," get-out-the-vote activity or "generic campaign activity," to the extent that these activities are "conducted in connection with an election in which a candidate for Federal office appears on the ballot." The terms in either category are further defined by rule, and those definitions are discussed below.

The rules adopted by the Commission to define "Federal election activity" produced considerable disagreement, just as its definitions of "soliciting" and "directing" had done. The point of contention is a familiar one. On one side are those anxious for a broad reading of the financing restrictions, while on the other are found those concerned to preserve more flexibility for political actors and also clear guidance for them in the conduct of their activities.

What is "Federal election activity"?
The significance of the dispute was brought out most clearly by the debate over the meaning of the term: "conducted in connection with an election in which a candidate for Federal office appears on the ballot." The

---

[28] 11 C.F.R. § 100.24.

FEC concluded that the wording of the term suggested a time limitation: in its view, Congress must have anticipated some period during an election cycle when there was no "election in which a candidate for Federal office appears on the ballot." On this basis, the Commission concluded that "Federal election activity" did not occur earlier than the date of the earliest filing deadline for access to the primary election ballot. In states without a primary for nominating candidates for federal office, the period for "Federal election activity" would commence January 1 of the even-numbered federal election year. The FEC acknowledged that this approach "may result in all fifty states having different time periods," but noted that uniformity would be achieved within each state.[29]

To emphasize: this question of when the "Federal election activity" period begins determines the source of funding allowable for the named activities. During this period, voter identification, get-out-the-vote and generic campaign activity financed by a state or local party must be paid exclusively from "hard" money— from funds that meet the source restrictions and the dollar limitations specified by the FECA. Prior to this period, however, the rules in effect prior to the enactment of BCRA apply: state and local parties may pay for these activities with a mix of hard and soft (state law-governed funds) in accordance with FEC rules for determining the correct ratio.

Even within the "Federal election activity" period, the statute provides for some clarification of the boundary line between federal and state laws. A state or local party committee can fund under state law advertisements that refer "solely" to state and local candidates, supporting, opposing, promoting or attacking them, so long as the communication does not also qualify as a "Federal election activity." For example, an advertisement that would qualify also as "GOTV activity" (see below) under the new law, does not slip out of the federal financing restrictions simply because it only refers to a state or local candidate. Yet such an advertisement could be funded with state "soft money"

---

[29] 67 Fed. Reg. 49,066 (July 29. 2002).

if, for example, it attacked a state or local candidate and did not otherwise fall within one of the "Federal election activity" categories. Other identified exceptions or clarifications include:

- A contribution to a state and local candidate so long as it is not "designated" for a Federal election activity. Neither the legislative history, nor FEC rules, explain the meaning of "designation." It may mean that a contribution to a state or local candidate is not subject to federal law, unless the contributor has an understanding with the state or local candidate that it will be spent for, say, an issue ad campaign that refers approvingly to a federal candidate along with the state candidate appearing in the ad. Of course, a state candidate cannot generally finance such an advertisement lawfully with soft money, and so it is not clear that prohibiting a contribution for this purpose is altogether necessary if the activity in question is illegal.

- The costs of a "political convention, meeting or conference" sponsored by a state or local party.

- The costs of "grassroots materials," such as pins or bumper stickers, that name only candidates for state and local office.

"Voter registration activity" (within 120 days of an election)

The Act treats as a Federal election activity "voter registration activity," prohibiting the use of soft money for this purpose within 120 days of the date of a regularly scheduled federal election.[30] At all other times, the state parties may pay for these activities under the "allocation" allowed under existing rules from both hard and soft funds.

The statute does not say more about what comprises voter registration activity, and the FEC went about the business of filling in the blank. The Commission rule defines this type of activity as "contacting individuals to assist them in registering to vote." Specific examples of this assistance include providing information and forms helpful or needed to accomplish registration, and also support in filling out any such forms. In adopting this approach to the rule—an approach not without its detractors—the Commission concluded that the Congress intended to reach "action rather than mere exhortation."

---

[30] 11 C.F.R. § 106.24(a)(2).

It is noted again that the rule contains within itself a time-limitation, 120 days within an election, and the activity in question is not among those subject to the special time limit for Federal election activities "conducted in connection with an election in which a candidate for Federal office appears on the ballot."

A local committee launches a door-to-door registration drive in September of an election year, which will involve the election of federal as well as other candidates. The local committee supplies forms, and the personnel distributing them are instructed to assist interested potential voters in filling them out. All the costs associated with this registration effort—the cost of personnel, materials, phones, and print advertising—would have to be paid under the Act with hard money. Assuming that the election is taking place on November 5th, the registration drive would have to be conducted on an all-hard basis for the period of 120 days beforehand, beginning with July 5th of that year.

The same local committee also finances a local radio drive to encourage people to take note of the pending election and to determine their registration status so that they can exercise their right to vote. Because this is exhortation, not specific action contacting individuals to assist them specifically with registration, the radio communications do not constitute "voter registration" activity subject to the "hard money" financing requirement within 120 days of an election.

The Act posed for local committees, in particular, a dilemma. Any number of them may have a local focus, yielding to their state committee's principal interest in federal races. The law has long recognized this local emphasis, by permitting such committees to engage in a limited amount of "exempt" federal election-related activities without registering as a "political committee" under federal law and becoming subject to federally imposed legal obligations.[31] It allows state and local party committees to fund up to $5,000 in a calendar

---

[31] Other committees are subject to registration as "political committees" when spending more than $1,000 in a year to influence federal elections. 2 U.S.C. §§ 431(4)(A) & (C).

year for these different kinds of "exempt activities," such as activities conducted with volunteers to distribute literature on behalf of federal and other candidates.

The Commission attended to these concerns by providing that the financing requirements of the Act applicable to "Federal election activity" would not now automatically catapult these committees into registration and reporting status under federal law. A state and local committee would still have to satisfy the financing requirements, demonstrating that it had sufficient "hard" or so-called Levin funds (see below) on hand to make the payments. If, however, the activities now treated as "Federal election activity" would also qualify as exempt activity, the state and local party could still have the benefit of the $5,000 allowance for avoiding full registration as a political committee under the federal law. Some organizations have challenged the FEC's statutory authority to create the $5,000 threshold.

"Voter identification" "Voter identification" also qualifies under the Act as a Federal election activity.[32] Parties using phones, mail, or volunteers to identify affiliated or sympathetic voters must pay the related costs with hard money. This requirement applies whenever such activity is "conducted in connection with an election in which a candidate for Federal office appears on the ballot": beginning the date of the earliest date of the filing deadline for access to the primary ballot (or if there is no primary in the state in question, beginning January 1 of the even-numbered federal election year).

The FEC defines voter identification to consist of "creating or enhancing voter lists" to identify voters on the basis of the likelihood of their voting, or voting for particular candidates. The sponsors took issue with what they viewed as too narrow a definition. They would have preferred a rule that treated "voter identification" and GOTV much the same, therefore placing under the all-hard money financing requirement "acquiring a voter list in and of itself." The FEC declined to extend the rule in this direction, concluding that the mere acquisition of a list, possibly solely to

---

[32] 11 C.F.R. § 100.24(a)(4).

support state and local candidate activity, did not have a sufficient connection to pure Federal election activity.

GOTV activity—the business of actually motivating voters and in some cases transporting them to the polls—also is a Federal election activity,[33] and the requirement of "all-hard" financing applies also to any of these activities within the time period specified for those conducted "in connection with" a federal election. The definition adopted by the FEC parallels that selected for "voter registration": it is concerned with action rather than mere exhortation. GOTV involves acts of "contacting registered voters...to assist them in engaging in the act of voting." The FEC offers as examples providing, within 72 hours of an election, information on elections dates and times, and the location of polling places. An offer of transportation to the polls, and any actual transportation provided, also constitutes GOTV activity payable within the prescribed time period with "hard money." **"Get-out-the-vote (GOTV)"**

Concerned throughout the rulemaking process to avoid what it called a "vast federalization of the political process," the FEC provided that the rule does not reach GOTV communications by state and local candidates, including associations or committees of such candidates, if the communications refer only to one or more of such candidates. Bear in mind, however, that this rule applies only to communications by state and local candidates themselves: it does not allow a state or local party to escape the all-hard financing requirements by only referring to state and local candidates.

All "hard" financing also is required for "generic campaign activity,"[34] conducted within the time period specified for activities conducted in connection with an election in which a federal candidate appears on the ballot. The statute defines such activity as "a campaign activity that promotes a political party and does not promote a candidate or non-federal candidate." The FEC rule implementing this provision makes clear that an "activity" for this purpose includes only "public **"Generic campaign activity"**

---

[33] 11 C.F.R. § 100.24(a)(3).

[34] 11 C.F.R. § 100.24(a)(b)(2)(ii).

communications": the purpose of this limitation is to assure that the financing restriction applies only to "external activities" of the party in communicating with the general public.

The two activities, GOTV and generic campaign activity, may be closely related in function, as in the case of appeals to the public to "Vote Democratic," or "Vote Republican." This relationship is not fixed, however, and a party also may advertise its virtues at some distance from an election to solidify party identification and for other political purposes.

> *A state party committee funds door hangers appealing to voters to "get out and cast your ballot for the Confused Party on Election Day. Vote Confused!" and providing a number voters can call to obtain free transportation to the polls. If the activity is conducted within the Federal election activity time period—beginning with the earliest date for primary ballot qualification, or in the case of a state without a primary election, January 1 of the election year—the Act requires that the attributable costs be paid with hard money only.*

> *The same state party also finances advertising on the time-honored right to vote, and the duty of citizens who value their heritage of freedom to vote. The advertisement contains only this message: it makes no mention of a federal candidate, or a political party. This is not a GOTV communication subject to the all hard money financing requirement for "Federal election activity."*

"Issue advertising" Then there is the matter of "issue advertising," described earlier as one of the controversial practices fueling support for the Act. The Act does not make specific mention of "issue advertising," but it does include within the term "Federal election activity," any

> [P]ublic communication that refers to a clearly identified candidate for federal office (regardless of whether a candidate for state or local office is also mentioned or identified) and that promotes or supports a candidate for that office, or attacks or opposes a candidate for that office (regardless

of whether the communication expressly advocates a vote for or against a candidate).[35]

The public communication described in this communication need not include "express advocacy"—the magic words that include "vote," "reject," "defeat," or the like. The provision turns instead on one objective factor, and another factor that is altogether subjective in nature.

The public communication must, in a relatively objective sense, "refer" to a clearly identified federal candidate. The term "clearly identified" encompasses the name of the candidate, a drawing or photograph, or some way in which her identity "is apparent by unambiguous reference."[36] More subjectively, the public communication also must then "promote or support," or alternatively "attack or oppose," that candidate.[37] The typical issue ad is rarely reticent in the expression of its views about a candidate. The reader is familiar with the standard approach—a grainy image, with a blurred black and white of the candidate, and a litany of appalling acts with which she is charged, followed by "Call Marcia Jones. Tell her that public office is a public trust, not a chance for her and her friends to feed at the trough."[38]

The Party, six months later and still Confused, runs ads intended to shore up the position of an incumbent Governor struggling with a legislature controlled by another party and contesting his leadership on a key public policy issue. The ads state that "The Confused Party is protecting your jobs and revitalizing the economy of this state. But the Simplistic Party, listening only to campaign contributions, refuses to enact desperately needed legislation to fund a true jobs program. Think about your future, then call Simplistic

---

[35] BCRA § 101; 2 U.S.C. § 431(20)(A)(iii). A "public communication" is "any form of general public political advertising," including broadcast and mail advertising, and communications to the general public through phone banks. BCRA § 101; 2 U.S.C. 431(22).

[36] 2 U.S.C. § 431(18).

[37] The Court found that this standard was not unduly vague. *McConnell*, at 62.

[38] Close to image of hog snorting with satisfaction over breakfast.

Party leaders and tell them—we want our government to help the people, not the special interests." Party lawyers argue over the question of whether the phrase "Simplistic Party leaders," a number of whom are federal officeholders running for reelection, "refers" to "clearly identified candidates," and therefore bars the use of soft money to pay for the ad.

The Confused Party decides to run the ad featuring a key supporter of the Governor, the senior U.S. Senator of the state who also is running for reelection. He appears on-camera to speak warmly of the Governor's leadership, and the Governor closes the ad, declaring that "I am proud of the help that Senator Smiles and I have been privileged to provide to the working families of this state." Opponents of the Governor and Senator Smiles file a complaint, alleging that the Party had financed with soft money a public communication, inasmuch as the closing remarks of the Governor are fairly taken as promotion or support of Senator Smiles.

Please note: This type of Federal election activity is <u>not</u> subject to a time limitation: it is not among the activities "conducted in connection with an election in which a Federal candidate appears on the ballot."

"Public communication" includes any "public political advertising"— but not the Internet

The term "public communication" is very inclusive, applying to any form of "general" public political advertising, including "broadcast, cable, or satellite communication, newspaper, magazine, outdoor advertising facility, mass mailing, or telephone bank to the general public." A mass mailing is a mailing of more than 500 pieces of mail "of an identical or substantially similar nature within any 30-day period," while a "telephone bank" is defined in similar terms involving more than 500 calls within the same 30-day time frame.

As the Commission debated the rules, it considered whether communications carried on the Internet should be included within the ambit of "public communications." The Congressional sponsors argued for its inclusion, but the FEC decided against it. The FEC, detecting no statutory basis for the inclusion, also found "no threat of corruption...in a medium that allows almost limitless, inexpensive communications across the broadest possible cross-section of the American public." More expansively, the FEC referred to the Internet as "a bastion of free political speech."[39]

Most federal officeholders are, in a technical legal sense, "candidates" throughout their term of office. The existing law requires any person who has raised and spent more than $5,000 on a campaign to file a Statement of Candidacy with the FEC or Secretary of the Senate; and most incumbent officeholders raise well beyond this amount within a short period after their most recent election and in anticipation of their next. So for federal officeholders, there is little space between their status as officeholders and their legal position as candidates.

The basic restrictions on "issue advertising"

As a result, party ads critical of their official actions, even ads with little clear-cut connection to their candidacies, must be paid under the restrictive "all-hard" rule. This restriction applies to ads run the year before an election—or in the case of a Senator, several years before an election—as well as the year of an election. It also applies to ads run against candidates unlikely to draw a strong opponent, or even any. By its terms, the provision makes no distinctions on content, which means that the ads replete with scurrilous personal attacks are treated no differently from the ads offering a more reasonable critique of the officeholder's position.

Issue advertising for purposes of state and local party activity shares many of the characteristics of "electioneering communications" by outside organizations as discussed in the next chapter. Like parties, these organizations also are subject to a prohibition on certain kinds of "issue advertising." Unlike the party issue advertising restrictions, those imposed on "outside groups" apply only to broadcast, cablecast, or satellite communications within 30 days of a primary or 60 days of a general election. Thus, these groups can run these ads freely at all other times; and they can, at all times, finance issue advertising in the mail or through telephone banking—in all media other than radio, television, or cable. Also, unlike the party issue

---

[39] 67 Fed. Reg. 49,072 (July 29, 2002).

advertising restriction, the prohibition on "electioneering communications" does not depend on whether the text of the communication could be said to promote, support, attack or oppose a candidate.

Powerful Corporation, enraged over the energy votes of Senator Smith, finances a slew of issue ads attacking him for his votes. The ads are run up to the 30th day period prior to his primary, and then up to the 60th day before the general election. Powerful also generates glossy, well-financed mail pieces intended to bring their criticism home, which are mailed out to the Senator's constituents within these 30 and 60 day periods. Powerful spends unlimited funds from its treasury coffers for these ads.

Senator Smith complains to his state party, and demands help in responding to these attacks. The Party develops an ad defending Senator Smith's record, citing his lifelong commitment to plentiful energy resources. The Party may not use soft money for these responses, but instead must pay only with "hard money." This "all-hard" requirement applies to all of its defenses of Senator Smith directed to the general public, whether by mail, broadcast media, or other means.

As will be noted below, the problems facing the state party in funding the defense of Senator Smith are not limited to the unavailability of soft money. The Act places limits on the amount of "hard money" for this purpose, by requiring that any expenditures of the party coordinated with Smith be treated as "contributions" to Smith's campaign. As "contributions," the spending is subject to dollar limits.

Keeping an eye on the help The Act also defines as "Federal election activity," the monthly services of a state, district, or local party committee employee who spends more than 25% of his "compensated" time in that month "on activities in connection with a federal election."[40] In other words, should an employee in any month exceed the 25% threshold for time spent on federal election-related activities, her entire salary for the month should be

---

[40] BCRA § 101; 2 U.S.C. § 431(20)(A)(iv).

paid for with hard money. The Act does not focus on activities that fall within the term Federal election activity, such as voter registration or issue advertising, but any activities by that employee conducted "in connection with a federal election." This "in connection with" formulation is not defined, and leaves the parties with an open question about the application of this provision. In any event, if an employee does not exceed the 25% threshold for federal election-related activities, then the state or local party can pay the entire salary cost for that month with funds allowable under state law—that is, 100% with "soft money," so long as the funds so spent comply with the requirements of state law.

Exception: the Levin Amendment

The Act also identifies specific activities of state, district, and local committees that may be paid with a "mix" of hard and soft funds. These are not simple exclusions; they are hedged in some cases with significant qualifications. The devil lurks in the details, or more to the point, the regulators do.

Of particular importance is an exception for certain Federal election activities conducted by state, district, and local party committees[41] under certain specified conditions. This exception was added to the bill in the Senate by amendment sponsored by Senator Carl Levin of Michigan—hence, the short name, also used here, of "The Levin Amendment."[42] Its purpose was to allow for some voter registration, GOTV, voter identification, and generic party activities that could be paid on a "mixed" or "allocated" basis with hard and soft funds. The Levin Amendment operates as an exception to the general rule that Federal election activities must be paid on an all-hard basis.

The Levin Amendment: some soft money and some Federal election activity

The Amendment's application is governed by certain conditions, which are designed to allow for soft money

But "some restrictions apply"

---

[41] Associations and similar groups of state and local candidates or elected officials that are otherwise treated the same as state and local party committees cannot take advantage of this exception.

[42] Changes to the Amendment were made following passage by the Senate, and prior to its consideration by the House, when it was incorporated into the House version of the Act known as Shays-Meehan.

financing of these activities without inviting much of the abuses of greatest concern to the drafters of the bill. Some of these conditions relate to the content of the activity, and others to the way the activity is conducted and financed.[43]

Don't mention the federal candidate

An activity funded under the Levin Amendment may not "refer to a clearly identified candidate for federal office."[44] Thus, a voter registration appeal funded under the conditions of the Amendment may urge "Vote Democratic," but it may not frame the appeal with a reference to a federal candidate, such as a candidate named Jones, as follows:

> *When you vote this November 5th, think about the jobs created by Jones' plan—and Vote Democratic.*

Or, stated differently, the Levin Amendment allows for some soft financing of these kinds of appeals when a federal candidate appears on the ballot—but not when that candidate, or any other federal candidate, is named.

Stay off the air

The Levin Amendment also excludes from its allowances activities conducted through "broadcasting, cable, or satellite communication." Voter registration activities, for example, may under this amendment be paid with soft and hard money, including within 120 days of an federal election, but only where these activities are conducted door-to-door, by mail, or by phone. The use of radio, TV or cable to fund these activities falls outside the exception. It is stressed that the party is not required to choose between one or the other means in conducting, for example, these voter registration or GOTV activities. It may fund under Levin the non-broadcast efforts with both hard and soft money, while paying on an "all-hard" basis the portion of the effort carried out through broadcast or cablecast facilities.

Limits on contributions for Levin Amendment activities

Restrictions on the financing of these activities are included among the conditions of the Amendment. The Amendment, as noted, allows for the use of both hard and soft monies for the Federal election activity conducted under its conditions. The soft monies paid for

---

[43] 11 C.F.R. § 300.32(c).

[44] 11 C.F.R. § 300.31(d).

this purpose must comply with the requirements of state law, which means that a state or local party may only raise for Levin Amendment purposes monies that it could otherwise lawfully raise under state law for state and local elections. Moreover, the party may not raise from any one "person" more than $10,000 in a calendar year for use in financing Levin Amendment activities. This limitation is among the more unusual features of the Act, without any precedent in the old law, and it deserves close attention.

Because state law controls in the first instance, this $10,000 limitation is a supplementary restriction added by the Act, but it does not supplant the state law rules. If a state's laws do not allow for corporate contributions to parties, then the Levin Amendment does not supersede the state restriction.[45] A party in a state that allows the contribution of corporate contributions may raise them for Levin Amendment activities, whereas a party operating in a state prohibiting corporate contributions is out of luck. As another example, if state law limits contributions to a party to a level below $10,000, then this lower limit—not the $10,000 limit established by the Act—applies to a contribution made for Levin Amendment purposes. If the state law limit is higher, then the lower federal $10,000 allowance applies. This is the key to understanding the $10,000 limit: that while it is a "soft money" allowance, it does not authorize a donor to extend or go beyond what state law would permit. And because the limit is set by federal law, it may allow for less—$10,000—than some state laws would authorize. State law controls source completely, but amounts only partially.

So, while existing law defines "person" broadly, to include corporations, unions, individuals, and partnerships, the availability of contributions from such persons for Levin Amendment activities depends on state law. State law determines who may be treated as a "person" who may contribute, and also how much they contribute.

---

[45] "Obviously, if a state prohibits corporate or labor union contributions to political parties, the Levin Amendment does not supersede that prohibition, and corporate or union contributions of Levin money would be banned." 148 Cong. Rec. H409 (daily ed. Feb. 13, 2002) (statement of Rep. Shays).

Enforcing the limit on contributions to Levin Amendment activities

The Amendment also limits the "persons" who may contribute in another way, by applying the limit collectively to that "person" and any other person "established, financed, maintained, or controlled by such person." The clearest example is a corporation and its parent, subsidiaries, or affiliates. In a state where corporations may otherwise contribute to state parties under state law, the entire family of related corporations may contribute only one $10,000 contribution to a national, district, or local committee for Levin Amendment activities.

At the same time the eligible contributor under the Amendment may make a contribution to each unit of a state party—the state committee, and any of the subordinate committees of the party at the local, municipal, or district levels.[46] The practical effect of this allowance may be limited, the reason being that the Act does not permit a local committee to accept such a contribution, and to then transfer it to the state party for use in funding the actual voter registration, GOTV, or similar Federal election activities. The unit of the party committee accepting the funds must make direct use of it for the specified Levin Amendment activities: Levin monies must be raised only by the committee spending them. Moreover, the sponsors of the bill stressed their intention that parties may not "create their own multiple subsidiary committees to raise separate $10,000 contributions under this provision."[47]

There is nothing in the Act, however, to prohibit the different units of the party from collaboratively committing the monies raised under the Levin Amendment to commonly conduct voter registration, GOTV, or other eligible activity.

Five different county committees raise $10,000 from the same Corporation X for Levin Amendment purposes—a GOTV drive conducted under the conditions of the Amendment. The committees may not transfer the funds

---

[46] 11 C.F.R. § 300.31(d)(3).

[47] 148 Cong. Rec. H410 (daily ed. Feb. 13, 2002) (statement of Rep. Shays).

from one to the other, but they could pool their resources and coordinate their direct expenditures of these funds in the implementation of a statewide GOTV drive.

The Levin Amendment calls for an allocation of funds, the special "soft" and the hard, to pay for Federal election activity. Now under FEC rules, the allocation has been established; the agency has fixed the "minimum" federal, hard money share of the expense, varying with the type of election year and the nature of the federal offices on the ballot.[48] These are the minimums by type of ballot:

Allocation: determining how much Levin funds may be used

Both Presidential and Senate candidate on the ballot	36%
Presidential candidate, but no Senate candidate, on the ballot	28%
A Senate candidate, but no Presidential candidate	21%
Neither a Presidential nor a Senate candidate	15%

These percentages represent the averages of ballot composition for parties in four selected state groupings; the groups were chosen on the basis of "size and geographic location, and for the particular elections held in each state in 2000 and 2002."[49]

Establishing the formulas for allocation in this way is a change from the type of allocation activity used by the FEC under the old "hard"/"soft" regime, prior to the enactment of BCRA. The formulas do not vary from state to state and they do not require measurements of time and space. Of course, the Levin activities may still be paid entirely with federal dollars. In the event that a party does have Levin funds available, raised as required in "homegrown" fashion, these formulas specify the minimum share payable with federal "hard" dollars.

---

[48] 11 C.F.R. § 300.33(b).

[49] 67 Fed. Reg. 49,098 (July 29, 2002).

Restrictions on fundraising under the Levin Amendment: hard money

Collaborative spending under the Levin Amendment appears permissible, but fundraising support from other parties or from candidates is not. One additional condition of the Amendment seeks to limit state and local parties to their own fundraising.[50]

As has been noted, the Amendment allows for "mixed" financing of these activities with both hard and a special form of soft money. The restrictions on raising this money extend to *both* the hard *and* soft money raised for this purpose. State and local parties must generally raise their own "hard money" for Federal election activities, paid under the Levin Amendment in some allocable share, but they may accept hard dollars raised by federal officeholders. They may not, however, accept funds transferred or received from national party committees, or other state and local party committees. It does not matter that the amounts so transferred were not "earmarked" for Federal election activity: the issue is only the use of the funds. Hence the party must either 1) establish a separate account for federal dollars used for Levin activities, so that it can easily establish their homegrown character; or 2) be able through "a reasonable accounting method" to establish that the amount of "homegrown" funds held in its general federal accounts was sufficient to cover the Levin-related expense.

These prohibitions do not apply only to direct assistance in the form of transfers or contributions. State and local parties, and also national party committees (and their officers or agents acting on their behalf), may also not establish joint fundraising ventures under which state and local parties raise hard money for their Levin Amendment purposes, while the other participants raise funds for other projects and purposes. Moreover, in still another example of the Act's focus on circumvention, the Act extends its prohibitions to any indirect support provided by national parties, or other state and local party committees, through "any entity directly or indirectly established, financed, maintained, or controlled" by any national, state, or local committee.

---

[50] 11 C.F.R. § 300.34.

Additional restrictions apply to the raising of Levin Amendment "soft" monies by state and local committees. National party committees—and once again, the officers and agents acting on their behalf—may not have any part in raising soft money for parties using them for Levin Amendment activities. The same restriction applies to federal candidates and officeholders. The Act will not allow any of these named committees or individuals to "solicit," "receive," "direct," or "transfer" soft funds to the state and local parties for these purposes. In fact, the Act takes the additional step of prohibiting fundraising for the parties under the Levin Amendment "in the name of" national party committees, candidates or officeholders.[51]

Levin Amendment: no help from federal candidates or officeholders, or the national parties, to raise "soft" funds

The Chair of the national Confused Party is asked by the state party to call major donors of the party, explain the Levin Amendment to them, and then solicit contributions directly to the state party for that purpose. The Chair of the national party may not agree to this request—or act on it. He also may not refer the request to the members of that state's congressional delegation with the intention that they would conduct this solicitation.

A friendly donor, interested in the state party's efforts, discusses the operation of the Levin Amendment with a U.S. Senator from that state, and then on her own initiative, contributes $10,000 to the party under her own name with a note: "Senator Jones advises me that your party could use these monies for the upcoming voter registration drive, and I am pleased to enclose a contribution for $10,000. Please make sure to credit the Senator internally for his efforts to bring this opportunity to my attention." Is this a prohibited contribution "in the name" of the officeholder? It is unclear.

State and local parties also may not collaborate in jointly raising their <u>soft</u> monies for Levin Amendment activities. They may not establish joint fundraising committees for this purpose, and a state or local party committee also may not solicit such funds for the

---

[51] 11 C.F.R. § 300.31(e).

Levin Amendment activities of other state and local committees.

These restrictions aim to enforce a "grassroots" or local "homegrown" character for the activities funded under the Levin Amendment. The Act's drafters appeared to believe that only "soft money" raised locally, for these state and local activities, avoids the danger of serving national or federal electoral purposes. While this concern is perhaps understandable where federal candidates, officeholders, or national committees propose to raise these funds, it may be less clear how the perceived danger is presented by state and local committees jointly raising these monies.

Accounts management for state and local party conduct of Levin and other "mixed" activity

The FEC provides by rule for complicated account structures intended to keep straight the dollars raised from different sources for different purposes.[52] State and local parties may establish generally these types of accounts:

- Federal accounts, for the receipt of hard or federal funds;
- Nonfederal accounts, holding funds permitted by state law; or
- "Levin" accounts, to hold funds of this nature.

The federal account may only contain hard money solicited with a clear statement of their use for federal election-related purposes. The nonfederal accounts holding state funds, received pursuant to state law, may also hold Levin funds. It is important to note that Levin funds need not be designated for this purpose: a contributor who has contributed funds within the $10,000 allowance, is a "Levin" contributor even if she or he is unaware of having achieved this distinction (such as it is). It is in the end a form of state law contribution, but it can only be expended for certain purposes specified under federal law—Levin Amendment activities to fund Federal election activities—if it meets the additional federal requirements, including the $10,000 limitation.

---

[52] 11 C.F.R. § 300.30.

If Levin dollars are held in a nonfederal account, used later for Levin Amendment activities, the state or local committee must be able to show once again through a "reasonable accounting method" that the account at the time of the expenditure held sufficient Levin-qualified funds. Alternatively, the party can hold Levin funds in a specific and segregated Levin account.

The state or local committee can use these various accounts to pay for allocable Federal election activity expenses, in one of two ways. The federal account may pay the expense, accepting reimbursement of its lawful share from the other affected accounts, nonfederal or Levin, pursuant to the allocation formulas discussed previously. A second approach for the payment of these expenses consists of the establishment of a "transmittal" or "allocation" account. A committee could establish multiple allocation accounts for different types of Federal election activity or other "mixed" activities payable with both hard and "soft" money, including Levin money.

Any transfer to a federal account cannot occur more than 10 days prior to the activity to be funded, nor more than 60 days thereafter. The time restrictions are intended to match transfers to specific payments, while avoiding any improper subsidy from improper sources for general federal account activity. FEC rules provide that any transfer outside these time limitations would constitute a "loan," not a transfer, and would violate the law.

Transfers into "allocation accounts" from the various other accounts need be only in the amount needed to meet the transferor's allocable share of the expenses. All expenses for this activity funded from the account must be paid from that account, and only that account, as long as it is maintained. Transfers are not allowed between allocation accounts.

Special reporting requirements and issues for state and local parties

An important question for local committees in particular is whether the new restrictions on their Federal election activity—a form of "federalization" of their activities—would affect their registration and related reporting obligations under the Act. The law compels any association raising or spending more than $1,000 to register with the Federal Election Commission as a "political committee," complying also with the relevant reporting requirements. The statute generally shows some mercy toward state and local committees: it allows them to engage in specific types of "grassroots" activity affecting federal elections, and to exceed the $1,000 registration threshold in doing so, without incurring federal registration and reporting requirements. For example, the law exempts from those expenditures that count toward the registration threshold, funds spent for certain Presidential and Vice Presidential voter registration and GOTV activities. A state and local committee operating under this exemption can spent up to $5,000 on such activities without triggering registration or reporting obligations.

The FEC took these policies embodied in the pre-BCRA statute into account when fashioning implementing rules under the new law. If a state and local committee has not already qualified as a political committee under the federal law, the amounts spent on "Federal election activity" are not expenditures—and do not count toward the registration and reporting thresholds—unless they would independently qualify as such expenditures. A Federal election activity that would count also as an exempt activity—such as the one conducted under the provision governing Presidential and Vice Presidential voter registration and GOTV—would still be treated as an exempt payment. So amounts spent for such a combined Federal election activity/exempt activity would count toward the $5,000, not the $1,000, registration and reporting threshold. This is the reporting effect of an exempt activity that is also a "Federal election activity": there is also the additional effect that amounts spent for this type of Federal election activity must still be paid with all hard federal funds, not with a mix of hard and soft money. Levin Amendment fundraising is not available. The committee spending the funds must also maintain records of federal receipts and disbursements, making them available to the FEC "upon request."

The FEC rules also establish two separate levels of reporting for state and local committees that are political committees and also spend funds on Federal election activity.[53] When a committee spends less than $5,000 in the aggregate in a calendar year on Federal election activity, the committee must report to the FEC all federal funds used, including the federal portion of any allocated expense. The reporting requirements are more extensive for political committees spending $5,000 or more on Federal election activities. These committees must report, for example, all federal funds used, including any Levin Amendment monies; the allocation percentage used for particular Federal election activities; and the category of Federal election activity for which each allocated disbursement was made.

Other exceptions

Apart from the Levin Amendment, there are other exceptions to the broad prohibition on soft money for state party "Federal election activity." One applies to any "public communication" that "refers solely to a clearly identified candidate for state or local office." There is here a BUT. Even if the communication refers "solely" to such a candidate, it may not qualify for the exclusion if the communication is a voter registration, voter identification, GOTV, or generic campaign activity that would otherwise be treated as a "Federal election activity." The law here has giveth, then immediately taketh away.

> **Exception: public communications referring to state and local candidates**

A state party advertises in a federal election year on behalf of a gubernatorial candidate, declaring in the ad devoted solely to that candidate that "Governor Wilson has made a difference for this state, battling the special interests and providing for more jobs to bring our economy to life. Call Governor Wilson—tell him to keep fighting for the people of this State."

So far so good—the exclusion of the Act applies, allowing the state party to fund this advertisement

---

[53] 11 C.F.R. § 300.36.

under the requirements and allowances of state law. But then the Party could modify the ad and take an additional step that negates the exclusion and brings the "all hard" financing rule into play.

"We need Governor Wilson's commitment to our state's workers and families. So on November 5th, take care of your family's future: Vote for Governor Wilson and the Confused Party."

By adding the appeal to support a particular party, the party has slipped away from the exception, that would have allowed for soft money financing under state law, and placed itself squarely within the all-hard financing requirement. The appeal here is a form of Federal election activity: a campaign message promoting a particular party, not just Governor Wilson.

It is noted that the various restrictions on the financing of Federal election activity apply "regardless of whether a candidate for state or local office also appears on the ballot." For example, a public communication or issue ad does not escape the Act's "all-hard" requirement simply because the advertisement discusses all senior officials of the state, including those who hold state, not federal, office.

"We need the leaders of the Confused Party to support a jobs program for our state's families. Call Governor Wilson and the elected leaders of our state and tell them—the time has come for the state to work for its workers."

The reference to the "elected leaders" of our state could spoil the fun for a party interested in operating within the exceptions to the all-hard financing requirements. An exclusive reference to Governor Wilson would allow the party to operate within the exception and pay with the funds allowed for these purposes under state law. But the broad reference to elected officials, including federal officeholders who also are candidates, may trigger the all-hard financing requirement. The ad may have become a "public communication" that "refers to a clearly identified candidate for federal office (regardless of whether a candidate for state or local office is also mentioned or identified)." ("May have become," because there is perhaps some question of whether the reference to "elected officials" is a reference to "clearly identified candidates," and the ad's wording may or may not rise to the level of an ad promoting, supporting, attacking or opposing a candidate.)

The complications of the exclusions also are apparent in the exception made for "a contribution to a candidate for state or local office." A party may make a soft money contribution to such a candidate, and nothing would seem more strictly nonfederal in character. The Act cautions that if the party asks that the money be spent for any of the activities defined to be "Federal election activities," then this "designation" means— well, something, though it is not clear what. That the contribution cannot be made at all? That it could be made but only with "hard money"? The Act does not say. But it is clear that the party should not designate a contribution in this way.

Exception: contributions to state and local candidates

A state party makes a soft money contribution to various state legislative candidates, but requests that each such candidate commit to the expenditure of a portion of these funds for party voter registration. If the state legislative races occur in a year in which federal candidates also appear on the ballot, the contribution may have been "designated" for a Federal election activity—voter registration— and the exception under the Act for this contribution does not apply.

Parties are able under this exception to pay with all soft funds under the allowances of state law for "the costs of a state, district, or local political convention." Because there is no qualification placed on this allowance, the party might somehow use publicity for the convention to plump for the party as a whole—to engage in some "generic" party advocacy, promoting a political party but not specific federal or other candidates. How far it might go in doing so may be tested in time; or parties may conclude that a convention is a convention, and that they may be unable to

Exception: conventions

make more of them than that. The FEC extended this exception to state and local political party conferences and meetings.

Exception: campaign materials

Another exclusion appears in the Act for the "costs of campaign materials," including but not limited to buttons, bumper stickers, and yard signs, but there is here, too, a BUT. Those materials may only name or depict a candidate for state and local office, and if they do, the parties may pay for them under state law, on an "all-soft" basis. This simple allowance may produce different results in different circumstances. If the materials refer to both federal and state candidates, then it would seem that the existing rules apply to allow for a "mix" of hard and soft money. If, however, the materials are produced for use in an activity that is treated under the Act as a Federal election activity—such as a GOTV—it is unclear whether this expense must be included among the costs, payable solely with hard money, of that Federal election activity.

Exception: building funds for state and local parties

A final allowance of note pertains to "building funds." While national party committees may not under the Act raise "soft monies" to construct or purchase office buildings, Congress elected to leave state and local parties free to do so. The monies they raise for this purpose, however, must satisfy the requirements of state law, and also one requirement of federal law: a party cannot accept monies from foreign nationals for this purpose. So if state law permits a party to collect corporate contributions for an office building, the party may raise such funds for this purpose under the Act. This is a major change in the law on this point. Under the old law, federal law controlled the question of what kind of money could be used for these building projects. Now the Act generally abandons the field, leaving the decision on the source of funding to the various states.

The Act also extends the right to fund these building projects to local as well as state parties. The FEC has since also confirmed that, as under the previous building fund provision available to national party committees, the state and local parties can finance under this provision capital requirements within the meaning of the Internal Revenue Code, such as equipment, and not only the core structure.[54] Parties can also enter into leases for space to generate income, but if the building was financed with nonfederal funds, then the nonfederal proceeds from the lease must be deposited only in the nonfederal account. By denying national parties the right to accept soft money for these projects, while providing for local parties to do so under state law, the Act takes the law on this point in divergent directions. The large national parties are limited in the funds available for their capital infrastructure, while much smaller local parties, with limited fields of operation, may, in many states, fund that infrastructure freely.

Other limitations on political parties
The Act is concerned with other activities of political parties, not only their soft money issue advertising. The restrictions imposed on these activities are generally intended to keep parties from operating as vehicles for circumvention of legal limits on contributions or other expenditures to influence elections. The various kinds of activities involved can be confusing to sort out, but they consist generally of

- "Independent expenditures" by parties which involve the express advocacy of a clearly identified candidate's election or defeat. This is different from "issue advertising," which does not include "express advocacy," but the practical differences for parties may be limited. The law on this issue is in flux.
- Independent expenditures by other political committees that are coordinated with parties.
- Other expenditures by political committees that are coordinated with parties—for example, expenditures for polling data, or for communications to the public on general political topics, or for voter registration or other voter contact activities.
- Coordination by parties with "outside groups" engaging in "issue advertising" or other forms of political action.

The Act intersects with the old law in various ways to limit the parties' actions in these various areas.

---

[54] FEC Advisory Opinions 2001-01 and 2002-12.

Party "independent" expenditures on behalf of their candidates

What is an "independent" expenditure? Party involvement in "independent expenditure" activity is one front in the reform war. An independent expenditure is one made by a political committee or individual to expressly advocate the candidate's election or defeat, but without the candidate's cooperation or consent, and not at her request or suggestion. There is no dollar limit on truly independent expenditures. The Supreme Court, as it worked through the metaphysics of its decision in *Buckley v. Valeo*,[55] concluded that if money was spent truly independently of a candidate, then limits were not needed to address the danger, associated with ordinary contributions, of an illicit bargain with the candidate—a trade of contributions for official action.

> *Furious is a committed activist with ample amounts of money who decides that he must do what is possible to end the political career of Senator Smith. Working from his basement apartment alone, and without contact with Smith's opponent, or any other agent of Smith's opponent, he places orders for and pays for $2 million in "independent expenditures" calling for the "end to Smith's disgraceful career as our Senator: Vote to Replace Smith on November 5." Furious may spend without limit (though he must report these expenditures to the Federal Election Commission under "independent expenditure" reporting requirements).*

Independent expenditures by political parties The Court also held in *Colorado Republican* that the parties, like individuals and other political committees, could make independent expenditures on behalf of their own candidates.[56] With these independent expenditures, the parties could escape the limits otherwise imposed on contributions made directly to their federal candidates, and "coordinated" expenditures made on their behalf. It appeared from the Court's rulings that parties could maintain independence from candidates for some purposes, and not for others. They might, for example, recruit candidates to run and train them, and offer them assistance along the way; but so long as they did not

---

[55] 424 U.S. 1 (1976).

[56] *FEC v. Colorado Republican Fed. Campaign Comm.*, 518 U.S. 604 (1996).

inform them or otherwise cooperate with them in planning and making a specific expenditure on their behalf, the expenditure was "independent" and the amount spent unlimited. The expenditure must be made from "hard" funds, and fully reported by the party.

A party recruits Congressional candidate Jackson. It meets with Jackson on her strategy for the race, helps her identify staff, and makes an early contribution to her campaign. In the general election, it becomes clear that Jackson is running into trouble, and needs more help than her campaign has funds to provide. The party, moreover, has little left under the limits for contributions to and coordinated expenditures on behalf of her campaign. So party officers meet without the knowledge of Jackson to plan a media campaign on her behalf, and fund it with $250,000 in "independent" expenditures. Jackson learns of the expenditures when the party's ads appear on the air, and its "independent" mail begins to arrive in mailboxes around the district. The party has made an "independent expenditure" and may spend freely in this way for Jackson without regard to the limit on contributions or party "coordinated" expenditures.

It is important to bear in mind how the Act has largely erased the once prominent distinction between an independent expenditure by a party and its "issue advertising." Under the old law, an "independent expenditure" must contain "express advocacy"—express advocacy of a clearly identified candidate's election or defeat—whereas an "issue ad" does not. The difference is between an appeal to "Throw Jones out" (independent expenditure) and "Call Jones and tell him that his bad votes on taxes are ruining our state"("issue ad"). Under the old law, the party running an issue ad of this kind could pay for it with both hard and soft money, while it must pay for an "independent expenditure" with hard money only. Under the new Act, both types of ads, if they refer to a clearly identified federal candidate, must be paid for with hard money. The only question is the one of coordination with the candidate: if the party has coordinated the ad with the candidate, then it must observe limits on how much it may pay for the ad under the law's "contribution" and "coordinated" spending limits.

Background: distinguishing "independent expenditures" from "issue ads"

An ad to the public states: "Congressman Jones lies like a rug. Call him and tell him to be honest for a change." This is not an independent expenditure. It is apparent that the ad sponsor dislikes Jones, but there is no mention in the ad of his election, or the wish of the sponsor, fairly inferred from the ad, that he lose it. A national or state party must pay for it with hard money. If the party had "coordinated" the ad with the candidate, then dollar limits on the amount spent for the ad would apply. If the party ran the ad without coordination with a candidate, then no limits would apply to its spending for the ad.

The ad is modified to read: "Congressman Jones lies like a rug. Call him and tell him that you think it is time to change the carpeting." The FEC has developed rules on "express advocacy"[57] which apply to an ad like this. After all, the agency reasons, who would not believe that the call to "change the carpeting," in an ad likening the candidate to a rug, is a call to remove him from office? The FEC has had limited success in persuading courts that this is "express advocacy": the Federal Circuit Court of Appeals for the Ninth Circuit agrees,[58] but other Circuits do not, and the Fourth Circuit has waged war on this view of the law.[59] The Supreme Court in McConnell concurred with the broader approach of the FEC, at least insofar as the question of "express advocacy" affected the decision on the constitutionality of the "electioneering communications" provisions. (See Chapter 2). Whether this decision suggests or ushers in a generally more flexible test for "express advocacy" remains to be seen.

The ad, modified once more, reads: "Congressman Jones lies like a rug. Call Congressman Jones and tell him to get out of town. And then, on November 5, make sure that he does." This is very likely express advocacy.

---

[57] 11 C.F.R. § 100.22.

[58] *FEC v. Furgatch,* 869 F.2d 1256 (9th Cir. 1989).

[59] *FEC v. Christian Action Network,* 92 F.3d 1178 (4th Cir. 1996).

Recognizing that parties may make independent expenditures, the Act's drafters were unhappy with the hybrid nature of the parties' relationship with their candidates—independent in some contexts, allowing for unlimited spending, while "coordinated" and subject to limits in other contexts. The Act therefore put parties to a choice as soon as their federal candidates had been nominated. A party could make coordinated expenditures for their general election nominee, or independent expenditures on her behalf, but not both. Moreover, the Act put this decision on the parties with some additional requirements intended to make it stick. It treated all committees of each party as a single committee for this purpose, and the FEC interpreted the law to enforce the choice made by any committee at any level within the political party structure, against all the other committees of the party. In addition, the Act provided that once a committee within the party structure decided to proceed with coordinated expenditures, it could not engage in certain transactions with another political party committee making (or intending to make) independent expenditures for the benefit of that candidate.

> **Trying to force parties to choose "independence"— the Court says "no"**

The *McConnell* Court, however, struck down the provision, holding that Congress could not condition or limit parties' exercise of their right to make independent expenditures. This was the only holding by the Court in the parties' favor, on the constitutional issues, and it affected hard, not soft, money activity.

It should be noted that the choice BCRA sought unsuccessfully to impose on parties left open another option for making a form of "independent" expenditure for candidates, even when the parties were also coordinating expenditures with that candidate. Parties may continue to finance "issue ads," albeit only with hard money. As noted, there is only one material difference between the issue ad and the independent expenditure: the presence or absence of "express advocacy." If an issue ad is not coordinated, no limits apply to monies spent to air it—just as there are no limits on independent expenditures. So a party might have elected to forego independence, and choose instead to make "coordinated" expenditures on behalf of its candidates, while also financing issue ads without limit for these same candidates' benefit. The issue ads would have to be paid for with hard money—but the same is true for any "independent expenditures" a party would finance.

Independent expenditures by national party committees on behalf of their presidential candidates

Since BCRA was enacted, the FEC has chosen by rule to clarify that national party committees could make "independent expenditures" on behalf of the party's Presidential nominees. This question had been left open by the *Colorado Republican* case.[60] Now under new FEC rules, a national party committee is barred by law from establishing independence from the Presidential candidate, only when the national committee is formally designated as the candidate's principal campaign committee. Yet the FEC has also suggested that national parties' success in establishing true "independence" in this context is unlikely. Generally, the interaction of the national committee and its Presidential candidate is so extensive that a claim of independence would be strained.

"Coordinated" party spending on behalf of its candidates

A party that coordinates an expenditure with a candidate or other person (like a political committee) is making a contribution to a candidate (or committee). Because the contribution is subject to dollar limitations, there is much at stake in the determination of whether a party expenditure is coordinated or independent.

An additional complication is that the FEC, pursuant to the command of Congress in BCRA, specifically defined "coordination" so that its more developed definition applies only to "public communications."[61] How "coordination" occurs when the object of the expenditure is other than a "public communication" is not

---

[60] *FEC v. Colorado Republican Fed. Campaign Comm.*, 518 U.S. 604 (1996).

[61] Congress directed the development of a new rule, having expressed some dissatisfaction with the pre-BCRA version.

clear. Any such expenditure, other than one for a public communication, is coordinated if "made in cooperation, consultation or concert with, or at the request or suggestion of," a candidate, the candidate's authorized committees or the candidate's "agents."

The coordination standard as it applies to party communications is much the same as that for outside groups planning communications while exchanging information or having contact with candidates.[62] This standard is also addressed at length in Chapter 2. For the immediate purpose here, a coordinated public communication is one that meets two tests: a "content" test and also a "conduct" test. Stated another way, it matters both what type of communication is involved, and then also how the communication was planned or developed.

Testing for coordination

The content of a communication subject to the coordination rules is one that

—contains express advocacy of a candidate's election or defeat;

—involves the republication or redistribution of a candidate's campaign materials; or

—qualifies as a "public communication," refers to a federal candidate, is directed to the candidate's electorate, and is distributed within 120 days of a primary or general election.

The "content" test

The conduct standard essentially looks to the role of the candidate in encouraging or developing the particular communication with the requisite content. To meet the conduct standard, the communication must have been

—created, produced or distributed at the request of the candidate or the candidate's agents;

—developed with the "material involvement" of the candidate, with specific attention to that involvement as it affected the content, intended audience, means of communication, choice of specific media outlet, or timing and frequency of the communication; or

—created, produced or distributed after "substantial discussion" with the candidate or the candidate's agents about the candidate's "plans, projects, activities,

The "conduct" test

---

[62] 11 C.F.R. §§ 109.37 and 109.21.

and needs," so long as the information conveyed is "material" to the development of the communication.

These "conduct" standards are concerned with contact between the candidate and the organization planning the public communication. The rules also consider the more indirect means by which this coordination may be accomplished. Coordination can occur through the use of common vendors, such as media consultants or pollsters, provided that in the course of concurrent services to the candidate and the organization, the common vendors convey material information about the candidate's "plans, projects, activities or needs." The potential effect of the use of common vendors is confined to concurrent services to the candidate and organization in the same election cycle. In addition, the rule also provides for a finding of coordination in certain circumstances, when a candidate's former employees or independent contractors come to provide service to the organization planning the communication. In this last instance, too, the rule does not consider prior employment or independent contracting relationships from the prior cycle, only the current cycle. As in other facets of the coordination rules, the triggering event is the conveyance of material information about the candidate's plans, projects, activities and needs.

Special liability rules for former employees and independent contractors

These indirect avenues to coordination can be traveled without the unfortunate candidate's knowledge or acquiescence. So what happens to the candidate if coordination is achieved through the carelessness or overt mischief of a common vendor or a former employee? Coordination can still occur, but in an odd twist, the contribution resulting from the coordination is deemed not "accepted" by the candidate. Should a party committee have made such a contribution as a result of coordination, then the party will have made an expenditure subject to the dollar limits that apply to party coordinated spending. The party may not have reported it, and the spending might also cause the party to exceed the applicable limit. The candidate, not having accepted the expenditure, does not share in the liability. The candidate does not enjoy this reprieve from liability if she or he had any substantial involvement in the expenditure, such as through the type of "substantial discussion" or "material involvement" described previously.

Finally, the rule recognizes that candidates do communicate with organizations about their positions on issues and their policies. A "response" by the candidate "to an inquiry about the candidate's positions on legislative or policy issues" does not, alone, create the conduct that serves as one of the predicates of liability under the rule.

A state party concludes that a Senate candidate, Lou Serr, could benefit from research into an opponent's record on federal regulation of salmon spread. The party purchases the research and donates it to the candidate. This is a contribution-in kind and not subject to the coordination rules discussed above, because the purchase of the research is not a "public communication."

The party, having purchased the research, finances an ad in the last two weeks of the election that promotes Lou Serr's position on the salmon spread issue and derogates that of his opponent, Winn Forshore. The ad meets the "content" test because it is a public communication that names a federal candidate in an ad directed toward the candidate's electorate within 120 days of an election. But it is not a coordinated communication, failing to satisfy the "conduct" test because Lou Serr had no role in the decision to run the ad or any aspect of developing or distributing it.

Now pretend that this last development never happened, and that instead, Lou Serr approaches the party and advises it of his view that the salmon spread issue was developing into a major issue in the campaign and a major tactical opportunity for his candidacy. He would like to run an ad on this issue, but he has run out of money. The party reassures him that it will run the ad—but the conversation is general, oblique, and in the view of all, cleverly unincriminating. Both the content and conduct tests have been satisfied, and a coordinated expenditure has been born.

Other "independent spending" issues

The Act seeks to tighten the requirements of true independence for "independent expenditures" by individuals and political committees. It provides that they are **No independence if a party is involved** not independent from candidates if they "coordinate" their spending with the candidate's political party.[63] Pre-BCRA law addressed only "coordination" with "any candidate, or any authorized committee or agent of such candidate." The Act brings parties explicitly into the picture, making clear that an expenditure cannot be independent if made "in concert or cooperation with or at the request or suggestion of…a political party committee or its agents." The drafters of the Act were apparently concerned to leave no ambiguity hovering over this point, and so it introduced parties directly into the definition.

Wealthy Wilson discusses Jones' candidacy with his State Chair, and the two note that Jones is running low on television ad money, while his opponent is spending to beat the band. The Chair suggests to Wilson that he consider running ads of his own lauding Jones' sponsorship of federally funded pigeon waste disposal in public parks, and calling for his election. Wilson funds those ads. Under the Act, the expenditure would not be independent.

But is this right? If one assumes that Jones is not privy to this discussion between the party Chair and Wilson, then the result wrought by the Act is a harsh one indeed. Jones is assumed to have received a contribution he did not request, as a result of a conversation that he did not authorize. The Act is more reasonably read to attribute Wilson's contribution to the party, not Jones. The unfairness is all the greater if the discussion between Wilson and the party Chair is less explicit than presented in the hypothetical. The Chair may note that Jones is running out of money, and he might also supply Wilson with a copy of the law governing the "independence" of expenditures under the Act. But he may never actually invite the expenditure. What then? Time and litigation may answer the question.

It is emphasized that these rules apply also to coordination with nonparty political committees. The law provides that expenditures—monies spent to influence the outcome of elections—will constitute contributions to candidates if made at their request or suggestion, or

---

[63] BCRA § 211; 2 U.S.C. § 431(17).

if made in cooperation, consultation, or concert with them. So if candidate Jones coordinates an expenditure with a political committee, in the hope, of course, that it will aid her candidacy, the expenditure when made would be treated as a contribution from the political committee to Jones.

The term "political committee" means a committee that makes "contributions" and "expenditures" within the meaning of the old law. Such a committee is registered with the FEC, discloses its finances, and complies with limits on what it receives and donates to candidates.

Candidate Jones approaches a political committee and proposes that it fund a mailing to residents of his district which would call into question the performance of Incumbent Gomes on budget policy. The law would suggest that any further expenditures made on this suggestion would result in a "contribution" from the committee to Jones. The committee, a multicandidate committee, may only make a contribution to Jones of $5,000 per election, and any such contribution must be reported.[64]

Political parties typically communicate with other political committees about the prospects and mutual support of candidates. The Act provides that should a political party committee enlist the aid of such a committee in its projects—that is, should the party coordinate with the political committee in making an expenditure—the expenditure will be treated as a contribution to the party under the federal law.[65]

Parties "coordinating" their spending with political committees

So in the last example, Jones might not make the request to the political committee, but instead a committee of his political party might choose to do so. In that event, a contribution would still occur, but it would be a contribution to the party, not to Jones. The limits that apply are the limits on contributions from the political committee to the party; and the dollar amount of those limits depend on whether the party

---

[64] 2 U.S.C. § 441a(7)(B)(i).

[65] BCRA § 214; 2 U.S.C. § 441a(7)(B)(ii).

involved is a national, state or local committee. Thus a political committee that is a multicandidate committee under existing law may contribute $15,000 per calendar year to a national party committee, and $5,000 per calendar year to a state political party committee.[66] These limits, if invoked by way of a finding of "coordination," may place real limits on communications and common action between and among the parties and all kinds of other political committees.

Party coordination with outside groups
The Act also takes up a large cause of recent years, that of the activities of outside groups—527s, or corporations, or tax-exempts—that benefit a candidate or party and may have been in some fashion "coordinated" with them. These groups are not political committees registered with the FEC and reporting under existing law. But they may produce voter guides, or "issue advertising," or other communications that plainly concern candidates and elections but are not treated as statutory campaign-related "expenditures." They may also propose these activities to candidates, or inform them of the activities; and the communications with the candidates may cover the content of the communications and the way they will be distributed. The coordination rules, as they apply to "public communications" by parties, apply also to such communications by outside groups coordinated with either 1) candidates, or 2) parties. A full discussion of these rules appears in Chapter 2 ("Outside Groups").

Coordinating "electioneering communications" with parties The Act also addresses coordination between parties and other outside groups in the making of "electioneering communications." In simplest terms, but as will be discussed at length in the following section, an "electioneering communication" is one that refers to a federal candidate and is broadcast to a candidate's electorate within 30 days of a primary or 60 days of the general election. This is "issue advertising" funded by 527s, corporations, tax-exempts or unions. The Act specifically provides that the "coordination" of these communications with parties will convert them into contributions

---

[66] These contribution limits are not changed under the Act.

to those parties.[67] Of course, such a contribution is illegal, which is the point of the provision: to prohibit this coordination with a party committee.

Very Bad Corporation funds an "issue ad" which states "Senator Jones is a bonehead. Call him and tell him that he's a dummy." The ad is run on cable in the Senator's state 45 days before the general election. It is an electioneering communication, and then the question is whether, in a meeting a day before the ad run, the corporation's lobbyist discussed the ad with the party affiliated with Jones' opponent. If the discussion produces coordination under Commission rules, then the electioneering communication by Very Bad is also an illegal contribution to the party with which the ad was coordinated.

Conclusion

All told, the Act administers a considerable beating to the parties' fundraising practices. Perhaps the parties may derive some comfort from the truth that this was not an accidental feature of the Act, but instead its primary purpose. At least, then, the Act does what those who wrote it intended for it to do. Their goal was to prohibit in some cases—those of the national parties— the raising and spending of soft money, and to severely limit this activity in other cases, namely, those of the state and local parties. Along the way, in the interest of tightening this soft money ban and guarding against loopholes, the Act places associated restrictions on fundraising and other actions of federal candidates and officeholders, party officers, and "agents" of parties.

A note on the background of legal restrictions on parties and their soft money

The very possibility of party "soft money," in theory, arises from the varied activities of political parties in supporting candidates at all levels of government— federal, state, and local. Federal law does not permit parties to spend certain kinds of monies, such as corporate monies, to support federal candidates, but state and local laws control the monies spent to support

"Hard" money for federal candidates... "soft" for the others

---

[67] BCRA § 202; 2 U.S.C. § 441a(7)(C).

state and local candidates. A number of states allow monies for state and local races that would be disallowed by federal law for federal races,[68] and impose different limits on contributions to candidates and parties than the ones in federal law. Parties, therefore, operate under different sets of laws for different activities, depending on where in the political process—federal, state, or local—they take place.

As a result, relatively early in the life of the "Watergate" reforms of the 1970s, parties established different accounts for these different activities. Federal accounts held the monies needed and allowed for federal races, while nonfederal accounts held the funds that state and local laws permitted for the support of state and local candidates. The operation of these different accounts was not controversial as long as parties simply contributed monies from these accounts directly to candidates. Controversy flamed into view as parties paid for "mixed activities"—activities that by their nature affected candidates throughout the ballot. A simple example: voter registration, which results in voters who, once registered, will cast a ballot up and down the ticket for federal, as well as state and local, candidates. Which monies in which accounts could be used?

FEC "allocation" rules The FEC concluded that parties could pay for these expenses out of each of their accounts, in some "mix" or predetermined portion. That portion was generally determined by the composition of the ballot for a particular election, and specifically by the relative number of federal and nonfederal candidates. If federal candidates made up 25% of the number of candidates on the state ballot, then the state party would have to finance 25% of the costs of "mixed" activity, like voter registration, with federal or "hard funds" subject to federal law limits. The balance of 75% could be paid with funds held in state and local accounts—with "soft money."

Critics concluded that these "allocation rules" allowed for "soft money" to underwrite too large a share

---

[68] For example, 29 states authorize corporate contributions to state and local candidates. States like Texas, Pennsylvania, and Illinois allow individuals to contribute substantially more to state and local candidates than they may contribute under federal law to federal candidates.

of the costs of these activities. State and local races outnumber federal ones, and so the percentage of the cost assigned to them will generally be higher—far higher—than that assigned to the federal races. Yet, the critics claimed, federal and state races should not be weighed on the same scale, that is, treated as equivalent. In their view, a race for the U.S. Senate mattered more than a race for county council, and so the decision to weight them the same in any formula simply allowed more "soft money" to seep into the parties' financing of federal races.

The critics sued, as critics often do, and a court agreed that the FEC had not adequately thought through how to handle the financing of these mixed activities.[69] The FEC was ordered to produce new rules, and after some time, it did. Under these new rules, federal races and others were not weighted the same, with the result, that while parties could still pay for "mixed activities" with both federal and nonfederal funds, the share paid from federal funds had to be higher than before. In addition to the assumption that federal offices counted more than others, it was assumed also that national parties, those directed at the federal level, cared less about state and local than they did about federal races. The rules established for these national parties fixed minimum percentages for the federal share of certain mixed activities—60% or 65%, depending on whether the committee was the national committee of the party or one of its congressional campaign committees, and whether the spending occurred in a presidential or nonpresidential year. Those rules were still more complicated, requiring a different approach to the financing of different mixed activities, such as "administrative," "fundraising," and "generic" party activities.

These rules were promulgated in 1991, but they did not quiet the critics for long. By 1995, the FEC had addressed the requirements for what has come to be known as "issue advertising." This advertising by parties and others lauds or attacks a federal candidate, or an officeholder who is a candidate, for a position on

Court to FEC: "Not good enough"

The advent of issue advertising

---

[69] *Common Cause v. FEC,* 692 F. Supp. 1391 (D.D.C. 1987).

an issue. These ads typically urge the viewers to call those officeholders to praise them or invite them to burn in hell. A telephone number typically, but not always, appears on the screen to facilitate the proposed contact with the named candidate-officeholder. What does not appear in the ad are words exhibiting a clear-cut intention to affect the outcome of an election—words like "vote," "defeat," "support," or "don't you wish that you would never see or hear from him again?" The FEC dutifully suggested that this could be an "administrative" expense of the party, payable on a "mixed" basis from both hard and soft money accounts.[70] Of course, only federal candidates or officeholders would generally appear in these ads, but the premise of the FEC's ruling was that the purpose of the ad was to influence opinion and action on issues, not elections.

A world gone mad... The unhappy critics of the early 1990s became the reform warriors of the late 1990s. To them, this latest development demonstrated that the election laws as envisioned in 1974 had collapsed. They believed that parties, on the thinnest of excuses, were spending soft money liberally for attack ads with the clear effect and the probable intent of influencing federal campaigns. Some of these kinds of ads appeared on the air, and others in the mail; but they appeared on the wings of some millions of dollars. "Special interests"—never clearly defined but meant to include anyone organized and well funded for political activity—provided the funds directly to federal candidates and officeholders who collected them for the parties. The sin lay in both directions—in the raising of the money by candidates and officeholders, and in the spending of the money by the parties to help them. If the old law had prohibited corporate and labor contributions to candidates, and also unlimited individual donations, what could explain the millions in this kind of money flowing through the parties—if not a breakdown in the law?

Outside groups joined the fray, first challenging the parties for dominance of the airwaves, then receding somewhat and focusing their "soft money" initiatives on

---

[70] 8 FEC Advisory Opinion 1995-25.

mailings and door-to-door mobilization of voters.[71] Republicans, generally suspicious of government interference in campaign finance, developed religion on the subject as they attacked the use of party soft money in supporting President Clinton's 1996 presidential re-election campaign.[72] Democrats pointed to the same use of soft money in the same presidential election year by the Republican nominee Robert Dole, but actively supported legislative reform.

Critics demanded legislation, but they also attempted litigation. The FEC, too, was drawn into the fight by the claims and counterclaims of the parties as each protested that their issue ads were legal while the other's were not.[73] All of these battles were fought to a stalemate. Only legislation remained to address the problem.

---

[71] David B. Magleby, ed., *Outside Money: Soft Money and Issue Advocacy in 1998 Congressional Elections* (2000).

[72] Investigation of Illegal or Improper Activities in Connection with 1996 Federal Election Campaigns, Final Report of the Comm. on Gov't Affairs, S. Rep. No. 105-167 (1998).

[73] Report of the Audit Division on Clinton/Gore '96 General Committee, Inc. and Clinton/Gore '96 General Election Legal and Accounting Compliance Fund; Report of the Audit Division on the Dole/Kemp '96 and Dole/Kemp Compliance Committee, Inc. (General).

Different Types of Political Actors: Different Legal Requirements [1]

	Reg. as "Political Committee" and Reporting to FEC	Limits on Contributions Received	Prohibitions on "Soft Money"	Reporting of Soft Money Activity to FEC
National Party Committees	YES	YES	YES	N/A – cannot accept any
State & Local Party Committees	YES – if active in federal elections	YES – under federal & state law	YES – for "Federal election activity"	YES
"527s"	NO – unless contributes to federal candidates or engages in "express advocacy"	NO – Unless contributes to federal candidates or engages in "express advocacy"	NO – except if incorporated, cannot make broadcast "electioneering communications"	YES – for broadcast "electioneering communications"
Tax-Exempts (501)(c)(4)s	NO	NO	NO – except if incorporated and making broadcast "electioneering communications"	YES – for broadcast "electioneering communications"
Federal Candidates Committees	YES	YES	YES	N/A – cannot accept any
State Candidate Committees	NO	YES – if imposed by state law	NO – except if engaged in certain "Federal election activity"	NO – but under state law
Corporations and Unions	NO – but their PACs might	NO – except their PACs	NO – except for broadcast "electioneering communications"	YES – for broadcast "electioneering communications"
Federally Registered Political Committees or PACs	YES	YES – under federal and state laws	Must allocate hard & soft money for get-out-the-vote & other activity under FEC rules	YES – under state laws and FEC rules

[1] General rules: there are always exceptions.

CHAPTER 2

OUTSIDE GROUPS

Issue ads and other such activities funded by "soft money" are not the sole province of parties, but also the handiwork of outside groups. These groups, including so-called "527s," but also corporations, unions and trade associations, seek to avoid activities prohibited by the law or regulated by the FEC—those conducted with "express advocacy" or coordinated with candidates. The field of activities open to them is still wide. Their soft-money funded communications may include on-the-air ads, but also phones, mail and even door-to-door advocacy on "issues" that may have a direct impact on voter choice in elections.[74]

The Act reflects a long-standing debate about the scope of permissible constitutional restraints on "outside group" political activity. Until the Supreme Courts decision in *McConnell*, the courts have shown a concern with the regulation of outside groups acting on their own and without express advocacy in funding "issue-related" communications. They have in general responded positively to the claim that these groups are engaged in speech, even if it is a form of speech effective in influencing collaterally the judgment of voters.[75] This position influenced the development of the Act. Its approach to the limitation of the soft money activities of these groups is, accordingly, narrow and hedged with qualifications of one kind or another. The approach is therefore also complicated.

"Coordinated" communications
An expenditure "coordinated" by an outside group with a candidate or party is a "contribution" to that candidate or party. This would be a problem generally for all concerned because, for example, corporations or unions cannot make contributions to federal candidates or to

---

[74] Magleby, *supra*, note 9.

[75] *FEC v. Central Long Island Tax Reform Immediately Comm.*, 616 F.2d 45 (2d Cir. 1980); *FEC v. Christian Action Network*, 92 F.3d 1178 (4th Cir. 1996); *Maine Right to Life Comm. v. FEC*, 98 F.3d 1 (1st Cir. 1996), *cert. denied*, 118 S.Ct. 52 (1997).

parties for federal election-related purposes. So if a corporation finances an ad complimenting a candidate on "a job well done," and the communication is "coordinated" with the candidate within the meaning of the FEC rules, the ad is, in a word, illegal.

The FEC had tried its hand at one rulemaking on coordination, fashioning a rule out of the body of a district court decision that grappled with this issue.[76] Congress, dissatisfied, directed the agency to try again.

The result is a new rule that is complicated in nature, but that in the main, is marked by three broad concerns. First, the rule is concerned with the coordination of "public communications," which means any

> Communication by means of any broadcast, cable or satellite communication, newspaper, magazine, outdoor advertising facility, mass mailing or telephone bank to the general public, or any other form of public political advertising.[77]

It should be noted that the rule specifically exempts "communications over the Internet." But of particular significance are those communications included within the rule: mail and telephone banks, which become public communications when more than 500 pieces of mail, or more than 500 calls, substantially similar in nature, are issued or placed within any 30-day period. This is a key difference between the public communications under the coordinated communication rule, and those communications deemed "electioneering communications" under the new law. The former include mail and phone communications, along with everybody's old favorite, broadcast ads; while the latter include only broadcast advertising.

Second, the presence or absence of express advocacy—the actual urging of a candidate's election or defeat—does not control the legal treatment of the communication. And third, the timing of the communication is a highly relevant consideration—and in some instances, decisive.

---

[76] *FEC v. Christian Coalition,* 52 F. Supp.2d 45 (D.D.C. 1999).

[77] 11 C.F.R. § 100.26.

As noted in the discussion of coordination by parties, a finding of legal coordination rests on three tests—1) a communication paid by some entity other than the candidate's committee; 2) a content test and 3) a conduct test. Much of the ground has been covered in the discussion of party coordinated communications. Moreover, there is little to be said about the first prong—that some organization other than the candidate's committee pay for the communication. But the essential tests—those involving "content" and "conduct"— bear repetition and elaboration.

The content test is one that looks to the nature of the **The "content"** communication: to the question of what it contains and **test** also when it is broadcast and distributed. The feature tying all of the covered types of content together is that they are all "reasonably related to an election."[78] An obvious example is a communication that contains "express advocacy" of a candidate's election or defeat. Another is a group's republication and redistribution of a candidate's previously published campaign materials. A third, discussed in the next section, is the "electioneering communication," which is a broadcast advertisement naming a federal candidate, and directed to her electorate, within 30 days of a primary election or 60 days of a general. The thread tying together these types of ads is some "reasonable relationship" to an election.[79]

The most novel approach adopted by the FEC in defining "content" is one that turns on both a reference to a federal candidate and on the timing of an ad. Hence a "public communication" that meets the content test is one that

—refers to a clearly identified federal candidate;

—is directed to the electorate of the candidate; and

—is publicly distributed or disseminated 120 days or fewer before an election.

It must be borne in mind that a communication meeting this definition is not "coordinated" under the rule unless it also satisfies the "conduct" test. But if it does, the rule suggests that a sponsor may coordinate every aspect of a television ad with a candidate, so long

---

[78] 68 Fed. Reg. 421, 427 (Jan. 3, 2003).

[79] *Id.* at 427.

as it is run more than four months—120 days—before an election. Indeed the Commission said as much when it explained the rules. "In effect, the [120 day rule] operates as a 'safe harbor,' in that communications that are publicly disseminated or distributed more than 120 days before the primary or general election will not be deemed to be 'coordinated' under this particular standard under any circumstances."[80] One outstanding question about the application of the 120 day rule is whether the window opens only with the advent of an election in which the named candidate is running—or does it open in advance of any federal election, whether the candidate is running or not? If Iowa's Presidential caucuses are in February and its Senate primary is in June, does the 120 day window open for the Senate candidate in October of the odd-numbered year? The rule does not say but Commission commentary strongly suggests that the 120 day rule applies only to an election in which the candidate is running.

The "conduct" test So much for the "content" portion of the test, and on to "the conduct" part. A request or suggestion by the candidate will meet this test. The candidate need not initiate the request; she may simply assent to the suggestion of the organization that proposes and eventually makes the communication. At the same time, the candidate may direct a suggestion to the public at large, advising the media that "I desperately need radio in the youth market," and avoid qualified "conduct." The FEC has offered the contrasting example of a "request posted…via electronic mail directly to a discrete group of recipients."[81]

"Material involvement" The candidate will also have satisfied the test with "material involvement" in decisions about content, intended audience, means or mode of communication, specific media outlet used, timing or frequency of the communication, or the size, prominence or duration of the communication. Under the old, now superseded rule, "material involvement," such as the delivery of polling results to the organization, may not have been enough to support a finding of coordination. Some substantial discussion would have been required. While, as noted

---

[80] *Id.* at 430, n. 3.

[81] *Id.* at 432.

below, a "substantial discussion" standard has been retained under the new rules, a separate test of "material involvement," not dependent on discussion or any other "interactive exchange,"[82] can also support a finding of coordination. The FEC has suggested that an involvement is material if it reflects in any way the "importance, degree of necessity, influence or the effect of involvement by the candidate or party."[83] This does not mean that the involvement was the deciding factor in—or the cause of—any public communication. The question is whether the involvement could be said to have had some significant effect or influence over the communication's planning, content or distribution.

The Commission has offered a hypothetical that illustrates this aspect of the rule. It is worth restating in full. Because it is long, the segment has been separated out into paragraphs for improved readability:

Candidate A reads in the newspaper that the Payor Group is planning an advertisement campaign urging voters to support Candidate A. Candidate A faxes over her own ad buying schedule to Payor Group, hoping that Payor Group will plan its own ad buying schedule around Candidate A's schedule to maximize the effect of both ad campaigns. The Payor Group subsequently runs ads that are all on NBC and ABC during the 6:00 news hour and during the most expensive weekday timeslot on NBC, whereas Candidate A's ads are run on CBS during the 6:00 news hour and during the most expensive time slot on CBS. When asked, Payor Group acknowledges that it received the fax from Candidate A, but says only that its plans for the timing of the campaign were in flux at the time they received the fax.

The analysis under the "materially involved" conduct standard focuses on whether the fax constituted material involvement by the candidate in a decision regarding the timing of the Payor Group communications. Significant facts might include that the Payor Group changed its previously planned schedule, or that Payor Group had not yet made plans and had factored in the fax in its decision to choose CBS and the same time slot, or show in some other way that the fax was

---

[82] *Id.* at 433.

[83] *Id.*

"important; more or less necessary, having influence or effect, [or] going to the merits" with respect to the Payor Group's decisions about the timing of its ads. The transmission and receipt of the fax in combination with the correlation of the two ad campaigns gives rise to a reasonable inference that Candidate A's involvement was material to the Payor Group's decision regarding the timing of its ad campaign.

If, on the other hand, the example is changed so that the Payor Group's ads run on the same channel right after the candidate's ads in a way that lessens the effect of both ad campaigns, it may be appropriate to conclude that Candidate A's involvement was not material to the Payor Group's decision regarding the timing of its ad campaign. In other words, the degree to which the communications overlapped or did not overlap is one indication of whether Candidate A's involvement was material to the timing of the Payor Group communications.

So in other words, one way to show that the information provided was not "material," is to establish that the public communication was stupidly planned or made. Coordination is disproved by foolishness, or by unhappy results.

Talking too much   Still the rule retains some notion of "substantial discussion" as one way that a candidate might coordinate with an organization the making of a public communication. The difference between the new and old rule is that the former requires that a substantial discussion involve a specific exchange of information about the candidate's plans, projects, activities and needs, and also that the information so conveyed be material to the creation, production or distribution of the communications. In other words, the information conveyed must matter to the making of the communication. Here we have some fairly inscrutable legal language from the Commission rules: "The substantiality of the discussion is measured by the materiality of the information conveyed...."[84]

A member of the staff of Jackson's campaign meets with an organization that would like to support Jackson in any

---

[84] *Id.* at 434-435.

way it can. The staff members relates that the principal difficulty facing the campaign is that Jackson and his spouse are endlessly bickering about the spouse's schedule, and that Jackson sets out each day on the campaign trail in a bad mood. His performances are suffering as a result, and the staff is attempting to persuade the candidate to arrange for the spouse to take a vacation for both their benefits. The organization then proceeds to run an advertisement, qualifying as a "public communication", touting the candidate's position on the environment. This communication has not been coordinated, for the information conveyed may well have included sensitive information about the state of the campaign, and even the state of mind of the candidate, but it is hardly material to the ad prepared and run by the organization.

The discussion of parties made note of the potential significance of common vendors, shared by the candidate and the spending organization, in analyzing the occurrence of "coordination." Three conditions determine whether coordination could result from the use of common vendors: **Caveat emptor**

—The vendor must be one whose services under the terms of the rule would support a finding of coordination. A shared plumber in the common sense of the term (not in the Nixon White House sense) would not present a problem under the rule. Yet consultants who provide or receive significant strategic information in the course of providing services would, if working for both candidate and organization, present all concerned with a threat of a finding of coordination. The key and common examples are pollsters, fundraisers, media consultants, general political consultants, time-buyers, mail consultants.

—The services must have been provided in the same election cycle. A candidate's pollster can bolt in the following cycle to an organization dedicated to making public communications, but the pollster, working for the organization and the candidate in different cycles, is not a "common vendor" under the rule.

—The vendor must have conveyed material information about the candidate's plans, projects, activities and needs to the spending organization. The mere sharing of the vendor is not enough; the inquiry for purposes of the rule is the information provided by the vendor to the organization.

Vendors naturally have expressed an interest in the permissibility of Chinese Walls—some arrangement by which the personnel involved with the candidate have no contact with the personnel who work with the organization. The Commission did not dismiss the possibility, but it also did not embrace it. It stated: "The Commission does not agree that the mere existence of a confidentiality agreement or ethical screen should provide a *de facto* bar to the enforcement of the limits...Without some mechanism to ensure enforcement, these private arrangements are unlikely to prevent circumvention of the rules."[85] So it depends, it appears, on whether the Wall is a true wall, built sturdily and regularly inspected for cracks.

"But she used to work for you ..." Former employees or independent contractors also present some challenges under the rules. The rule once again is concerned only with the case of former employees or independent contractors who, having worked for the candidate, wind up on the payroll of the organization in the same election cycle. Moreover, it is not enough that they do appear on the payroll of the latter, having worked in the same cycle for the former: material information must pass to the organization planning or developing a public communication. It is worth noting that liability does not depend on the former employee acting as an "agent" for his former candidate-employer, under the former employer's continuing control. The rule looks to the information carried by the employee from his former position: its materiality, and its "use and conveyance," in the fashioning of the public communication for the benefit of the candidate.

Congress made clear in its directive to the agency to develop new coordination rules, that it would not countenance any rule requiring formal agreement or collaboration as a condition of "coordination." So none of the elements of coordination specified by the rule require or depend upon any such agreement. This means, among

---

[85] *Id.* at 437.

other things, that parties to illegal coordination can stumble into it, rather than have plotted actively to sneak around the federal campaign finance laws. They need not have "planned or systematically approved or executed the plan";[86] nor need there even be a "mutual understanding or meeting of the minds."[87] The Court in *McConnell* considered a challenge to this aspect of the law—insofar as it eliminated a formal agreement as a legal condition for finding coordination—but the Court upheld the law.

Franklin the Pollster works with both a candidate and the National Association for the Promotion of White Teeth, for which he provides general public relations consulting. In the course of a meeting with executives of the Association, Franklin chats informally about the Senate races that year and the chances of the party with which he is associated to win the Senate. Asked specifically about his candidate-client, Franklin expresses some concern about the race, noting that in his polling, the candidate is losing ground on national security issues. He thinks nothing of it. The Association, however, goes on the air within one month of the election with an ad lauding the candidate for his stand on national security. The expenditure appears to have been "coordinated."

"Electioneering communications"

The Act proposes to impose certain disclosure requirements, but also some outright prohibitions, on "electioneering communications" by outside groups. The Act defines the term, and it makes clear that this is a special form of communication—made in a certain way, with a certain content, and directed toward a particular audience. The complete statutory definition:

> (i) The term "electioneering communication" means any broadcast, cable, or satellite communication which
> (I) refers to a clearly identified candidate for Federal office;

Electioneering communication defined

---

[86] *Id.* at 440.

[87] *Id.*

> (II) is made within-
>> (aa) 60 days before a general, special, or runoff election for the office sought by the candidate; or
>> (bb) 30 days before a primary or preference election, or a convention or caucus of a political party that has authority to nominate a candidate, for the office sought by the candidate; and
> (III) in the case of a communication which refers to a candidate for an office other than President or Vice President, is targeted to the relevant electorate.[88]

These types of communications are subject to two different requirements. First, as a general matter, they are reportable, regardless of which type of organization finances them (with the exception of political committees, as discussed further below). When financed by a corporation or a union—or with the funds supplied by a corporation or a union—electioneering communications may not be "made"—meaning, publicly distributed—within 30 days of a primary election or 60 days of a general.

Sponsors of the Act made two principal arguments in support of these restrictions aimed at "electioneering communications" or "issue advertising." First, they argued that the prohibition on corporate and union "electioneering communications" has "a basis in law extending back to 1907," when Congress imposed the standing prohibition on corporate spending in federal elections.[89] Second, they argued that these issue ads had a clear connection to federal elections: they pointed to the frequency of such ads immediately before elections and to studies purporting to show that viewers interpreted these ads as intended to influence elections. Hence the argument is one of both purpose and effect: the timing and frequency of ads demonstrates their election-influencing purpose while the reaction of viewers

---

[88] 2 U.S.C. § 434(f)(3)(A).

[89] 147 Cong. Rec. S3034 (daily ed. Mar. 28, 2001) (statement of Sen. Snowe).

establishes their election-influencing effect. Because the ads "are ultimately engulfing the political process," indeed "having a greater impact than the ads the candidates run themselves,"[90] the sponsors believed that the prohibitions and disclosure requirements are necessary to the enforcement of the campaign finance laws. The Congress compelled disclosure of these ads in all instances and prohibited them in others where corporate and union funds were involved.

The definition of "electioneering communication" does not include any particular content—other than that the ad "refer" to a "clearly identified candidate for federal office." The reference may be visual, or by name. The FEC rules provide that the reference need not be explicit: any unambiguous reference will do, such as references to "Your Congressman," or "the incumbent." There is, however, only three modes of communication affected by the provision—"broadcast, cable, or satellite communication." The restrictions attached to these "electioneering communications" do not apply, therefore, to a host of communications, such as those effected through the mails, the Internet or the phones. Yet the restrictions do apply to the full range of broadcast communications. The FEC specifically declined to exempt by rule Low Power FM Radio, Low Power Television, or Citizens Band Radio.

Broadcast communications only

In this respect, electioneering communications are more narrow in scope than the public communications at the heart of the rule governing "coordination." The effective time period for these restrictions and prohibitions has been narrowed to 30 days prior to a primary and 60 days prior to the general, on the theory or assumption that ads of this kind "close" to an election have the undeniable purpose to influence the voters, and certainly that effect. Under the Act, a communication is targeted to the relevant electorate if it is received by 50,000 or more persons in the state or Congressional district of the candidate "referred to."

There are additional issues of interest in the FEC's development of the rule since the enactment of

---

[90] *Id.*

the statute. The statute defines an electioneering communication as one that is "made" with a certain content and within a specified period of time. The FEC, however, noted that the term "public distribution" better captured Congress' purpose: in the Commission's words, "the operative event is the dissemination of the communication, rather than the disbursement of the funds."[91] The FEC also concluded that the distribution in question was distribution for a fee. It assumed, no doubt rightly, that broadcasters would not soon escape the inclination to charge organizations for airing their political or public policy advertisements.

Targeted communications   In determining for purposes of the definition whether a communication can be "received" by 50,000 or more in a Congressional district, the question is the number of potential viewers or listeners, not the actual number who tune in. The Commission noted but could not solve another related problem of so-called "adjoining markets." An organization might direct an ad to a Congressional district or state in one media market, where no election is pending, but the broadcast market might include at least 50,000 potential viewers in an adjacent state or district where there is such a primary on the horizon. The communication is still an "electioneering communication," the FEC concluded, and this is not because the result is a sound or good one, but instead because the language of the statute leaves no other choice. In somewhat the same vein, it also does not matter that the candidate running in the state or district, also named in the ad, has no opposition. The reference to the candidate is still sufficient to create the electioneering communication.

The FEC also struggled with the difficulties presented by Presidential primaries. There is no "target" electorate, and hence no related requirement under the law. Yet the problem presented is that an ad naming a Presidential candidate could be directed to a state that already held its primary, or would not do so for months, but could somehow be considered an electioneering communication because it is run within 30 days of a primary in some other state altogether.

---

[91] 67 Fed. Reg. 65,191 (Oct. 23, 2002).

"Such a sweeping impact on communications," the FEC declared, "would be insufficiently linked to pending primary elections, may not have been contemplated by Congress, and could raise constitutional concerns."[92] The FEC chose the common sense route of finding that the provision did not apply unless 1) the ad could be received by 50,000 or more people in a state with a primary within 30 days, or 2) it could be received by 50,000 or more people nationwide—anywhere in the country—30 days before the first day of the national nominating convention and during the period of the convention. The FEC will publish on its website for each state and for each political party, the triggering event, such as a caucus or primary, for the application of the 30-day electioneering communication ban.

The law clearly applies to electioneering communications financed by a corporation or union, but also by another entity drawing on corporate or union funds. The Commission did conclude, however, that so-called "MCFL" corporations could not be subject to the prohibition. Those corporations, recognized by the Supreme Court and then by FEC rules, are organized for ideological purposes and do not accept corporate or union funds.[93]

"MCFL" exception

The FEC also considered the circumstances in which the corporation or union might be liable for another entity's decision to fund a communication with funds supplied by either. The rule adopted by the agency provides for liability when the corporation or union "knows, has reason to know, or willfully blinds itself to the fact that the person to whom the funds are given, disbursed, donated, or otherwise provided, intended to use them to pay for an electioneering communication."[94] Willful blindness for this purpose may be found where the corporation or union becomes aware of facts that should have led any reasonable person to inquire about the intent of the person receiving the funds for their use, but elects not to inquire.

---

[92] 67 Fed. Reg. 65,193 (Oct. 23, 2002).

[93] *FEC v. Massachusetts Citizens for Life,* 479 U.S. 238 (1986); 11 C.F.R. § 114.10.

[94] 11 C.F.R. § 114.4(a)(2).

What is not an "electioneering communication"?

The law provides for some exclusions, ruling out the Internet as an "electioneering communication," along with news stories, commentaries and editorials. Political committees making statutory "expenditures"—payments for the purpose of influencing a federal election—are not required to report them as electioneering communications, provided that the committees making them are registered political committees that are required to report them otherwise to the FEC.

The FEC, however, concluded that additional exemptions were necessary to protect spending that nominally might fall within the applicable definition, but that would not be properly treated as an "electioneering communication." One such exemption was necessary to harmonize the electioneering communication provision with the allowance for state and local candidates to run ads referring to a federal candidate so long as they did not "promote, support, attack or oppose" that candidate. Since under the laws of some states, such candidates might well lawfully use corporate or union funds for such ads, the FEC has determined to exempt them from possible prohibition as "electioneering communications."

A similar effort to reconcile seemingly conflicting statutory enactments lay at the root of the Commission's exemption of advertisements by 501(c)(3) organizations. These organizations are prohibited from intervention in any political campaigns by the terms of their exemptions. The Commission concluded that ads by these organizations, if operating in accordance with the conditions of their exemption, should not be treated as election-related—that is, as electioneering communications. Incorporated state candidate and party committees that are not "political committees" registered and reporting under federal law are also removed from the types of organizations that must comply with the restrictions on "electioneering communications."

Of equal interest, however, were the FEC's decisions declining to create exemptions for certain types of advertising that could be treated as "electioneering communications." Including in an ad the name of a piece of legislation that carried the name of sponsor who is also a federal candidate—such as the "McCain-Feingold" bill? The FEC concluded that an exemption for this type of reference to a federal candidate would invite evasion. Advertising by a candidate to promote the candidate's business, when the ad cites the name only in connection with the business? Once again, the FEC, concerned with evasion, declined to craft an exemption.

Wilson runs a steak house and also is running for the Senate. His company runs, as it has for years, a cheesy advertisement promoting his steak house, which is named "Wilson's Beef and Barbecue Mansion." The ad refers to Wilson by name, but otherwise touts only the fare served and the ample parking available. Within 30 days of the primary, the ads run. Wilson's company has made a prohibited "electioneering communication." Wilson's competitors denounce the ad, then take their beef about this ad to the FEC and seek to drive a steak through the heart of his candidacy.

The same concern with evasion persuaded the FEC to deny an exemption to advertising on ballot initiatives that would involve reference to a federal candidate. The Commission specifically stated that as "ballot initiatives or referenda become increasingly linked with the public officials who support or oppose them, communications can use the initiative or referenda as a proxy for the candidate, and in promoting or opposing the initiative or referendum, can promote or oppose the candidate."[95]

Reporting of "electioneering communications"

The Act broadly requires reporting by any person who disburses monies for the "direct costs of producing and airing electioneering communications" which, in the aggregate, exceed $10,000 per year.[96] The report will have to identify the person making the "disbursement" for this purpose, but also any person "sharing or exercising direction or control over the activities" of the organization and "the custodian" of the organization's

Reporting "direct" costs

---

[95] 67 Fed. Reg. 65,202 (Oct. 23, 2002)

[96] BCRA § 201; 2 U.S.C. § 434(f).

books and accounts. Under the rules promulgated by the FEC, the individuals deemed to share or exercise "direction or control" would include officers, directors, executive directors, partners or owners.

The report will also include:

• The organization's principal place of business;

• The amount of each disbursement of more than $200 for the "direct costs" of producing and airing the communication. The FEC concluded that a binding and exhaustive statement of the costs subject to disclosure was required, and it adopted a rule that included within the definition

—vendor costs

—studio time

—material costs

—cost of a broker to purchase the airtime

—the cost of the airtime

• The identification of the persons to whom the disbursements were made, which could include, for example, those engaged to produce the ad and the stations paid to air it;

• The names and addresses of all contributors of an aggregate amount of $1,000 or more to the organization making the disbursement in the period from the beginning of the preceding calendar year to the date of disclosure; and

• The "elections" to which the "electioneering communications pertain" and the names (if known) of the candidates.

Other costs considered by the Commission were expressly excluded from the scope of the rule. The disclosure requirement does not reach "in-house costs" such as staff compensation and other overhead, nor the costs of polling or focus groups which were considered insufficiently connected to the resulting communication to be considered "direct costs."[97]

Different reporting requirement for the use of only individual funds

The Act also adjusts the reporting requirements so that they apply more narrowly where the organization or association has established a "segregated bank account" to hold individual funds contributed for the purpose of financing these kinds of communications.[98] In that case,

[97] 68 Fed. Reg. 410 (Jan. 3, 2003).

[98] BCRA § 201; 2 U.S.C. § 434(f)(2)(E).

the report need disclose only the names and addresses of contributors to that account who contributed a total amount of $1,000 or more over the period from the preceding calendar year through the date that the $10,000 threshold for reporting was reached. Only American citizens or individuals admitted to permanent residency may contribute to this account.

The significance of this provision is that the organization may maintain other accounts for other purposes, but the amounts paid into and from those accounts would not be disclosed in the reports of electioneering communications. The segregated individual account would not be limited to the payment of electioneering communications, and could be used for other purposes, but it would be the only account whose contributors would be publicly disclosed in a report under the Act.

The Citizens for a Happier and More Fulfilling Existence fund electioneering communications lauding Senator Jones in TV ads within 20 days of his primary election in his state. The organization pays $50,000 for the ads. The Citizens maintains a number of accounts and fund a number of activities, but for purposes of these ads, it maintains an account into which only individuals may contribute and from which these ads are financed. Its report to the FEC of these activities discloses only the activity from this account, and then only the amounts paid from the account for the "direct costs" of airing and producing these ads.

Later in the election, within 45 days of the general election, Citizens has run out of money in the segregated account, and draws funds for more of these ads from another account used for other organization activities. The next report filed under the Act must disclose all contributors to the organization, from all of its accounts, including others on which it did not draw for these electioneering communications.

Why all of this trouble? The sponsors were sensitive to the criticism that these reporting requirements fall on organizations that may, in fact, seek only to comment on issues, albeit issues involving officeholders who are also candidates in a pending election. Their ads do not include "express advocacy," and the circumstances may be such that they are motivated by concerns other than that election. So the Act is limiting the range of disclosures which need to be made, focusing on "direct costs" and also affording organizations the opportunity to structure their accounts to limit the range of their finances subject to public disclosure.

Citizens for a Happier and More Fulfilling Existence is troubled by legislation sponsored by Senator Gloom brought to the floor for debate late in the Congressional session. As it happens, the debate and vote will occur within 60 days of the general election in which Gloom is standing for reelection but without an opponent. The Citizens begins to run advertisements intended to pressure Gloom into acceding to a particular, brightening amendment. The ad states: "Call Senator Gloom—Tell him to cheer up, and support the Goodcheer amendment." The ad cannot affect Gloom's reelection one way or other, and the organization's ad has been aired to advance a legislative objective. It must, however, file a report under the Act if the direct costs of the ad exceed $10,000.

Timetable for reporting "electioneering communications"

Reports of "electioneering communications" must be filed within 24 hours of crossing the $10,000 threshold.[99] The "disclosure date" from which the 24 hours begins to run is the first time in the calendar year that a communication is publicly distributed. It is this distribution—not the date when contracts were executed, or disbursements were made—that triggers the period when the filing must be made. The 24 hours extend from the date of public distribution to midnight of the day following disclosure, to account for the difficulty in always determining precisely when an ad began to air.

Subsequent reports are filed for each additional spending in excess of each subsequent $10,000 trigger. The reports are filed with the FEC, which compiles the relevant information and makes it available on its website.

---

[99] BCRA § 201; 2 U.S.C. § 434(f)(1).

The Citizens Committee finances research into Senator Jones' position on an issue. It expands the exercise to a full "opposition research report" which a consultant prepares for a cost of $15,000. So far no obligation to report has been incurred: the monies spent so far, though they may be used later for electioneering communications, do not include the "direct costs" of producing and airing any such communications.

On the basis of this research, the Citizens Committee enters into a contract with a media firm to prepare and produce, and then buy the time for, electioneering communications. Those communications will state that Jones has a long history of sponsoring stupid legislation, and that those hearing or seeing the ad should call him and tell him to "wise up." If the agreement with the media firm calls for fees and costs exceeding $10,000, the Citizens Committee must prepare a report for filing with the FEC within 24 hours of the public distribution of the communication. A subsequent additional payment for airtime will generate another requirement for a report, also to be filed within 24 hours, if that additional payment exceeds $10,000.

Prohibiting corporate and union "electioneering communications"

As noted, the Act prohibits some "electioneering communications," while compelling disclosure of all others. The prohibition is placed on those entities, and most pertinently corporations and unions, subject to the existing prohibitions on spending "in connection with a federal election." These entities may not fund electioneering communications, nor donate funds to another organization to finance them.[100]

This prohibition raised the constitutional stakes of the Act considerably higher. The disclosure requirements present potential constitutional issues of their own, but here the Act absolutely prohibits a corporation or union from financing any broadcast, cable or satellite ad within the 30- and 60-day limits that refers to a federal candidate and is directed to the "relevant electorate." It is noted, however, that within these 30- and 60-day periods, the corporations and unions remain

---

[100] BCRA § 203; 2 U.S.C. §§ 441b(a) and 441b(c).

free to fund ads through other media, such as mail and telephone banks. The Supreme Court in the *McConnell* case upheld this prohibition.

Powerful Corporation is angry over the proposed repeal of a tax provision which would have a significant impact on its business. As the fall Congressional session winds down in an election year, Powerful launches advertisements in 15 states, attacking federal lawmakers from those states who have expressed support for the bill. The ads begin within 60 days of the general election.

Some the candidates named in the ad are running for reelection, though two are not: one announced her retirement, and the other lost in the primary. Some number of ads have run in states other than ones represented by these candidates, as part of the Company's interest in publicizing the issue. Those ads mention some of the candidates. Moreover, two of the candidates are United States Senators representing the same state, but only one is running this year, while the other—though a candidate for reelection—will not face the voters for another four years.

As it happens, moreover, Powerful has supported seven of these candidates earlier in the year with contributions from its PAC. The company releases a statement announcing the ads which states that while it will continue to support most of these candidates for reelection, it is financing the ad blitz to focus their attention on the Company's extreme dissatisfaction with the tax measure. Under the Act,

- *Powerful may run the ads in states other than ones represented by the candidates appearing in them. An electioneering communication is by definition one directed to the relevant electorate—a requirement not met by these ads.*

- *The Company may also run ads in states where the named federal officials are not candidates for reelection, either because of retirement or primary defeat.*

- *The Company, though otherwise Powerful, may not run the ads in states where the lawmakers mentioned are federal candidates, even if Powerful is otherwise supporting them for reelection.*

- *The Company may not run the ad that refers to the United States Senator who is running for election in that year, but it may include in those ads his colleague who is a candidate but not on the ballot for another four years.*[101]

The Act anticipated litigation, providing that if its definition of "electioneering communication" "is held to be constitutionally insufficient by final judicial decision," another definition, believed to be safer, should take its place. This alternative was similar to the structure of the restrictions on party "issue advertising," requiring not only the mention of a federal candidate but also language indicating support for or opposition to the candidate. Yet the Court in *McConnell* upheld the primary definition, centered on the simple identification of the candidate to her voting constituency within specific periods before elections. Hence, the alternative definition was not needed, and has passed into history. Powerful Company will remain unhappy.

It is emphasized that the prohibition on "electioneering communications" falls on unions and corporations, or on communications paid with union or corporate funds. An *unincorporated* 527 or tax-exempt organization is not subject to the prohibition, so long as neither a corporation or a union "directly or indirectly disburses any amount for any of the costs of the communication." An unincorporated 527 or tax-exempt could accept union or corporate funds for other purposes, and pay the costs of any "electioneering communication" out of individual funds held in a separate segregated account, but the electioneering prohibitions still apply if the communication is targeted to the candidate's electorate. It is clear that individuals and federal political committees spending only hard money may pay for ads in the form of "electioneering communications" at any time.

Exempting 501(c) and 527 organizations using individual funds?

---

[101] "The reference to a clearly identified candidate is intended to mean a candidate who is up for election in that two-year cycle. Therefore, if one Senator is up for election in a cycle, an ad that appears within 60 days of an election and mentions only the second Senator for that state is not an electioneering communication, even though the second Senator is also technically a candidate for election some years hence." Statement of Supporters of the Bipartisan Campaign Reform Act of 2001 Concerning Intent of Certain Provisions. 147 Cong. Rec. S3245 (daily ed. Apr. 2, 2001).

CHAPTER 3

LESS SOFT MONEY, MORE HARD MONEY: INCREASES IN THE FEDERAL CONTRIBUTION LIMITS

As originally introduced in the Senate, the Act did not provide for any broad adjustment upward in the limits on "hard money" or federal contributions. It did raise the limit on contributions from individuals to state parties from $5,000 to $10,000 per calendar year. This increase was fashioned in the belief that as national party committees lost their "soft money" sources, the state parties would be compelled to "pick up the slack"—to raise more money for various activities that national parties for some time had funded. Supporters also noted that inflation had severely eroded the effective purchasing power of the $1,000 per election contribution limit for individuals, enacted into federal law in 1974.[102] With greater responsibilities, the state parties would need more resources, and as the overall emphasis of the bill is to restrict all party soft money activities, the Act sought to provide those additional resources in the form of increased "hard" contributions.

The Senate debate resulted in two amendments which substantially broadened that approach, increasing contributions across-the-board from individuals to Senate candidates and party committees and increasing them still more in one special case. The special case was that of the Senate candidate facing an opponent who commits substantial amounts of his or her own money to the race. In that latter case, the Senate adopted a "millionaire's amendment," modified and passed also by the House for Congressional races as well, intended to provide increased limits for a candidate facing heavy personal spending by a wealthy opponent. The House also increased the individual

---

[102] "Thirty years ago, a car cost $2,700. Now it costs $22,000. The cost of campaigning has risen even more dramatically....Virtually every aspect of campaigning, from the salaries for consultants to the paper on which you write—all of it is much more expensive today." 147 Cong. Rec. S2459 (daily ed. Mar. 19, 2001) (statement of Sen. Feinstein).

Increases in the contribution limits

FROM ∨ TO->	Senate cand	House cand	Presidential cand	Nat'l party cmte	State party cmte	PAC	Annual agg limit
Individual	$2,000/elec	$2,000/elec	$2,000/elec	$25,000/cal yr	$10,000/cal yr	$5,000/cal yr	$95,000/2 yrs [2]
Multicandidate PAC	$5,000/elec	$5,000/elec	$5,000/elec	$15,000/cal yr	$5,000/cal yr	$5,000/cal yr	n/a
Non-multicandidate PAC	$2,000/elec	$2,000/elec	$2,000/elec	$25,000/cal yr	$10,000/cal yr	$5,000/cal yr	n/a
National party committee	$35,000 [1]	$5,000/elec	$5,000/elec	Unlimited	Unlimited	$5,000/cal yr	n/a
State party committee	$5,000/elec	$5,000/elec	$5,000/elec	Unlimited	Unlimited	$5,000/cal yr	n/a
Non-individual "person" (e.g., partnerships, Indian tribes)	$2,000/elec	$2,000/elec	$2,000/elec	$25,000/cal yr	$10,000/cal yr	$5,000/cal yr	n/a

[1] Specifically, the DSCC/DNC and NRSC/RNC may respectively give a combined $35,000 to each Senate candidate during the calendar year in which the election is to be held.

[2] The application of this limit is complex: see discussion at pages 91-92.

contribution limits, and so the bill provides for increased limits for both House and Senate candidates.

Increases in the contribution limits

The chart on the opposite page sets out the changed limits. It also notes that the Act "indexed" some of the limits for inflation, but not others: the indexed limits appear in italics. The chart does not address the significant additional limit increases provided for under the millionaire amendment, but these are discussed below, with examples.

More money for candidates and parties— and to battle millionaires, too

Candidates and parties make off with the prize, while PACs—political committees established by unions, corporations, and trade associations, and other political committees which are not political party committees—did not receive a raise in their limits. Limits on individual contributions to candidates and state parties are doubled—to $2,000 per election in the first case, and to $10,000 per calendar year in the second. The contribution limit for individuals contributing to national party committees was increased by 25%, from $20,000 per calendar year to $25,000.

The Act also raised the aggregate annual limit for contributions, from $25,000 per calendar year now, to $95,000 over a two-year election cycle, running from January 1 of an odd-numbered year through December 31 of the next, even-numbered year.

The complicated aggregate limit on individual contributions

Of the $95,000
- $37,500 may be contributed to candidates (in amounts of $2,000 per candidate per election)
- the balance of $57,500 is available for contribution to other committees, such as party committees, or political committees established by corporations, unions, or just citizens banding together to express a common political agenda (e.g. Citizens Banding Together to Express a Common Political Agenda). BUT...
- ONLY $37,500 of the balance of $57,500 may be contributed to political committees which are not national party committees.

Donor Wilson wishes to give as much she possibly can in the 2004 cycle. To do so, she cannot exceed $37,500 in contri-

butions to candidates, and she must make at least $20,000 in contributions to national party committees.

Donor Smith is a party enthusiast. He makes the full amount of contributions he is allowed to candidates. Now he wishes to contribute the balance available under the aggregate limit, $57,500, to national party committees. He may do so. Of the $57,500, $20,000 is reserved for the national party committees; but he could contribute the full amount of $57,500, if he wished, to national party committees.

The statute appears to require that a contribution counts against the limit for the two-year cycle in which it is made. The old law applied a different rule: a contribution to a candidate counted for the year in which the election was scheduled. So a contribution to a candidate seeking election in 2006 would count toward the 2006 annual limit, even if made in 2004.

The FEC has confirmed the new rule after some initial confusion. It regulations now make clear that a contribution applies to the limit of the election cycle when made: for example, a contribution made to a congressional candidate in 2004 counts for the 2004 cycle limit, "regardless of the year in which the particular election is held."[103] Out of concern for the initial confusion over the requirements of this counting rule, the rule applies only to contributions made on or after January 1, 2004.

The timing of indexing
There are other complexities, perhaps also anomalies, in the construction of the revised contribution limits. As noted, certain of the limits are indexed for inflation. These include the limits to candidates and national party committees, and also the aggregate limit of $95,000 per two-year election cycle on all individual hard money federal contributions. These increases become effective in January of the odd-numbered year—2003 for the 2004 election cycle. The FEC does not normally have the Consumer Price Index data until March following an election. So some period of time will pass after each election when the limits will, for legal purposes, have increased, but the

---

[103] 11 C.F.R. § 110.5 (c)(1).

precise amount of the limit will not be known.

Differences in indexing may also have other effects of interest. Under the law governing public funding of presidential candidates, the government may match $250 of an individual contribution received by an eligible presidential candidate. This amount is not, however, indexed, and so as the individual contribution limits increase, the "matchable" amount for presidential candidates seeking public funds will decline as a percentage of the total contribution made.

Another result of the approach to indexing is the difference in the treatment of "multicandidate" and regular political committees. A multicandidate PAC is a committee that qualifies by the breadth of its activities for a higher limit on contributions to candidates: $5,000 rather $1,000 per election. It qualifies for the special limit by filing with the Commission a certification that it has been registered with the Commission as a political committee for at least 6 months, that it has made contributions to at least 5 federal candidates and that it has received contributions from more than 50 persons. A committee that does not so qualify is limited to the $1,000 per election limit. The Act indexes the non-multicandidate limit and increases it to $2,000 per election, but not the multicandidate limit, with the result that at some time in the future indexing may power an increase in the lower, non-multicandidate limit beyond the limit enjoyed by the multicandidate committee.

The increase in limits also affects "persons," as well as individuals. Persons (other than candidate committees) as defined under the law may contribute up to $2,000 per election to any candidate, and they also enjoy the same authority as individuals to give under the increased limits of $25,000 in a calendar year to national party committees and $10,000 to state parties. Under the law, "persons" include partnerships, certain limited liability companies, Indian tribes, and non-multicandidate political committees. The terms under which these "persons" may contribute are not the same, though the subject is not one for treatment here. Certain of these "persons" run up against other limita-

> **Indexing:**
> **No help to**
> **presidential**
> **public funding**
> **system**

> **Indexing some**
> **PACs, but not**
> **others**

> **"Persons"**
> **have their**
> **own limit**

tions in making federal contributions, and some—like certain limited liability companies that are taxed as corporations and thus treated like corporations for purposes of the campaign finance law—may not contribute at all.

Protection against millionaires?

The individual limits—and also in some instances the party spending limits—have also been increased under the "millionaire's" amendment, to lighten the stresses on a candidate faced with a wealthy opponent willing to commit substantial sums of money to the competition. The sponsors of the amendment in the Senate acknowledged, rightly, that the provision is "very complicated."[104] There are, moreover, different provisions affecting Senate and House candidates, though they are structured conceptually much the same.[105] The similarities in approach are critical to appreciating what the amendment is designed to accomplish, and how it works.

First, each of the provisions provides a method for determining when the potential increase in the contribution limits is triggered. In both cases, this trigger is spending by a wealthy opponent from personal funds in excess of a "threshold amount." This amount is calculated differently, as one would assume, for the House and Senate: in the House, the number is $350,000, while the Senate provision keys the amount to the voting age population of the state.

Second, each of the provisions makes the increase of the contribution limit depend, in part, on how much money the candidate facing the wealthy opponent has committed from her own personal funds and how much she maintains in the way of an advantage in cash from other contributors. These calculations are intended to gear the relief to the candidates who really need it—not candidates who, in some combination of personal spending and fundraising, remain competitive even with a wealthy opponent.

---

[104] 147 Cong. Rec. S2542 (daily ed. Mar. 20, 2001) (statement of Sen. Domenici).

[105] BCRA §§ 304, 316 and 319; 2 U.S.C. §§ 441a-l; 11 C.F.R. Part 400, subpart D.

Third, each of the provisions identifies different amounts of contribution limit increases available to candidates with "millionaire" opponents. The House offers a tripled limit ($6,000 per election), and also removes the limit on party "coordinated" spending for the candidate with a wealthy opponent. The Senate provides for a graduated series of increases, and only for an exemption from party committee spending for the candidate facing the most massive level of personal spending by a wealthy opponent.

Fourth, each of the provisions defines the terms under which the increased limits are suspended. The suspension of the limit in both instances occurs when the wealthy candidate withdraws, or if the amount of contributions received under the increased limits exceeds a percentage of the wealthy candidate's spending,[106] or if the candidate's own personal spending increases to a certain level.

Fifth, each of the provisions compels the candidate who receives increased limits to return to the donors, after the election, the amounts raised under these limits that have not been used.

Sixth (and last), each provision has a related provision that prohibits a candidate who spends more than $250,000 from his personal funds in an election from raising contributions after the election to repay himself.

This is the basic scheme. The FEC made an attempt to show how these provisions might work in practice, by developing a lengthy hypothetical and publishing it in the Federal Register. This appears in the Appendix. Working through this hypothetical should put those facing wealthy opponents, who are spilling their personal funds in all directions, in good fighting trim and able to claim what is owed them.

The following sections offer a shorter explanation, also with some hypotheticals, discussing separately House and Senate races and their related rules. The provisions use specialized terms for some of the key

---

[106] The sponsors of the amendment term this limit a "proportionality provision," which is a means of "ensuring that a wealthy candidate is not punished by the less wealthy candidate's ability to raise funds" under increased contribution limits. 147 Cong. Rec. S2542 (daily ed. Mar. 20, 2001) (statement of Sen. DeWine).

steps, and these are mentioned if only to introduce them to readers who may hear them uttered in the future.

Senate elections. The "threshold amount" is the amount spent by an opponent of personal funds that brings into play the potential for an increase in the limits for the affected candidate. A candidate determines this amount by multiplying $0.04 times the relevant state's voting age population, and adding $150,000.

Notification of spending

Within 15 days after becoming a candidate, the wealthy opponent must file a declaration with the FEC and with the other candidates in the race, stating the amount of personal funds she intends to spend in excess of the threshold amount. "Personal funds" includes bank loans secured against a candidate's personal assets, and it also covers any legally enforceable obligation to spend personal funds. Moreover, under FEC implementing rules, "personal funds" includes all income, from employment or investments, received in the current cycle, and gifts of the kind "customarily" received in prior cycles.

This first notification is simply a declaration of intention, which does not trigger access to the higher limits. But at the time the opponent makes or obligates to make expenditures from personal funds totaling more than two times the "threshold amount" in any particular election, she must file another notification, with the FEC and with the opposing candidate, within 24 hours. Additional notifications are required within 24 hours after each additional $10,000 in expenditures from personal funds. Candidates must ensure that their committees make timely filings, and the filings are effected through email and fax to assure some measure of dispatch upon which the effectiveness of the provision, and the relief it provides, depends. Senate candidates must file reports with the Secretary of the Senate, the FEC, and each opposing candidate, while House candidates report to the FEC and each opposing candidate. Parties affiliated with candidates are also entitled to notification, so that they can spend the additional funds over the limit.

Now that the battle lines are drawn, and the wealthy

opponent has made her move by the requisite amount over the threshold, the candidate may proceed to calculate the increase in the contribution limit to his campaign from individuals. Two key points need to be made about the opponents whose spending authorizes the affected candidate to calculate his statutory advantage of increased limits. This relief is available, of course, if the candidate is facing more than one opponent who expects to spend over the threshold. In calculating his statutory entitlement, the candidate can the use the opponent whose spending is the highest, and whose spending would trigger either benefits, or in the case of the Senate, the highest level of benefits. But the FEC limits the relief to spending by the candidate running in the same election: unfair as it may seem, if a candidate running in one primary spends heavily to influence the outcome in another for the same office in order to encourage the success of the weakest possible general election opponent, the millionaire's amendment does not apply. Its benefits are only available in head-to-head contests.

The calculations occur in several steps:

1. The candidate must calculate the so-called "opposition personal funds" amount. This is the largest total of personal fund expenditures made in the election by the wealthy opponent, MINUS (a) the amount of personal funds the candidate has used in the same election and (b) any additional advantage the candidate with the wealthy opponent may have in other fundraising. This fundraising advantage is known in the Act as the "gross receipts advantage." It is calculated from June 30 and December 31 off-year fundraising totals, and it is the difference between 50% of the candidate's cycle-wide gross receipts and 50% of the opponent's (not including personal funds).

Calculating the disadvantage

The June 30 calculation of gross receipts advantage is effective from July 16 through January 31 of the year before and then the first month of the election year, while the December 31 calculation holds from February 1 of the election year through election day. The reason simply is that the opponent reports on which the calculations are based are only available July 15 of the year before the election and then January 31 of the election year. The gross receipts advantage is not a factor, and it is not calculated, for the period through June of the year before the election: only the sheer differences in personal funds, without adjustment for the fundraising differential, controls the availability of relief in that early period. The calculation of gross receipts advantage occurs twice a cycle, but the calculation of "opposition personal funds" is required of the candidate on each occasion that the opponent files notification of another $10,000 in personal spending.

The FEC rules provide for candidates to file reports on which the calculation of "gross receipts advantage" depends. These special reports provide information on their funding in a "concise and comprehensive manner," and all candidates filing reports with the FEC for Senate and House campaigns must file them. The gross receipts reporting includes, comprehensively, itemized and unitemized contributions; political party contributions and expenditures for their benefit; loans; and other receipts, including interest income and dividends.

Wealthy Wilson has raised $1.8 million by the end of the off-year, that is, as of December 31, while her opponent, Modesty Means, has raised $4.0 million. In determining the so-called "opposition personal funds amount"—which in turn will decide the availability and amount of increased limits for Modesty Means—the $1.1 million advantage Modesty Means enjoys in general fundraising is debited against Wilson's personal spending (50% of Modesty's $4 million minus 50% of Wealthy's $1.8 million, or $2 million minus $900,000). This lower net number will reduce the availability and amount of increased contributions limits for Means, because while she is being outspent in personal funds, she is making up the difference to the some extent with her general fundraising advantage.

Calculating the increased contribution limit for responding to the millionaire

2. Now the candidate may proceed to calculate the level of increased contribution limit by figuring out the multiple by which the "opposition personal funds" amount exceeds the "threshold amount":

- if the "opposition personal funds" amount is 2

times to 4 times the "threshold amount," then the limit is multiplied by 3 ($6,000 per individual per election);

• if the "opposition personal funds" amount is 4 times to 10 times the "threshold amount," then the limit is multiplied by 6 ($12,000 per individual per election); or

• if the "opposition personal funds" amount is 10 times or more the "threshold amount," then the candidate's party may make unlimited coordinated expenditures on his behalf.

The FEC directs candidates to the use of a table or chart provided for under the rule, enabling the ready identification of the relief to which they may be entitled. This is that table:

If the opposition personal funds amount is more than–	But less than or equal to–	The increased limit for contributions by individuals is–	The amount limitation on coordinated party committee expenditures is–
(i) ($0.08 x VAP) + $300,000	($0.16 x VAP) + $600,000	3 x applicable limit	The limitation set forth in 11 CFR 109.32(b)
(ii) ($0.16 x VAP) + $600,000	($0.40 x VAP) + $1,500,00	6 x applicable limit	The limitation set forth in 11 CFR 109.32(b)
(iii) ($0.40 x VAP) + $1,500,000		6 x applicable limit	The limitation set forth in 11 CFR 109.32(b) does not apply subject to the provisions of 11 CFR 400.31(d)

When the limit comes down again....

The candidate provided with these increased limits is not, once qualified, perpetually eligible to raise at the higher limits and benefit from unlimited coordinated expenditures. The limits decline from the higher level when: (i) the candidate spends personal funds in a way that would change the calculations, (ii) the opponent who triggered the higher limits drops out, or (iii) the amount by which the candidate benefited from higher individual contribution limits or party spending limits exceeds 110% of the "opposition personal funds" amount.

Candidates and parties have the responsibility to "monitor" the changing facts as they would affect the continuing eligibility for the higher limits. This is one of the reasons why a party must monitor the status of the "opposition personal funds" calculation applicable to each opposing candidate. This calculation must be done on the occasion of each notification of additional personal spending. Likewise, the candidates and parties must monitor the 110% threshold—that is, the threshold of 110% of the opposition personal funds amount—after which further contribution and party expenditure relief is no longer available. Once this threshold is exceeded, the candidate must notify within 24 hours both the Commission and their national parties. For purposes of the rule, withdrawal of the opponent, also resulting in suspension of relief, occurs with the public announcement of withdrawal, or the date of ineligibility by law for nomination or election.

Giving back after the election what was not spent

When the election is over, the candidate must determine the amount raised but not spent under increased limits, and then refund the excess portions to the original donors within 50 days after the election. For purposes of this rule, any run-off is part of the election to which it relates. The refunds must be made to the original contributors; and any refund check not cashed within six months must be disgorged to the Treasury within nine months. The committees disposing of excess funds must report the disposition to the Commission. It should be noted that the refund requirement does not apply to any amount of a contribution that could have been accepted under the regular limit. So if the candidate raised $6,000 from Smith, who had not given before, and now must refund excess unspent monies to Smith upon the withdrawal of his opponent and the cessation of entitlement to the higher limit, the candidate may retain $2,000 of the $6,000—the amount Smith could have donated regardless of the allowances of the millionaire's amendment.

Booker, a librarian, is running for Senate in Bedford Falls against Potter, a wealthy banker. The state's voting age population is 100,000, making the "threshold amount" for personal spending $154,000.

Both Booker and Potter win their primaries. Shortly thereafter, Potter puts $2 million of his own funds into the race, and files a notice with Booker and the FEC. Booker pulls out her adding machine. So far, she has put none of her own money into the campaign, and Potter has outraised her. As a result, the "opposition personal funds" amount is $2 million, or more than 10 times the "threshold amount" of $154,000. Booker can thus accept up to $12,000 for the general election from an individual. Her party can also make unlimited coordinated expenditures on her behalf.

Yet before Booker can spend any of the extra money she has raised, Bedford Falls is rocked by an embezzlement scandal at Potter's bank. Potter withdraws from the race after being forced to admit that he perjured himself before federal regulatory authorities.

After watching Potter's press conference on TV, Booker immediately directs her campaign to stop raising funds at the higher limits, and the national party stops making coordinated expenditures above the normal limit. An unknown and poorly funded candidate replaces Potter on the ballot in November, and Booker wins overwhelmingly without having to spend much money at all. Before Christmas, her campaign issues refunds to the donors who contributed at the higher limits that she briefly enjoyed because of Potter's personal funds.

House elections. The differences between the House and Senate approaches are straightforward, even if in application, the Amendment is complex. The House threshold amount is $350,000 in any particular election, and the candidates planning to spend in excess of this amount must file a notification with the FEC, the opponent, and each national party within 24 hours. They must file additional notifications within 24 hours after each additional $10,000 in expenditures.

The calculation of opposition personal funds is the same for House and Senate candidates, and if it exceeds $350,000 for the House candidate, the individual limit is tripled for that candidate, and her party may also make unlimited coordinated expenditures on her behalf. Continued eligibility for the increased limits will depend, as in Senate elections, on the candidate's use of her own personal funds, and on the continued candidacy of the wealthy opponent. The House provision, like the Senate provision, also limits the amount of monies raised under the increased limit to a specified percentage of the wealthy opponent's "opposition personal funds" amount. The House limit, however, is lower—100%, rather than the 110% limit set by the Senate provision. As with the Senate, the House candidate, like the Senate candidate, must also calculate after the election the amount raised under the increased limits but left unspent, and then refund the excess portions to the original donors within 50 days.

Jed Leland, a former reporter, is running for Congress in New York City in the Democratic primary against Charles Foster Kane, a wealthy publisher. In the closing days of the campaign, Kane takes a $500,000 personal loan, secured against his lavish Florida vacation home, and puts the funds into his campaign. He files the required notice with Leland and the FEC.

As of December 31 of the previous year, Leland had raised $1,000,000 to Kane's $900,000. The son of wealthy parents himself, Leland had also loaned $100,000 to his campaign. As a result, Leland's "opposition personal funds" amount is $350,000: Kane's $500,000 in personal spending, minus the sum of: (a) Leland's $50,000 gross receipts advantage (50% of Leland's $1 million raised minus 50% of Kane's $900,000, or $500,000 minus $450,000) and (b) Leland's own $100,000 in personal spending.

Because Leland's "opposition personal funds" does not exceed $350,000, he cannot raise at higher limits. Kane crushes Leland in the primary.

Personal loan repayment restrictions

Candidates may not raise more than $250,000 in contributions after the election to repay personal loans made to their campaign.[107] This restriction applies to all federal candidates, including Presidential candidates. It also applies, on an aggregated basis, to all loans combined that may be outstanding after the election.

---

[107] BCRA § 301; 2 U.S.C. §§ 441a-1(j).

This is only a post-election restriction. Repayment may be made of any loan, in any amount, with contributions "made on the date of the election or before." The cash-on-hand of the committee as of the day after the election may be applied to all loans outstanding, which may be paid in full, but such payment must be completed within 20 days of the election. All contributions received after the election may be applied to the loans only in an aggregate amount up to $250,000.

No doubt, FEC will arbiter disputes over compliance with these "millionaire" provisions. Has the person planning large personal expenditures made timely notification of the intent, and then also of the expenditures? Has a candidate raised more money under increased limits than the eligibility rules allow? Did a candidate properly calculate monies received under these increased limits and make timely post-election refunds to the donors?

Conclusion on the "millionaire" amendment

Critics may also question how the Act might plausibly limit contributions to $2,000 per election, on the grounds that a larger amount would risk corruption, while authorizing contributions substantially larger for a candidate facing a millionaire. If a contribution exceeding $2,000 risks corruption, then, they would argue, it will presumably do so regardless of the reasons why a candidate needs the money. In fact, a candidate, who urgently needs the money to counter the resources of a wealthy opponent, stands to incur an even larger measure of indebtedness to the donor who lends a monied hand in the hour of need. And still another question of interest may be whether Congress can enact special provisions designed to discourage, or mitigate the impact, of personal spending for election-related purposes that the Supreme Court has held to be constitutionally protected.

Other contribution or fundraising limits and prohibitions

The Act makes some other changes to the rules governing the making and solicitation of contributions in federal elections. They are varied, unified only as parts of an overall attempt by the drafters to plug up one perceived hole or the other in the old law.

One provision amends a longstanding prohibition of the criminal code on "fundraising on federal property." The old law stated that

> It shall be unlawful for any person to solicit or receive any contributions...in any room or building occupied in the discharge of official duties [by any Members of Congress, candidates for Congress, officers or employees of the United States, or persons receiving any salary or compensation for services from the U.S. Treasury], or in any navy yard, fort or arsenal.

Fundraising on federal property

The provision was amended in 1979 to allow Congressional staff to accept contributions sent to them in their offices, but not solicited for delivery there, provided that the contributions were transferred within seven days to their employers' political committees.

For some time, it lay dormant, surfacing from time to time when the Justice Department would address apparent violations resulting from "computer-generated direct mail campaigns in which solicitation letters are inadvertently sent to prohibited areas."[108] The Department, concluding that "such matters do not warrant prosecution," would simply advise the mailer that its fundraising lists should be purged of federal government addresses. Attention turned back to this provision, however, when allegations were made against the reelection effort of President Clinton, focusing specifically on the alleged use of White House "coffees" and other events and facilities to raise funds.[109]

The Act amended the provision to clarify the different paths taken by the prohibition.[110] First, it prohibits "any person" from soliciting or receiving contributions from a person located in a federal government office. Second, it turns in the other direction and applies the

---

[108] Craig C. Donsanto and Nancy S. Stewart, U.S. Department of Justice, *Federal Prosecution of Election Offenses* at 68-69 (6th ed. 1995).

[109] Investigation of Illegal or Improper Activities in Connection with 1996 Federal Election Campaigns, Final Report of the Comm. on Gov't Affairs, S. Rep. No. 105-167, at 191-223 (1998).

[110] BCRA § 302; 18 U.S.C. § 607.

prohibition to an individual who is an officer or employee of the federal government, barring them from such solicitations or receipts "while in any room or building" used for federal government business. This revised provision removes any confusion about the applicable legal authority, which had been read to prohibit solicitations only when the prospective donor was on government property.

The amended prohibition retains the prospects for both a criminal penalty and fine, but limits the fine to $5,000. The amendment also retains the allowance for inadvertent receipt of monies on federal property, conditioned on their transfer within seven days to a political committee, and it extends the allowance to contributions received in the Executive Office of the President.

Contributions by foreign nationals

The 1996 Presidential election fundraising controversies make their appearance also in a provision strengthening the ban on foreign nationals in all elections. For some time, some question was raised and debated about the scope of the prohibition, and specifically about whether it extended to contributions of "soft money" to political parties.[111]

The strengthening amendment of the Act is meant to leave no doubt about the breadth of the prohibition.[112] The foreign national prohibition now applies to "donations," not only to "contributions"—so it is not relevant that the foreign national or party claims that the purpose of the funds was to influence a nonfederal rather than a federal election. The Act specifically applies the prohibition to contributions or donations to political party committees, or to expenditures or independent expenditures, or to disbursements for "electioneering communications."[113]

Good times again on Sesame Street

The Act amended the old law by absolutely prohibiting contributions, hard and soft, by minor children (17 years old or younger). Previous law allowed minors

---

[111] A District Court held that it did not apply to soft money, only to "hard money" contributions to candidates or to the hard "federal" accounts of parties. A Court of Appeals reversed on this issue. *United States of America v. Kanchanalak*, 192 F.3d 1037 (D.D.C. 1999).

[112] BCRA § 303; 2 U.S.C. 441e(a).

[113] An "electioneering communication," it will be recalled, refers to a federal candidate in any broadcast, cablecast or satellite media within 30 days of a primary or 60 days of a general election.

under 18 to contribute, on the condition that 1) the contribution decision was made knowingly and voluntarily by the minor child; 2) the funds (or goods and services) contributed are the minor child's, such as funds from a trust established for and in the child's name; and 3) the contribution was not made from a gift donated to the child to make the contribution possible, or from other funds controlled by another person. Under the Act, a minor could not contribute at all, under any circumstances, to a candidate or to a political party. The *McConnell* Court struck down these restrictions, finding that there was "scant evidence of this form of evasion."[114]

Fraudulent fundraising

A final change of interest is the Act's amendment of the old law's prohibition on "fraudulent misrepresentation of campaign authority."[115] This provision dates back to early Watergate controversies, and it is concerned with "dirty tricks" which occur when a candidate for federal office, or the employee or agent of such a candidate

> Fraudulently misrepresent[s] himself or any committee or organization under his control as speaking or writing or otherwise acting for or on behalf of any other candidate or political party...on a matter which is damaging to such other candidate or political party....

The Act does not change this prohibition, but it adds another one intended to prevent the fraudulent solicitation of funds. This change is concerned with individuals and organizations carrying or using the name of candidates or parties without their permission to conduct fundraising appeals.[116]

---

[114] *McConnell* at 10 (delivered by Chief Justice Rehnquist with respect to BCRA Titles III and IV).

[115] BCRA § 309; 2 U.S.C. § 441h.

[116] *See Friends of Phil Gramm v. Americans for Phil Gramm in '84*, 587 F. Supp. 769 (E.D. Va. 1984).

CHAPTER 4

RESTRICTIONS ON FEDERAL CANDIDATES AND OFFICEHOLDERS

In the chapter on parties, there appeared some discussion of the prohibitions on federal candidates' and officeholders' solicitation, receipt, direction, transfer, or expenditure of "soft money" in connection with an election for federal office. Those prohibitions apply to the candidates' fundraising for national, state and local political parties, and for 501(c) organizations engaged in election-related activity. There are exceptions, some of which have been noted, such as the allowance for federal candidates or officeholders to speak, attend or be a featured guest at a state party event held to raise "soft money," or to raise money under restrictions for tax-exempt organizations engaged in election-related work, such as GOTV and voter registration. Restrictions apply to:

- "Agents" of candidates and officeholders; and
- An entity directly or indirectly established, financed, maintained, or controlled by or acting on behalf of one or more candidates or individuals holding federal office.

These restrictions and others affecting federal elections and officeholders have introduced a major change in federal campaign law that typically did not threaten politicians with liability. Under BCRA, their liability is now potentially very significant. The law, moreover, has become still more complex since the enactment of the statute. The FEC, in major advisory opinions, has answered significant questions about the scope of the restrictions—such as their application to fundraising for state and local candidates, or to fundraising for ballot initiatives. This chapter reviews additional law on these and other points affecting the fundraising and other activities of federal officeholders and candidates.

Who is the "agent" of a federal officeholder or candidate?

A key term is "agency" and the FEC, as discussed earlier, defined it to include actual authority to act on behalf of the candidate or officeholder in raising "soft money." In the first edition, the following hypothetical appeared:

"Stanley is the administrative assistant to Congressman Jones, and maintains strong ties to state party organizations in the Congressman's state. For years, he has moonlighted as an adviser to the party on fundraising and strategy. After the Act passes, it appears that Stanley may not encourage party supporters to make soft money contributions to the party. It may not matter whether Congressman Jones has directed his aide to encourage these contributions: as an agent of the Congressman, he may be separately enjoined from the same activities forbidden to his boss."

"Multiple hats" allowed
This now appears incorrect in light of the FEC's choice of the definition of the term "agent." The Commission specifically sanctioned "multiple hats," and also focused on the issue of actual authority—on whether the candidate or officeholder authorized, expressly or by implication, the fundraising on his or her own behalf. So it does matter whether "Congressman Jones has directed his aide to encourage these contributions." This is, in fact, the whole game. Of course, there is law and there is prudence; and some officeholders may be unwilling to invite an argument over whether actual authority was given, even by implication alone. This is, after all, a question of fact, and questions of fact are settled typically by challenges followed by investigations. Some Members of Congress may well direct their aides to refrain from any fundraising activity that their employer has not specifically authorized.

The Commission had occasion to consider the scope of the concept of "agency" in replying to a request for an Advisory Opinion from the son of a United States Senator.[117] The Senator's son is a state official, and also the former Chair of the state party. The question before the agency was whether the son could raise "soft money" for his state party, while also periodically raising, as he had in the past, hard money for his father's reelection campaign. Here the agency had to consider the "multiple hats" notion, but also the complicating factor of the blood relationship between the possible

---

[117] FEC Advisory Opinion 2003-10.

principal and agent. The FEC concluded that a filial tie did not alone establish "agency."

"Leadership PACs"

Then there is the matter of "leadership PACs," which are multicandidate committees closely associated with and typically led by federal officeholders. Those PACs, unlike the personal campaign committees of these officeholders, do not expend funds to support their reelection, but rather raise funds with their assistance for distribution to other candidates. These PACs often used to have both federal and nonfederal accounts, drawing on the nonfederal accounts for contributions under state law to state and local candidates. Those soft accounts would also defray a part of the costs of the administration and fundraising of these PACs.

Under the Act, a federal officeholder would be prohibited from soliciting or directing soft money contributions to these leadership PACs. These leadership PACs, moreover, appear to constitute under the Act "entities" which are "directly or indirectly established, financed, maintained, or controlled by" a federal officeholder or candidate. As such, they are separately prohibited from solicitation, receipt, direction, transfer or expenditure of these funds. In addition, the prohibition on the conduct of these activities by an "agent" of candidates or officeholders would seem to cover members of the leadership PAC staff, such as staff raising funds.

No soft money for Leadership PACs

In the first edition, some question was raised about the application of the fundraising limits to monies raised for both the federal and nonfederal—the hard and soft—accounts of a leadership PAC. The legislative history reflected some Congressional intention to allow officeholders with leadership PACs to raise separate amounts, up to the hard money limit, for both the federal and nonfederal account of the PAC.[118] The FEC

---

[118] Hence Senator McCain stated on the floor of the Senate:
"A federal officeholder or candidate is prohibited from soliciting contributions for a Leadership PAC that do not comply with federal hard money source and amount limitations. Thus, the federal officeholder or candidate could solicit up to $5,000 per year from an individual or PAC for the federal account of the Leadership PAC and an additional $5,000 from an individual or PAC for the non-federal account of the Leadership PAC."
148 Cong. Rec. S2140 (daily ed. Mar. 20, 2002) (statement of Sen. McCain).

considered, and rejected, this possibility in the course of developing its implementing rules. An officeholder or candidate can still raise funds for the nonfederal account, for use in state and local elections, but only one limit, the federal limit, is available in the aggregate to any fundraising for the two accounts. So if the officeholder were to raise $5,000 in the course of the calendar year from a particular individual for the nonfederal account, no more could be raised in that year from the same individual for the federal account.[119]

How these limits work may be illustrated by the example of contributions raised by a federal officeholder or candidate for a state party, rather than a "leadership PAC." The officeholder or candidate may raise from an individual $10,000 per calendar year for the party "hard" money account, and also the same amount for the party's nonfederal account. (As noted previously, however, the federal officeholder or candidate may not raise any amount for a state party for use for certain "Federal election activity" under the allowances of the Levin Amendment.) The federal limit applies in both instances. In the case of a leadership PAC, the officeholder could only raise a single contribution, up to the $5,000 annual limit, for all of its accounts combined.

Congressman Jones is approached by the state party for fundraising support for state and local elections. Jones' state places no limit on corporate contributions to the party for those purposes. Jones, however, may only raise funds under federal limits for the party "nonfederal account": $10,000 from an individual per calendar year, and $5,000 per calendar year from a political committee.

---

[119] The FEC has also grappled for some years with a hard money question: whether "leadership PACs" should be considered "affiliated" with the personal "authorized" campaign committees of the candidate who established or directs both committees. If affiliated, the committee should share the same contribution limits: they would cease operating as wholly independent committees. The FEC has since promulgated a new rule that it would not find affiliation in these circumstances. 68 Fed Reg. 47386 (Aug. 8, 2003). The two types of committees are bound by the contribution limit in supporting each other: the leadership PAC may not make contributions, in cash or in kind, exceeding $5,000 a calendar year to the authorized committee.

Jones, by now exhausted, is asked some weeks later for assistance once more by the same state party seeking funds for Levin Amendment get-out-the-vote activity. Jones may not raise funds for this purpose.

Raising money for state and local candidates

May a federal candidate or officeholder raise money for a state or local candidate, as when a member of the Congressional delegation solicits contributions for a candidate for Governor in her state, or when the Congresswoman who heads the ticket raises funds for candidates "down ballot"? She may, but only under federal law limits and source restrictions.[120] Under this provision, federal campaign finance law supplants state law as it would otherwise apply to contributions raised for a state or local candidate. The federal candidate or officeholder may only raise $2,000 per election from an individual for any state or local candidate, and $5,000 a calendar year to that candidate from a PAC, even if state law were to provide for more generous limits for those candidates. Moreover, while the FEC rules are silent on this point, the Act's legislative history indicates the Congressional sponsors' intent that federal candidates or officeholders raising money from a single individual for state and local candidates may have to observe the aggregate limit on that individual's contributions. Specifically—

> A federal candidate or officeholder may not ask a single individual to donate amounts to all state candidates in a two-year election cycle that in the aggregate exceed $37,500, which corresponds to the aggregate amount of "hard money" that individuals may donate to all federal candidates over a two-year cycle.[121]

Regardless of the allowances of state law, the federal candidate or officeholder could not raise monies from corporations or unions for state and local candidates.

---

[120] BCRA § 101; 2 U.S.C. 441(e)(1)(B).

[121] 148 Cong. Rec. S2140 (daily ed. Mar. 20, 2002) (statement of Sen. McCain).

These restrictions illustrate the determination of the drafters that federal candidates or officeholders not have anything to do with large or unlimited amounts of "soft money"—or perhaps more to the point, that donors have no more opportunity to buy favor with those candidates and officeholders by putting in their hands or at their disposal large sums of soft money.[122]

Fundraising for state candidates

The FEC has also ruled that federal candidates may appear at fundraising events for state and local candidates. "Mere attendance" poses no problem. A problem arises only if the officeholder (or candidate) is assisting in the actual fundraising for those candidates. A candidate or officeholder may speak at such an event, soliciting contributions generally. But when he or she does so, the party sponsor or candidate must arrange for notices limiting the scope of the candidate's solicitation to hard money. These may be written notices, "clearly and conspicuously displayed," confirming that the officeholder or candidate is only soliciting funds that fall within federal law limits and source restrictions. A written notice replaces the need for any oral representations to the same effect. Conversely, if there is no written notice, the candidate may make the requisite representation, saying:

"I am only asking for $2,000 from individuals and I am not asking for corporate, labor or union funds."

This curious oral notice need only be provided once, which should help greatly with the rhythm and interest of the balance of the speech. Later, when the officeholder or candidate is mingling with the attendees at the event, many of whom may be donors or potential donors, the officeholder or candidate may mercifully avoid repeating the statement on a "one-on-one" basis. On the other hand, the officeholder and candidate may not recite in "rote" fashion the disclaimer of any intention to

---

[122] Some federal officeholders may become candidates for state office, and the Act makes some allowance for them to raise and spend money for their own state and local purposes under the limits of state and local, rather than federal, law. The exception requires that the solicitation of the funds, and their later expenditure, refer "only to such state and local candidate" or her opponents for state or local office.

raise funds other than federal funds, while "encouraging the potential donor to disregard the limitation."

What if those hearing the appeal disregard the limitation and contribute soft money anyway, inspired by the rhetoric of the speech, or blinded by ignorance, or determined to violate at least the spirit of the law? The candidate is not liable. She has discharged the relevant legal obligation with the sincerely delivered "oral" representation. The remaining question for the FEC has been the circumstance in which a "solicitation" has occurred, requiring the various representations, either written or oral. Mere "publicity" for an event is not in and of itself a solicitation. But if the publicity includes clear language of solicitation—as distinguished from a general "save the date" announcement—and the candidate consented to being named in or featured in the material, then solicitation has occurred and triggers a corresponding requirement for a representation of intent to solicit only federal or hard funds. In this same vein, the FEC has held that a candidate's appearance in event materials, as a member of the "host committee," constitutes a solicitation. The FEC could not decide whether the position of Honorary Chairperson of the event would also be treated as a solicitation for these purposes.[123]

The FEC considered the questions raised by a federal candidate or officeholder fundraising in the very different setting of support for a state ballot initiative.[124] The outcome turned on the issue of candidate control: on whether the candidate had established, financed, maintained, or controlled the committee for which monies were raised, one devoted to overturning by initiative a state campaign finance law. The federal officeholder in question had organized the committee, then served as its first Chair; and after a period when he was not associated with the committee, he sought to return as its Chair and raise funds for it, assisted by others involved with his Congressional office and campaigns.

The element of "control" by the federal officeholder or candidate

The first question is whether a ballot initiative committee is engaged in election-related activity, since

---

[123] FEC Advisory Opinion 2003-3.

[124] FEC Advisory Opinion 2003-12.

it is concerned with influencing the passage of legislation and not the election of public officials. The FEC held that the committee was somehow both involved and not involved in election-related activity. How is that, you ask? The FEC concluded that in the period before the initiative qualified for the ballot, all the activities conducted to achieve qualification were not, yet, election-related. Once qualification was successfully achieved, the funds spent to influence voter approval of the initiative would be election-related. So as a general rule, the fundraising restrictions of BCRA—limiting the officeholder to federal limits and sources in raising funds—would be triggered in the post-qualification period. The ballot initiative would be treated as a nonfederal election for purposes of the new law and the related officeholder and candidate fundraising restrictions.

For the hapless officeholder who establishes or controls a committee, however, this bifurcated treatment of the initiative would be of little help. The FEC held that he could raise funds for the committee only under BCRA restrictions throughout the entire period, both before and after qualification for the ballot. This is because he had "established" the committee, and still clearly controlled it. This special relationship meant that, in raising funds for the committee, he could solicit only individuals and federal political committees, and any contributor was limited to $5,000 per calendar year. Moreover, any "Federal election activities" conducted by the committee would be subject to other BCRA requirements. An example would be "issue advertising"—any public communications naming the federal official in ads directed to his Congressional district and appearing to promote or support him. Such a public communication would have to be paid for entirely with federal or "hard" money.

Jones is a federal candidate, and he would like to raise funds for a 501(c) organization dedicated to promoting the virtues of eternal bliss and discouraging melancholy and ennui. Since the organization is a tax-exempt entity not engaged in election-related activities, he may solicit funds

*from any person, in any amount, so long as he does not spec-
ify to the organization how the funds raised would be spent.*

*Later, Jones decides to organize his own version of the
tax-exempt, now seeking to discourage alienation as well as
melancholy and ennui. The legal outcome here is different:
since the organization is one he controls, he cannot raise
funds from persons other than individuals and registered
political committees, or in amounts other than $5,000 per
calendar year. Upon hearing from counsel about this rule,
Jones becomes at once both melancholy and alienated.*

While federal candidates may not raise "soft
money" for party voter registration and GOTV
programs, federal candidates and officeholders may do
so for 501(c) tax-exempt organizations engaged in
these activities. A number of conditions and requirements apply, resulting in significant limitations on the
kind of nonprofit tax-exempt fundraising, related to a
federal election, that these candidates and officeholders may do. The Act distinguishes between two kinds
of nonprofits—those whose principal purpose is to
engage in these election-related activities and those
who may conduct such activities but not as their "principal purpose."[125]

**Different
rules when
soliciting for
tax-exempt
organizations**

501(c) nonprofits *without* a principal purpose of
funding registration and GOTV activities. Candidates
and officeholders may raise funds without limit for
these kinds of organizations, so long as they make only
a "general solicitation" of the money and do not "specify
how the funds will or should be spent." If the solicitation is specific, seeking funds for election-related activity, then only individual contributions to the
organization may be solicited, and only in amounts of
$20,000 per individual per calendar year.

*A federal candidate chooses to raise money for the Red
Cross, and she directs solicitations to a wide range of potential donors, looking for as large a contribution as any one
donor can provide. The Act does not restrict this activity.*

---

[125] 11 C.F.R. § 300.65.

The same candidate raises money for the NAACP, which conducts a wide range of activities, including, but not as one of its "principal purposes," voter registration. The candidate may conduct a solicitation without limit on the amount raised from each donor, so long as the candidate does not suggest the monies raised will or should be spent for voter registration. If the candidate does make a statement to that effect, then the solicitation must be limited—to individuals, and to an amount requested from each individual not to exceed $20,000 per calendar year.

501(c) nonprofits *with* a principal purpose of funding registration and GOTV activities. Federal candidates and officeholders may raise money for nonprofits with this principal purpose. But if they do, the Act limits the scope of the solicitation and the amount that may be solicited. The candidates or officeholders may solicit donations in these circumstances only from individuals, and then only in amounts from each donor up to $20,000 per calendar year.

As in the case of national party committees, a candidate or officeholder may seek and rely upon a certification from a nonprofit that it is not, in the current cycle, engaged in federal election-related activities. The requirements for such a certification are the same for candidates and officeholders as they are for parties: the certification must be in writing, signed by an officer or authorized representative with "actual knowledge" of the activities, and the candidate or officeholder may not rely on any such certification if she knows it to be false.

When someone gives more than asked

What happens if a federal officeholder solicits an individual, and seeks only a $20,000 contribution, but the individual makes a contribution in a larger amount? The officeholder is not liable in this circumstance: the prohibition applies to a "solicitation," and the officeholder's solicitation conformed to the limitations of the Act. It is also true, however, that the question of what was solicited is a question of fact; and if the contributor, following a conversation with an officeholder, contributes more than $20,000 to the tax-exempt, a question about the understanding between the two could be raised. For this reason, as federal candidates and officeholders consider the additional liability they face under these new solicitation restrictions, they may prudently confirm all solicitations in writing.

The national parties may encourage their federal candidates and officeholders to engage in these activities. Nothing in the Act suggests, much less states clearly, that these exceptions do not apply because of the involvement of a national party committee. Hence:

When parties encourage solicitations...

The national party requests that federal officeholders affiliated with the party assist with a major national fundraising campaign to raise tax-exempt funds for GOTV and voter registration in minority areas. The officeholders may do so, if they comply with the requirements stated previously. They also may do so at the request of candidates who would benefit from these activities, and of the charities engaged in the registration and GOTV work.

Summary of restrictions on federal candidate/officeholder fundraising

Generally:

1. May not "solicit, receive, direct, transfer," or spend soft money for any political organizations:
   a. National parties;
   b. State and local parties [including for Levin Amendment activities];
   c. 527s;
   d. Leadership PACs or other multicandidate committees.
2. Prohibition applies to:
   a. Their "agents";
   b. Entities they directly or indirectly establish finance, maintain, or control.

Examples:
   - "527s";
   - Leadership PACs.
3. Exceptions:
   a. May solicit generally for a 501(c) organization if:
      i. Organization not engaged principally in certain election-related activities like voter

registration; and the candidate does not control the organization or specify how the monies would be spent;

ii. Organization principally engaged in these activities but officeholder or candidate only
    (a) Solicits individuals;
    (b) Solicits from each individual no more than $20,000 in a calendar year.

b. Organization not engaged principally in certain election-related activities, but the officeholder or candidate seeks to solicit funds specifically for those activities—and then may only solicit individuals for contributions of no more than $20,000 a calendar year;

c. May also run for a state office and solicit funds only for that office under state law;

d. May attend, speak, or be a featured guest at a state or local party "fundraising event."

Liability of federal candidates and officeholders

The provisions attaching personal liability to federal candidates and officeholders mark a sharp departure from the traditional approach of campaign finance laws. Those laws have generally operated to insulate candidates who have been treated as "agents" of their own committees, and liability for illegal contributions received or expenditures made has typically fallen on those committees.

In any event, the risks to the officeholder must be evaluated also in light of the sharply increased criminal exposure provided by the Act for "knowing and willful" violations. As discussed further below, the Act provides for the criminal enforcement of certain "knowing and willful" violations involving the "making, receiving, or reporting" of contributions or donations. The term "solicitation" does not appear in the language of this provision; but the act of solicitation is integrally related to the "making" of contributions. So it is possible, perhaps even likely, that a candidate found to have solicited soft money "knowingly and willfully" would be subject to criminal penalties.

It was noted earlier that the Act provides an exception from its broad prohibition on "soft money" fundraising for federal officeholders or candidates who "attend, speak, or [are]... featured guest[s] at a fundraising event for a state, district, or local committee of a political party." The party may also publicize appearances by the officeholders or candidates, including promoting their involvement in pre-event materials. When speaking at the event, the candidate may do so "without restriction or regulation."

Restrictions on state and local candidates

State and local candidates are not home free under the Act. They, too, are subject to a prohibition on "soft money" fundraising, even if state law would otherwise permit it. A state candidate may not fund a "public communication" which in some way "refers" to a federal candidate, and also supports or opposes, or promotes or attacks, that candidate.[126] A "public communication" includes the broadest range of communications, including broadcast, satellite and cablecast communications, as well as the use of mass mailings, phone banking, or any other form of "general public political advertising."[127] If the state candidate wishes to fund the communication, he must use only funds that meet federal law requirements for contributions—no union or corporate general treasury monies, and no contributions from individuals that exceed $2,000 per election—and also comply with federal law reporting requirements.

The restrictions on the source of funds are reasonably clear. A state or local candidate should be able to show that he has on hand in his political committee sufficient funds that meet federal law standards. Yet the additional requirement that the expenditures be reported in accordance with federal law erects a very specific hurdle. It suggests that the candidate should register the state committee as a federal "political

---

[126] BCRA § 101; 2 U.S.C. § 441i(f).

[127] A mass mailing, as noted earlier, means more than 500 pieces of identical or substantially similar mail pieces sent out within a 30 day period, while a phone bank means more than 500 calls of an identical or substantially similar nature over a period of 30 days.

committee," at least long enough to file a public report of the federal candidate related expenditures. The FEC rules are silent on how in practice this would work. State candidates will be concerned more with avoiding expenditures that even raise the issue—at least those state candidates fortunate enough to be aware of the issue at all.

But federal candidates can say nice things about state and local candidates

The FEC has addressed the question of whether a federal officeholder creates legal problems for a state candidate when appearing in an "endorsement ad" for the state candidate.[128] The FEC held that it did not: the endorsement ran in only one direction, from the federal candidate to the state candidate, and could not be said to support, oppose, promote or attack the federal candidate. The FEC also found that the ad did not constitute an illegal coordinated expenditure, because it did not satisfy the "content" standard. (See Chapter 4.) It is noteworthy that the FEC based its decision on the text of the ad submitted by the state candidate for agency review. The FEC decision is consistent with the legislative history.

Governor James is running for another term on the same ticket with popular Senator Jones who is seeking reelection in the same year. Governor wishes to fund an ad through his gubernatorial committee featuring his relationship with Jones, and noting his share in major achievements by Jones in bringing development money to the state. James may not run this ad, unless his campaign pays for it with monies that meet federal limits and restrictions on source. But if the ad only speaks to the Governor's achievements, with Jones appearing only to praise the Governor, the ad may be funded under the state law.

But state and local candidates are OK—if they keep quiet about federal candidates

The Act does allow the hapless James to run such an ad if it "is in connection with an election" for his state office—and refers "only" to him, or any other state and local candidate running for the same state and local office. This is a curious exception, seemingly premised on the mistaken belief that without it, there would be some question of whether an ad by a state candidate, mentioning only a state candidate, could be financed

---

[128] FEC Advisory Opinion 2003-25.

under state law. Federal law, however, could not purport to restrict the financing of such an ad in any event.

Candidates' "personal use" of campaign funds

So much for federal candidates and officeholders and their "soft money." The Act makes some other adjustments in the federal law affecting federal candidates. It codifies much of the existing rulebook, developed by the FEC, defining and prohibiting candidates' "personal use" of their campaign funds.[129] The law stated only that "personal use" was prohibited, but the FEC has in the past developed rules with considerably greater detail. The basic FEC scheme has been adopted in the Act, making these restrictions a matter of federal law—and emphasis—and not merely regulatory fiat. The Act states, as do the current FEC rules, that a candidate has made a prohibited "personal use" of her campaign funds if those funds are used to "fulfill any commitment, obligation, or expense of a person that would exist irrespective of the candidate's campaign...."[130]

The Act reworked the regulatory language, and did not delve into qualifications and exceptions, though it is not clear that there is any intention to deprive the FEC of the continuing authority to provide for such qualifications and exceptions. Thus, for example, personal use under the Act includes payment of campaign funds for "a clothing purchase." The FEC rules set out the same prohibition, but with an exception for "items of *de minimis*" value that are used in the campaign, such as campaign T-shirts or caps with campaign slogans. The Act's drafters were stressing that clothing could not be bought with campaign funds, but not expressing an objection to campaign T-shirts. The FEC rules will still govern the precise contours of each of the exceptions, and there also is a significant body of interpretations by the FEC over the years that still should be consulted.

All the same, the Act stresses the key prohibitions, defining "personal use" to include

"**Personal use**" **of campaign funds**

---

[129] BCRA § 301; 2 U.S.C. § 439a.

[130] An officeholder may also use campaign funds to pay for certain expenses associated with his duties as a holder of federal office, subject to other statutory restrictions and the rules of the House and Senate.

- Home mortgage, rent, or utility payments;
- Clothing purchases;
- Noncampaign-related automobile expenses;
- Country club memberships;
- Vacation or other noncampaign-related trips;
- Household food items;
- Tuition payments;
- Admission to a sporting event, concert, theater, or other form of entertainment not associated with an election campaign; and
- Dues, fees, and other payments to a health club or recreational facility.

The FEC appears likely to construe the allowances for the use of campaign finds strictly. In a recent Advisory Opinion, the FEC would not allow a federal officeholder to refund from his federal committee improper contributions originally made to his state committee.[131] The FEC noted that the original contributions related to a state, not a federal candidacy, and that the officeholder was not in any event legally obligated to refund the money.

What candidates may do with their campaign funds

At the same time, the Act identifies the exclusive uses to which campaign funds may be put.[132] Other than expenditures "in connection with" their campaigns, the Act leaves in place the allowance under the prior law for the payment with campaign funds of ordinary and necessary expenses incurred in connection with the candidate's duties as "a holder of federal office." The officeholder considering payments for this purpose must, however, also consult the "ethics rules" of the House and Senate which control how officially related expenses are paid. The candidate may contribute with campaign funds to 501(c) charities, as recognized under the Internal Revenue Code, and she also may contribute without limitation from those funds to national, state, or local party committees.

---

[131] FEC Advisory Opinion 2003-26.

[132] The FEC rules implementing the old law sanctioned other uses of campaign funds that were permissible if otherwise "lawful." The Act did not retain this general catch-all provision.

CHAPTER 5

DISCLOSURE

The Act amends the old law to supplement and improve its various disclosure requirements. Previously noted has been the special disclosure of "electioneering communications." In addition, the Act promotes greater frequency of reporting by candidates and national party committees, and expands the range of reporting required of committees or individuals that make "independent expenditures." Another provision adds considerably to the requirement under the old law for "disclaimers" to be attached by political committees, candidates, and others to their general public political advertising for the purpose of disclosing the sponsorship of their ads. That provision also compels candidates and others who finance television and radio ads, including "negative ads," to include in those ads statements of responsibility or approval of their content. In support of these disclosure requirements, the Act mandates that the FEC direct the development of new reporting software, and also assure prompt distribution to the public via the Internet of reports filed with the FEC.

More frequent filings for national party committees and candidates

The simplest provisions are those that mandate greater frequency of reporting by candidates and national party committees. Under the old law, candidates could elect in their off-years (years other than the year in which the election is scheduled) to file reports twice yearly of their receipts and disbursements. The Act eliminates this option, and imposes on them for those years—as well as for the actual election year—quarterly reporting.[133] National party committees also are required to file monthly in place of quarterly reports.[134] State and local party committees that engage in Federal election activity must also file monthly.

---

[133] BCRA § 503(a); 2 U.S.C. § 434(a)(2)(B).

[134] BCRA § 503(b); 2 U.S.C. § 434(a)(4)(B).

Sponsorship identification—and candidate approval of ads

The law before BCRA provided for certain disclosures—popularly referred to as "disclaimers"—that require "general public political advertising" to carry a statement of who paid for communications and whether a candidate authorized them. The Act adds to these requirements to assure the same disclosures for soft money activities, and also to compel the inclusion of statements of approval or responsibility by candidates or others who financed the ads. Certain of these requirements apply specifically to "negative" campaign ads.

Disclosing sponsorship of "soft money" communications

Political committees financing these ads with soft money—in whole or in part—must make a clear statement identifying who paid for and authorized them. A political committee is a committee registered with the FEC, but still able to spend "soft money" for some purposes. An example would be a state party, or a nonparty political committee, which unlike national party committees may maintain under the new law "soft money" accounts for some purposes. The Act provides that if such a political committee makes a soft money "disbursement" for "general public political advertising" allowed under the Act, the communications must carry the required statement of sponsorship.[135] Public communications for this purpose includes a political committee website, and also 500 substantially similar unsolicited emails. The same requirement holds for any "person" financing "electioneering communications," and in this instance, the Act also requires, in addition to disclosure of the person paying for the communication, additional information in the form of a "permanent street address, telephone number, or World Wide Web address."

Printed sponsorship notices

Printed "disclaimers" are subject under the Act to more exacting standards for presentation.[136] The Act provides that these printed disclaimers shall

(1) be of sufficient type size to be clearly readable by the recipient of the communication;

---

[135] BCRA § 311; 2 U.S.C. § 441d(a).

[136] BCRA § 311; 2 U.S.C. § 441d(c).

(2)   be contained in a printed box set apart from the other contents of the communication; and

(3)   be printed with a reasonable degree of color contrast between the background and the printed statement.

Candidates are subject under the Act to a new type of "disclaimer" for radio and television advertisements.

Radio ads must carry "an audio statement by the candidate that identifies the candidate and states that the candidate has approved the communication." Television ads must also include such a statement, but the Act imposes some particular requirements, namely, that the statement:

(i)   shall be conveyed by

   (I)   an unobscured, full-screen view of the candidate making the statement, or

   (II) the candidate in voice-over, accompanied by a clearly identifiable photographic or similar image of the candidate; and

(ii) shall also appear in writing at the end of the communication in a clearly readable manner with a reasonable degree of color contrast between the background and the printed statement, for a period of at least 4 seconds.[137]

Statements by candidates and others of their "approval" of TV and radio statements

The FEC has added more specific requirements to assure the visibility and clarity of these statements. The rules provide for a safe harbor of sorts for candidate voiceovers accompanying a still picture: 80% of screen height. For the printed statements, a candidate can operate safely by assuring that they appear at no less than 4% of screen height, for a period of no less than 4 seconds, and with a reasonable degree of color contrast.

What about committees other than candidate committees. The FEC has indicated that it believes that these types of approval—"stand by your ad" statements—may be required for phone banks conducted by political committees other than candidate committees, or other non-candidate organizations.

---

[137] BCRA § 311; 2 U.S.C. § 441d(d).

Disclosure for "electioneering communications"

This requirement applies to persons other than candidates, including entities making "electioneering communications."[138] The Act requires an audio statement about the political committee or other person paying for the ad, in the form of "[name of person] is responsible for the content of this advertising." The disclosure must also include the name of any "connected organization" of the payor. Thus, if the payor is a political committee of a trade association, for example, then the disclosure must include the name of the trade association, as well as its political committee. Television statements of approval are required of these organizations, as they are for candidate committees: a "representative" of the sponsoring organization must appear in an "unobscured, full-screen view," and the same statement must appear at the end in a writing with the requisite readability and reasonable color contrast.

"Certifications" and disclaimers for "negative ads"

An additional control on content imposed by the Act on candidate ads takes aim at the "negative ad," the customary attack launched by one candidate at an opponent in paid advertising.[139] The Act does not specifically refer to "negative" ads, but instead to ads in which the candidate makes a "direct reference to another candidate for the same office"; but the legislative history makes clear the intent.[140] Under the Act, candidates are not entitled to the benefits of the "lowest unit rate" under federal law for their purchase of broadcast time unless they certify to stations, in writing, that ads with this "direct reference" will carry certain statements of approval by the candidate. This requirement appears to overlap with the broad "disclaimer" requirement mentioned earlier, which also compels candidates to appear in those ads, by voice or image, to accept responsibility for them.

In the provision conditioning access to the lowest unit rate, the candidate must, in television ads, include

---

[138] BCRA § 311; 2 U.S.C. § 441d(2).

[139] BCRA § 305; 47 U.S.C. § 315(b)(2).

[140] The provision will "help slow the explosive growth of negative political commercials that are corroding the faith of individuals in the political process." 147 Cong. Rec. S2692 (daily ed. Mar. 22, 2001) (statement of Sen. Wyden).

in the ad, for a period of no less than 4 seconds:
  (i)   a clearly identifiable photographic or similar image of the candidate; and
  (ii) a clearly readable printed statement, identifying the candidate and stating that the candidate has approved the broadcast and that the candidate's authorized committee paid for the broadcast.

A radio broadcast would include a "personal audio statement by the candidate" identifying herself, the office she seeks, and stating that she has approved the broadcast.

Should the candidate file a certification under this provision, but not meet these requirements in ads with a "direct reference" to another candidate, the candidate loses her entitlement to the "lowest unit rate" for all ads placed with the station within the periods before elections when the rates are in effect. Should the candidate decline to file the certification, then the candidate is also ineligible for the rate.

It is not clear how the statement required for an ad with a "direct reference" to another candidate would differ from, or be added in some way to, the statement of approval candidates are required to make in TV and radio broadcasts of any kind. The statements are different; but the general one, applicable to all ads, would meet the requirements for the more specific one needed for a "direct reference" ad.

Independent expenditure reporting

The Act 's disclosure provisions also affect the reporting of independent expenditures, and expand the reporting requirement of those making them.[141] Under the old law, the disclosure involved a statement of whether the expenditure supports or opposes the candidate, and under penalty of perjury, whether it was in fact made without the request or collaboration of the candidate. Contributors to the committee or person making the expenditure would have to be identified, if their contributions exceeded $200.00.

---

[141] BCRA § 212; 2 U.S.C. § 434g.

These requirements are left in place, but the Act amends the requirement of a filing within 24 hours with the FEC of any independent expenditure aggregating $1,000 or more after the 20th day, but more than 24 hours before, the date of an election. The Act provides for additional reports, also filed within 24 hours, each time an additional expenditure of $1,000 or more is made. It also requires, as existing law does not, reports to be filed within 48 hours at any time up to the 20th day before an election, for any independent expenditure aggregating $10,000 or more. Additional reports are required on a 48-hour basis for each additional aggregate expenditure of more than $10,000 in that election.

Access to broadcast station records of requests to buy political advertising

The Act promotes a different type of disclosure through an amendment to the Federal Communications Act, assuring public access to records of requests to broadcasters to purchase time for various kinds of political ads.[142] These ads include those by or for candidates, but also by persons wishing to place ads on "a message relating to any political matter of national importance." Such messages are, for example, those popularly associated with "issue ads." They may refer to a candidate for public office, but they need not: the Act also secures access to records of requests for time for ads on "a national legislative issue of public importance."

The Act requires that broadcasters maintain records of these requests in some detail, including information on whether requests were rejected or accepted; the rate charged; the date and time of airing of the ads; and the name of the candidate or issue involved in the communication. The records must also contain, for ads other than those paid for by candidates, information about the person purchasing the time, including the name, address, and phone number of a contact person, along with a list of the chief executive officers or members of the executive committee or board of directors of the organization.

These requirements are intended to help trace the

---

[142] BCRA § 504; 47 U.S.C. § 315(e).

flow of "issue advertising" dollars. They apply to 527 or tax-exempt spending for election-related advertising, but do not depend on whether a candidate is named in the ad. Nor is there any connection to periods immediately before elections: the access is guaranteed at all times, and the stations are required to maintain records for a period of not less than 2 years. The organizations engaged in advertising subject to these requirements must disclose their officers or representatives. The real "interests" behind such ads are, as a result, more readily identified.

Reports under the Millionaire's Amendment

A variety of disclosure requirements have emerged from implementation of the "millionaire's amendment" (See Chapter 4). Candidates must file special forms reporting on their committees' finances, so that other candidates can complete the calculation of their possible entitlement to contributions relief. Notifications of personal spending are required, as are notices to the Commission and political parties of both the entitlement to relief and also the suspension of benefits upon certain triggering events, such as the withdrawal of an opponent. The hypothetical developed at length by the FEC and contained in the Appendix notes the various different disclosures that this provision requires.

Getting information, fast and on the web, through the FEC

The Act places new responsibilities on the FEC to assure improved, speedier public Internet access to reports filed with the agency, and to develop special software that candidates would use to facilitate virtually instantaneous disclosure. The agency is mandated to make reports "accessible" to the public not later than 48 hours after receipt by the Commission, or within 24 hours if the report is one filed electronically. It must maintain a "central site" on the Internet for public access to reports and other election-related information maintained by the Commission. Since the IRS receives the reports from "527s," it processes information that is "election-related," and the Act requires the two agencies,

IRS and FEC, to coordinate in making their reports available through or posted on the FEC site.

Reporting software for candidates—and instant reporting

The FEC is also mandated to promulgate standards for use by vendors in developing special reporting software. The software would be designed to more easily record information on receipts and disbursements while transmitting the recorded information immediately to the Commission and facilitating immediate Internet posting by that agency. The FEC would provide the software, once available, to all candidates or committees filing under the Act. Candidates would be required to use this software for their reporting. The Act does not establish a timetable for the completion of this project. In light of the steps required—promulgation of standards and vendor development—some time may be required to bring it to fruition.

Inaugural committees

The Act also provides for one additional disclosure requirement, somewhat off the subject of campaign finance: donations to Presidential Inaugural Committees. For purpose of federal law, an "Inaugural Committee" is the committee appointed by the President-elect to "be in charge of the Presidential Inaugural Ceremony and functions and activities connected with the ceremony."[143] The Act conditions recognition of such a committee on its compliance with a requirement that it report donations of $200 or more to the Federal Election Commission within 90 days of the Inauguration. Beyond this reporting requirement, the Act prohibits acceptance by these committees of donations from foreign nationals.

---

[143] 36 U.S.C. § 501(1).

CHAPTER 6

ENFORCEMENT

The Act makes significant changes in the basic approach to enforcement of the federal campaign finance laws. It increased the penalties for some violations, changed the statute of limitations for criminal enforcement, mandates the development of criminal sentencing standards for campaign finance violations, and appears to have generally motivated more of a focus on criminal enforcement of matters previously left to civil disposition.

Knowing and willful violations

The law allows for two classes of civil violation. One, for want of better terms, is the garden-variety violation, while the other is one found to have been committed "knowingly and willfully." Under existing laws, knowing and willful violations are subject to heightened penalties; and they may also be referred to the Justice Department (DOJ) for criminal prosecution.[144]

The Act provides that any person—candidate, committee, or other—who is found to have knowingly and willfully violated the law in "making, receiving, or reporting" any expenditure or donation aggregating $25,000 or more during a calendar year is subject to felony prosecution: either criminal fine, or imprisonment of not more than five years, or both fine and imprisonment. "Knowing and willful violations" aggregating at least $2,000 but less than $25,000 are also enforceable criminally, as misdemeanors, with fines or imprisonment for not more than one year, or both.[145]

Criminal penalties for "knowing and willful" violations

The question of which violations of a "knowing and willful" nature would be prosecuted civilly, and which criminally, has been more or less governed for a number of years by a "Memorandum of Understanding" negotiated by the FEC and DOJ in 1975. The MOU acknowl-

---

[144] In some cases, the Department may elect against proceeding with prosecution in the first instance, and refer the matter to the FEC for consideration under a "knowing and willful" standard.

[145] BCRA § 312; 2 U.S.C. § 437g(d)(1)(A).

edges that some knowing and willful violations would not be the "proper subject" for criminal prosecution. The MOU attempted to establish, in broad terms, the standards for determining knowing and willful violations of a criminal nature. These would be violations that were 1) significant and substantial; and 2) aggravated in the intent with which they were committed, or in monetary amount.

The relevant "factors" cited in the analysis of when such a violation occurred would include:

—their repetitive nature

—the existence of a prior practice or pattern

—prior notice of potential liability

—the "extent of the conduct," determined by the number of locations affected by the violation; the number of persons involved; and the monetary amount.

The MOU also allowed for the possibility of "other proper considerations," all unspecified, that might bear on the decision. As a practical matter, the FEC took on the burden of enforcing even "knowing and willful" campaign finance violations. This is not to say that the Department of Justice was altogether silent: over the years, it prosecuted federal campaign finance violations, but the numbers were relatively small and the cases by and large minor, with the exception of some high-profile prosecutions in the wake of the intense attention to alleged financing irregularities in the 1996 Presidential election.[146]

Still the FEC held center stage in the enforcement of cases involving apparent "knowing and willful" misconduct. This was in part a function of uncertainties about the law and its interpretation. On issues like party "soft money," which involved some considerable disagreement about what the law was, the Department did not seem the appropriate forum for the resolution of the question.

BCRA's impact on the MOU or its application in practice has been perhaps in some sense indirect. The new law reflected a Congressional concern with more aggressive criminal enforcement or focus. As discussed below, the statute of limitations was extended, and

---

[146] *See, e.g., United States of America v. Kanchanalak,* 192 F.3d 1037 (D.D.C. 1999).

Congress also directed the development of sentencing guidelines for campaign finance violations. Whether Congress intended a more thoroughgoing revision of criminal enforcement policy is less clear. In any event, the FEC and DOJ have since concluded that the long-standing 1975 MOU is outdated and a new protocol for determining their respective responsibilities is required. As of the date of this edition, they are renegotiating its terms, with the expectation that they can conclude their effort successfully by mid-2004. It has become clear from the public comment of senior DOJ officials that they anticipate a more robust or assertive role for the Department. They are looking for more reliable, timely notification of possible criminal conduct that comes to the attention of the agency. Their assertiveness in taking up cases with possible criminal dimensions—rather than yielding ground in the first instance to the FEC—seem likely also to increase.

"Conduit" contributions

Another type of violation singled out for criminal enforcement is the prohibition on "conduit" contributions.[147] Section 441f of the law provides:

> No person shall make a contribution in the name of another person or knowingly permit his name to be used to effect such a contribution and no person shall knowingly accept a contribution made by one person in the name of another person.

The conduct addressed in the provision takes the form of A, the true source of the funds, providing the money to B who then contributes the money in her own name. The making of conduit contributions came to widespread attention in enforcement actions arising out of the 1996 Presidential campaign. The Act reflects the intention to sharply increase the consequences for these violations.

"Conduit" contributions: your name, my money

The Act raises the penalty level for "knowing and willful" violations of the "conduit" provision in two ways. First it increases the fines that may be imposed

Civil penalties for conduit violations

---

[147] BCRA § 315; 2 U.S.C. § 437g(d)(1)(D).

by the FEC—or by the courts upon suit by the FEC—for these kinds of violations. The violation is still "knowing and willful," but the penalty may be a civil one if the amount of money involved in the violation is less than $25,000. Under the old law, a "knowing and willful" violation could be punished by a civil penalty not to exceed the greater of 1) $10,000, or 2) an amount equal to 200% of any contribution or expenditure involved in the violation. The Act raises these penalty levels for conduit contributions, to not less than 300% of the amount involved in the violation, and not more than the greater of 1) $50,000, or 2) 1,000% of the amount involved in the violation.

Criminal penalties for conduit violations

Second, the Act includes the application of criminal penalties for violations of this "conduit" prohibition aggregating more than $10,000 in a calendar year. The penalties include imprisonment, or a criminal fine, or both. The term of imprisonment is not to exceed two years; but it should be noted that if the amount involved is $25,000 or more, the term of imprisonment under the Act's general "knowing and willful" criminal penalty provisions could extend to five years. Alternatively, a criminal fine is mandated at the levels previously described for civil violations: not less than 300% of the amount involved in the violation, and not more than the greater of $50,000 or 1,000% of the amount involved in the violation.

Criminal sentencing standards

The commitment to increased criminal enforcement is also reflected in a mandate to the United States Sentencing Commission to promulgate or amend guidelines for criminal penalties for violations of the federal campaign finance laws, and to submit to Congress recommendations on improved enforcement. The Sentencing Commission has developed these guidelines, which begin at so-called "base level 8"—2 points higher than the base level for fraud. The Commission noted that while election-related offenses were similar to fraud, they are "generally...more serious due to the additional harm, or the potential harm, of corrupting the elective process."

The guidelines adjust upwards for specific offense characteristics:
- amount of the funds involved in the offense;
- involvement of a foreign national or foreign government;
- involvement of government funds or an effort to secure a federal benefit; and
- involvement of intimidation, threats of harm, or coercion.

Another upward departure may be warranted where a defendant's conduct was "systematic or pervasive corruption of a governmental function....that may cause a loss of confidence in government."

The Act also mandates the Commission to provide for "sentencing enhancement"—not a good thing—for certain kinds of violations. These are:
- foreign national contributions;
- "a large number of illegal transactions";
- a "large aggregate amount" of illegal spending;
- the receipt or disbursement of government funds; or
- "an intent to achieve a benefit from the federal government."

This last ground for sentencing enhancement is of some interest. By and large, the criminal laws have not focused successfully on whether a campaign contributor, in violating the Act, sought effectively an illicit advantage in influencing the official action of a candidate. It mattered only whether the law was violated; and the question of motivation was largely irrelevant. The consideration in sentencing of whether there was "an intent to achieve a benefit from the federal government" means that this issue of motivation has entered, in a sense, by the backdoor—not in the theory of prosecution, but in the determination of sentence in the event of a conviction.

A factor in sentencing: were you trying to buy something from the government?

Another similar question is raised by the consideration of whether the violation involved the receipt or disbursement of government funds. Existing law does not, by a specific exclusion, apply to the receipt or expenditure of federal government funds. For example, an officeholder who directs the use of government property to conduct campaign activity is violating other

Or were you using government property?

statutes and Congressional rules, but she is not committing a violation of the Federal Election Campaign Act. It is possible that the sentencing guideline mandate is intended to make this factor relevant by the "back door"—by making some use of government resources relevant to sentencing, even if it is not as a matter of law relevant to the theory of the prosecution or to the grounds for conviction.

Overall, the purpose of the amendments concerned with criminal penalties and enforcement is to encourage criminal prosecution of violations of the campaign finance laws, and to insure imprisonment in virtually all cases concluding in a conviction. The old law had been seen to have "structural flaws...that make it difficult for the more conscientious prosecutors to adequately pursue their cases"; the Act provides those prosecutors "with the tools they need to investigate and prosecute those who violate our campaign laws and attack the integrity of our electoral process."[148]

Statute of limitations

The old law prohibited prosecution, trial or punishment for any criminal violation, "unless the indictment is found or the information is instituted within 3 years after the date of the violation." The Act extends this statute of limitations to 5 years,[149] so that "prosecutors are [not] denied the time they need to pursue complex crimes."[150]

FEC rulemaking under the Act

Enforcement under the Act will also occur through rules promulgated by the FEC after enactment. The Act contemplated these rules, and mandated their initial completion within specified periods of time. The FEC was directed to promulgate rules on the provisions governing political parties within 90 days of enactment, and on all other provisions within nine months (270

---

[148] 147 Cong. Rec. S3128 (daily ed. Mar. 29, 2001) (statement of Sen. Thompson).

[149] BCRA § 313; 2 U.S.C. § 455(a).

[150] 147 Cong. Rec. S3128 (daily ed. Mar. 29, 2001) (statement of Sen. Lieberman).

days). As noted throughout this book, the FEC has issued scores of rules pursuant to this provision.

Nothing in the Act would prohibit those affected by the Act from initiating their own proposals for rule-making. It can be expected, in fact, that there will be such proposals to supplement whichever ones the FEC concludes that it should develop. Moreover, as noted, candidates and other may file—and so far have filed—requests for Advisory Opinions seeking interpretations of the law as applied to a particular proposed activity.

A note on the effective date for the Act

The Act took effect generally on November 6, 2002, with some variations.

The party soft money provisions became effective on November 6, 2002, except that national party committees could use soft money on hand as of that date through January 1, 2003, to retire debts and obligations incurred solely in connection with the November general elections, or incurred after the date of those elections solely in connection with runoffs, recounts or election contests resulting from the November 2002 general elections. Those debts and obligations could be paid until 2003 with funds allocated between hard and soft accounts under the rules prescribed by the Federal Election Commission under the old law.

All the other provisions of the Act became effective November 6, 2002, with the exception of the modification in the "hard money" contribution limits. Increases in those limits took effect January 1, 2003.

CHAPTER 7

THE SUPREME COURT DECIDED: A NOTE ON *McCONNELL v. FEDERAL ELECTION COMMISSION*

Having heard the case on September 8, 2003, the Supreme Court issued its decision almost exactly 90 days later, on December 10. By a 5-4 vote, the Court sustained the constitutionality of most of the material provisions of the law. The majority offered broad support for the soft money-related provisions of the law, finding them fully grounded in Congressional authority to regulate campaign finance and consistent with constitutional precedent. The exceptions have been noted, as appropriate, elsewhere in this book. The key points and themes of the majority opinion are as follows:

(1) Congressional Authority to Regulate Campaign Finance. The Court strongly endorses Congress' authority to determine needed controls on funds spent to influence federal elections. The majority says much about the history of Congressional regulation of political money, beginning with the Progressive Era controls imposed on corporate political spending. Congress, the Court claims, is owed a substantial measure of "deference" to these efforts to protect the political process from the corruptive effects of interested money.[151] In fact, the Court states, this deference is justified by "Congress' ability," in enacting and enforcing contribution limits, "to weigh competing constitutional interests in an area in which it enjoys particular expertise."[152] This is a strong claim for Congressional authority to strike the relevant constitutional balance, and it pervades the majority's support for the constitutionality of BCRA's core soft money-related provisions.

This claim rests also on the additional position that Congress, when legislating limits on political money to

---

[151] *McConnell*, at 6.

[152] *Id.* at 27.

attack "corruption" or its appearance, need not limit its effort to instances of bribery or comparable "sale of office." The Court stresses that the more insidious effects of money to win "access" support aggressive Congressional controls.[153] The Court cites also the potential use of money to more subtly affect the course of legislative affairs, such as in "manipulations of the legislative calendar" to discourage the progress of particular bills.[154]

(2) Prohibitions on National Party Soft Money. The Congress' attempt to address national party soft money is described by the Court as both its "main goal" and also a "modest" one.[155] It finds that the potential for corruption accomplished through soft money received and spent by the parties—or solicited by them for use by others—is supported by "common sense," and also by the "ample record" before the Court as developed in the litigation and also in Congressional investigations into 1996 Presidential election financing practices.[156] The close relationship between parties and candidates is a key factor in the Court's analysis: this relationship allows the parties to act as the link between donors seeking legislative advantage and candidates seeking electoral benefits.[157]

The Court does make some room for the national parties in two respects. First, it chooses to avoid a reading of the law that would prohibit national party committees from donating "hard money" to tax-exempt organizations engaged in Federal election activity, and also "527" political organizations.[158] It concludes that so broad a restriction would be "constitutionally questionable."[159] Moreover, the Court rejects the suggestion that

---

[153] *Id.* at 18, 20, 40-45.

[154] *Id.* at 40.

[155] *Id.* at 32.

[156] *Id.* at 12, 35.

[157] *Id.* at 41, 45.

[158] *Id.* at 73.

[159] *Id.*

the restrictions are so broad that national parties could not cooperate with state and local parties in planning for the state and local parties' own raising and spending of soft money.[160] The national parties' officers need avoid only direct "personal" involvement in the raising and spending of state and local party soft money.[161]

(3) Restrictions on State and Local Party Financing of "Federal Election Activity." The Court credits the Congressional regulation of state and local party "Federal election activity" as a critical means of avoiding evasion of the statute.[162] As the majority sees it, Congress could conclude on the record that state and local parties were used for this purpose of circumvention, but also that they might be exploited for these purposes in the future.[163] Of some comfort to the Court are the various "temporal and substantive limitations" built by Congress into the state and local party provisions. The Court cites as one example that certain "Federal election activity" provisions are triggered only when the spending "occurs in connection with an election in which a Federal candidate appears on the ballot."[164] The Court notes approvingly that the FEC has defined the term to defer the effective application of the soft money restriction for GOTV, voter identification, voter registration and generic campaign activity, to the earliest date for qualification for the primary ballot under state law, or January 1 of the election year in states without a primary.[165]

The Court also upholds the various restrictions on the raising of Levin monies. It describes these restrictions as "minor,"[166] and as "justifiable anticircumvention

---

[160] *Id.* at 51.

[161] *Id.*

[162] *Id.* at 56-57.

[163] *Id.*

[164] *Id.* at 60-61.

[165] *Id.*

[166] *Id.* at 63.

measures."[167] The Court is similarly unconcerned that there is any vagueness associated with the prohibition on the use of soft money by state and local parties to finance "public communications" that "promote, oppose, attack or support" an identified federal candidate.[168] The Court believes that those of ordinary intelligence will be able to readily identify communications of that nature, and that any doubt may be dispelled by seeking an Advisory Opinion from the FEC.

Finally, the Court takes on the objection that parties stand to suffer treatment more harsh than that facing "interest groups." The Court agrees that this may be so, but that the "disparate treatment" of parties and these groups does not violate the Constitution. The Court cites to the "real-world difference" between parties and interests—differences apparently having to do with the close involvement of elected officials with the former.[169]

(4) <u>Restrictions on Soft Money Solicitations by Federal Candidates and Officeholders.</u> The Court upholds these as "valid anticircumvention measures."[170]

(5) <u>The Prohibitions on Union and Corporate-Paid "Electioneering Communications."</u> The Court defends these provisions by refuting any notion that Congress is limited to regulating advertising that includes "express advocacy": that is, words like "vote," "defeat" or "reject." The Court states that the "express advocacy restriction was an endpoint of statutory interpretation, not a first principle of constitutional law."[171] Advertisements naming, and either praising or attacking, a federal candidate within 60 days of a general election reflected typically an intent to influence a federal election. Congress could recognize the evident purpose of such ads, in prohibiting their payment with corporate and

---

[167] *Id.*

[168] *Id.* at 62, n. 64.

[169] *Id.* at 80.

[170] *Id.* at 75.

[171] *Id.*at 83.

union funds within specific pre-election periods.[172] The Court did conclude, as did the FEC in its implementing rules, that the class of corporations subject to the prohibition did not include so-called "MCFL" corporations. (See Chapter 2.)

(6) Forcing Parties to Choose Between Independent and Coordinated Spending for a Candidate. The Court affirmed the lower court's rejection of this forced choice.[173] Parties therefore are able to make both types of expenditures for the benefit of their candidates: a "coordinated expenditure" subject to limits, in full cooperation with the candidate; and also limitless independent expenditures so long as they are planned and made without the candidate's agreement or consent. Both types of expenditures, of course, must be paid with hard money.

(7) Minor Children. The Court found "scant evidence of this form of evasion"—the attempt by parents and perhaps others to make their contributions in the name of minor children.[174]

---

[172] *Id.* at 100.

[173] *Id.* at 107-113.

[174] *Id.* at 10 (delivered by Chief Justice Rehnquist with respect to BCRA Titles III and IV).

CONCLUSION

The Congress has spoken, and also the Supreme Court; and so the development of the law will now follow the adaptation of the regulated community and the FEC. The courts will also soon rejoin the battle as challenges are brought (as some already have) to FEC rules and enforcement actions. The history of campaign finance before the Bipartisan Campaign Reform Act suggests a long and complex evolution in the application—and hence, the settled meaning—of the new law.

Some hint of what lies ahead can be gleaned from the rulemaking of the FEC under the new statute. The agency has turned out hundreds of pages of rules and explanations. A number of them, discussed in this book, involve highly intricate tests for determining "coordination" or simple but controversial definitions of terms like "solicit." The agency has already been sued over some of these decisions. The Advisory Opinions the FEC has issued have also presented complex interpretations of the law—about the specific conditions under which federal candidates and officeholders may raise funds for state candidates, or for ballot initiative campaigns. As the Commission noted at various points throughout the recent rulemaking, the answer to specific questions may depend wholly on specific facts, and the Commission's application of the law to the specific questions brought before it cannot fail to produce surprises. In its decision in *McConnell*, the Supreme Court noted the role of the FEC at various points in its decision, and approvingly cited to the Advisory Opinion process as an important venue for resolving claims about ambiguities in the law.

The purpose here is not to review or critique *McConnell*, or the result in any agency decision. It is to stress that with the enactment of the new law, and the successful defense of its constitutionality, we have embarked on the beginning—not reached the destination—of the latest phase in the long-running campaign to reform the political process. The *McConnell* Court concluded its opinion with the acknowledgment that the new law would not quiet the controversies about the uses and influence of political money. It wrote: "Money, like water, will always find an outlet."[175] The Court's decision approving the major provisions of the law was premised on the need for Congress to anticipate and address means of circumventing campaign finance controls. For this reason, the law does not for the most part (with the exception of provisions like the "electioneering communication" provision) depend on "bright lines," but instead on adjustable ones. With time, regulatory experience, and litigation, BCRA in its actual application and effect ten years from now will seem very different from the text that emerged in 2002 from the Congress. We can also assume from the history of campaign finance reforms before BCRA that the impact of the law on various types of political organizations and actors may also take surprising turns, in directions different from those forecast upon enactment.

Finally, it is worth noting that the Court in *McConnell* did not question that BCRA will directly affect core political conduct. It concluded, however, that Congress could judge the legislative interests, in protecting the "integrity" of the electoral process, to be worth the constitutional costs to free speech and association. The very margin of the decision, 5-4, with strong views expressed on both sides, mirrors the same intense divisions on this fundamental choice among elected officials, the parties, academicians, reporters, and other observers of the political process. *McConnell* does not settle this dispute, any more than the original Federal Election Campaign Act silenced the same type of arguments when it was enacted some thirty years ago. By upholding this new law, however, the Supreme Court has changed in real and significant ways the terms of this old conflict. Now the argument will continue, on these new terms, before the FEC and in the courts. If the historical pattern holds, the Congress will be called back into the fray in another 30 years or so.

---

[175] *Id.* at 118.

APPENDIX

Bipartisan Campaign Reform Act of 2002

PUBLIC LAW 107-155—MAR. 27, 2002   116 STAT. 81

Public Law 107–155
107th Congress

An Act

<table>
<tr><td>To amend the Federal Election Campaign Act of 1971 to provide bipartisan campaign reform.</td><td>Mar. 27, 2002
[H.R. 2356]</td></tr>
</table>

Be it enacted by the Senate and House of Representatives of the United States of America in Congress assembled,

SECTION 1. SHORT TITLE; TABLE OF CONTENTS.

(a) SHORT TITLE.—This Act may be cited as the "Bipartisan Campaign Reform Act of 2002".

(b) TABLE OF CONTENTS.—The table of contents of this Act is as follows:

<table>
<tr><td></td><td>Bipartisan
Campaign
Reform Act of
2002.
2 USC 431 note.</td></tr>
</table>

116 STAT. 82   PUBLIC LAW 107–155—MAR. 27, 2002

TITLE I—REDUCTION OF SPECIAL INTEREST INFLUENCE

SEC. 101. SOFT MONEY OF POLITICAL PARTIES.

(a) IN GENERAL.—Title III of the Federal Election Campaign Act of 1971 (2 U.S.C. 431 et seq.) is amended by adding at the end the following:

2 USC 441i.

"SEC. 323. SOFT MONEY OF POLITICAL PARTIES.

"(a) NATIONAL COMMITTEES.—

"(1) IN GENERAL.—A national committee of a political party (including a national congressional campaign committee of a political party) may not solicit, receive, or direct to another person a contribution, donation, or transfer of funds or any other thing of value, or spend any funds, that are not subject to the limitations, prohibitions, and reporting requirements of this Act.

"(2) APPLICABILITY.—The prohibition established by paragraph (1) applies to any such national committee, any officer or agent acting on behalf of such a national committee, and any entity that is directly or indirectly established, financed, maintained, or controlled by such a national committee.

"(b) STATE, DISTRICT, AND LOCAL COMMITTEES.—

"(1) IN GENERAL.—Except as provided in paragraph (2), an amount that is expended or disbursed for Federal election activity by a State, district, or local committee of a political party (including an entity that is directly or indirectly established, financed, maintained, or controlled by a State, district, or local committee of a political party and an officer or agent acting on behalf of such committee or entity), or by an association or similar group of candidates for State or local office or of individuals holding State or local office, shall be made from funds subject to the limitations, prohibitions, and reporting requirements of this Act.

"(2) APPLICABILITY.—

"(A) IN GENERAL.—Notwithstanding clause (i) or (ii) of section 301(20)(A), and subject to subparagraph (B), paragraph (1) shall not apply to any amount expended or disbursed by a State, district, or local committee of a political party for an activity described in either such clause to the extent the amounts expended or disbursed for such activity are allocated (under regulations prescribed by the Commission) among amounts—

"(i) which consist solely of contributions subject to the limitations, prohibitions, and reporting requirements of this Act (other than amounts described in subparagraph (B)(iii)); and

"(ii) other amounts which are not subject to the limitations, prohibitions, and reporting requirements of this Act (other than any requirements of this subsection).

"(B) CONDITIONS.—Subparagraph (A) shall only apply if—

"(i) the activity does not refer to a clearly identified candidate for Federal office;

"(ii) the amounts expended or disbursed are not for the costs of any broadcasting, cable, or satellite communication, other than a communication which refers solely to a clearly identified candidate for State or local office;

"(iii) the amounts expended or disbursed which are described in subparagraph (A)(ii) are paid from amounts which are donated in accordance with State law and which meet the requirements of subparagraph (C), except that no person (including any person established, financed, maintained, or controlled by such person) may donate more than $10,000 to a State, district, or local committee of a political party in a calendar year for such expenditures or disbursements; and

"(iv) the amounts expended or disbursed are made solely from funds raised by the State, local, or district committee which makes such expenditure or disbursement, and do not include any funds provided to such committee from—

"(I) any other State, local, or district committee of any State party,

"(II) the national committee of a political party (including a national congressional campaign committee of a political party),

"(III) any officer or agent acting on behalf of any committee described in subclause (I) or (II), or

"(IV) any entity directly or indirectly established, financed, maintained, or controlled by any committee described in subclause (I) or (II).

"(C) PROHIBITING INVOLVEMENT OF NATIONAL PARTIES, FEDERAL CANDIDATES AND OFFICEHOLDERS, AND STATE PARTIES ACTING JOINTLY.—Notwithstanding subsection (e) (other than subsection (e)(3)), amounts specifically authorized to be spent under subparagraph (B)(iii) meet the requirements of this subparagraph only if the amounts—

"(i) are not solicited, received, directed, transferred, or spent by or in the name of any person described in subsection (a) or (e); and

"(ii) are not solicited, received, or directed through fundraising activities conducted jointly by 2 or more State, local, or district committees of any political party

PUBLIC LAW 107–155—MAR. 27, 2002

or their agents, or by a State, local, or district committee of a political party on behalf of the State, local,
or district committee of a political party or its agent
in one or more other States.

"(c) FUNDRAISING COSTS.—An amount spent by a person
described in subsection (a) or (b) to raise funds that are used,
in whole or in part, for expenditures and disbursements for a
Federal election activity shall be made from funds subject to the
limitations, prohibitions, and reporting requirements of this Act.

"(d) TAX-EXEMPT ORGANIZATIONS.—A national, State, district,
or local committee of a political party (including a national congressional campaign committee of a political party), an entity that
is directly or indirectly established, financed, maintained, or controlled by any such national, State, district, or local committee
or its agent, and an officer or agent acting on behalf of any such
party committee or entity, shall not solicit any funds for, or make
or direct any donations to—

"(1) an organization that is described in section 501(c)
of the Internal Revenue Code of 1986 and exempt from taxation
under section 501(a) of such Code (or has submitted an application for determination of tax exempt status under such section)
and that makes expenditures or disbursements in connection
with an election for Federal office (including expenditures or
disbursements for Federal election activity); or

"(2) an organization described in section 527 of such Code
(other than a political committee, a State, district, or local
committee of a political party, or the authorized campaign
committee of a candidate for State or local office).

"(e) FEDERAL CANDIDATES.—

"(1) IN GENERAL.—A candidate, individual holding Federal
office, agent of a candidate or an individual holding Federal
office, or an entity directly or indirectly established, financed,
maintained or controlled by or acting on behalf of 1 or more
candidates or individuals holding Federal office, shall not—

"(A) solicit, receive, direct, transfer, or spend funds
in connection with an election for Federal office, including
funds for any Federal election activity, unless the funds
are subject to the limitations, prohibitions, and reporting
requirements of this Act; or

"(B) solicit, receive, direct, transfer, or spend funds
in connection with any election other than an election
for Federal office or disburse funds in connection with
such an election unless the funds—

"(i) are not in excess of the amounts permitted
with respect to contributions to candidates and political
committees under paragraphs (1), (2), and (3) of section
315(a); and

"(ii) are not from sources prohibited by this Act
from making contributions in connection with an election for Federal office.

"(2) STATE LAW.—Paragraph (1) does not apply to the solicitation, receipt, or spending of funds by an individual described
in such paragraph who is or was also a candidate for a State
or local office solely in connection with such election for State
or local office if the solicitation, receipt, or spending of funds
is permitted under State law and refers only to such State

or local candidate, or to any other candidate for the State or local office sought by such candidate, or both.

"(3) FUNDRAISING EVENTS.—Notwithstanding paragraph (1) or subsection (b)(2)(C), a candidate or an individual holding Federal office may attend, speak, or be a featured guest at a fundraising event for a State, district, or local committee of a political party.

"(4) PERMITTING CERTAIN SOLICITATIONS.—

"(A) GENERAL SOLICITATIONS.—Notwithstanding any other provision of this subsection, an individual described in paragraph (1) may make a general solicitation of funds on behalf of any organization that is described in section 501(c) of the Internal Revenue Code of 1986 and exempt from taxation under section 501(a) of such Code (or has submitted an application for determination of tax exempt status under such section) (other than an entity whose principal purpose is to conduct activities described in clauses (i) and (ii) of section 301(20)(A)) where such solicitation does not specify how the funds will or should be spent.

"(B) CERTAIN SPECIFIC SOLICITATIONS.—In addition to the general solicitations permitted under subparagraph (A), an individual described in paragraph (1) may make a solicitation explicitly to obtain funds for carrying out the activities described in clauses (i) and (ii) of section 301(20)(A), or for an entity whose principal purpose is to conduct such activities, if—

"(i) the solicitation is made only to individuals; and

"(ii) the amount solicited from any individual during any calendar year does not exceed $20,000.

"(f) STATE CANDIDATES.—

"(1) IN GENERAL.—A candidate for State or local office, individual holding State or local office, or an agent of such a candidate or individual may not spend any funds for a communication described in section 301(20)(A)(iii) unless the funds are subject to the limitations, prohibitions, and reporting requirements of this Act.

"(2) EXCEPTION FOR CERTAIN COMMUNICATIONS.—Paragraph (1) shall not apply to an individual described in such paragraph if the communication involved is in connection with an election for such State or local office and refers only to such individual or to any other candidate for the State or local office held or sought by such individual, or both.".

(b) DEFINITIONS.—Section 301 of the Federal Election Campaign Act of 1971 (2 U.S.C. 431) is amended by adding at the end thereof the following:

"(20) FEDERAL ELECTION ACTIVITY.—

"(A) IN GENERAL.—The term 'Federal election activity' means—

"(i) voter registration activity during the period that begins on the date that is 120 days before the date a regularly scheduled Federal election is held and ends on the date of the election;

"(ii) voter identification, get-out-the-vote activity, or generic campaign activity conducted in connection with an election in which a candidate for Federal office appears on the ballot (regardless of whether a candidate for State or local office also appears on the ballot);

"(iii) a public communication that refers to a clearly identified candidate for Federal office (regardless of whether a candidate for State or local office is also mentioned or identified) and that promotes or supports a candidate for that office, or attacks or opposes a candidate for that office (regardless of whether the communication expressly advocates a vote for or against a candidate); or

"(iv) services provided during any month by an employee of a State, district, or local committee of a political party who spends more than 25 percent of that individual's compensated time during that month on activities in connection with a Federal election.

"(B) EXCLUDED ACTIVITY.—The term 'Federal election activity' does not include an amount expended or disbursed by a State, district, or local committee of a political party for—

"(i) a public communication that refers solely to a clearly identified candidate for State or local office, if the communication is not a Federal election activity described in subparagraph (A)(i) or (ii);

"(ii) a contribution to a candidate for State or local office, provided the contribution is not designated to pay for a Federal election activity described in subparagraph (A);

"(iii) the costs of a State, district, or local political convention; and

"(iv) the costs of grassroots campaign materials, including buttons, bumper stickers, and yard signs, that name or depict only a candidate for State or local office.

"(21) GENERIC CAMPAIGN ACTIVITY.—The term 'generic campaign activity' means a campaign activity that promotes a political party and does not promote a candidate or non-Federal candidate.

"(22) PUBLIC COMMUNICATION.—The term 'public communication' means a communication by means of any broadcast, cable, or satellite communication, newspaper, magazine, outdoor advertising facility, mass mailing, or telephone bank to the general public, or any other form of general public political advertising.

"(23) MASS MAILING.—The term 'mass mailing' means a mailing by United States mail or facsimile of more than 500 pieces of mail matter of an identical or substantially similar nature within any 30-day period.

"(24) TELEPHONE BANK.—The term 'telephone bank' means more than 500 telephone calls of an identical or substantially similar nature within any 30-day period.".

SEC. 102. INCREASED CONTRIBUTION LIMIT FOR STATE COMMITTEES OF POLITICAL PARTIES.

Section 315(a)(1) of the Federal Election Campaign Act of 1971 (2 U.S.C. 441a(a)(1)) is amended—

PUBLIC LAW 107–155—MAR. 27, 2002   116 STAT. 87

(1) in subparagraph (B), by striking "or" at the end;

(2) in subparagraph (C)—

(A) by inserting "(other than a committee described in subparagraph (D))" after "committee"; and

(B) by striking the period at the end and inserting "; or"; and

(3) by adding at the end the following:

"(D) to a political committee established and maintained by a State committee of a political party in any calendar year which, in the aggregate, exceed $10,000.".

SEC. 103. REPORTING REQUIREMENTS.

(a) REPORTING REQUIREMENTS.—Section 304 of the Federal Election Campaign Act of 1971 (2 U.S.C. 434) is amended by adding at the end the following:

"(e) POLITICAL COMMITTEES.—

"(1) NATIONAL AND CONGRESSIONAL POLITICAL COMMITTEES.—The national committee of a political party, any national congressional campaign committee of a political party, and any subordinate committee of either, shall report all receipts and disbursements during the reporting period.

"(2) OTHER POLITICAL COMMITTEES TO WHICH SECTION 323 APPLIES.—

"(A) IN GENERAL.—In addition to any other reporting requirements applicable under this Act, a political committee (not described in paragraph (1)) to which section 323(b)(1) applies shall report all receipts and disbursements made for activities described in section 301(20)(A), unless the aggregate amount of such receipts and disbursements during the calendar year is less than $5,000.

"(B) SPECIFIC DISCLOSURE BY STATE AND LOCAL PARTIES OF CERTAIN NON-FEDERAL AMOUNTS PERMITTED TO BE SPENT ON FEDERAL ELECTION ACTIVITY.—Each report by a political committee under subparagraph (A) of receipts and disbursements made for activities described in section 301(20)(A) shall include a disclosure of all receipts and disbursements described in section 323(b)(2)(A) and (B).

"(3) ITEMIZATION.—If a political committee has receipts or disbursements to which this subsection applies from or to any person aggregating in excess of $200 for any calendar year, the political committee shall separately itemize its reporting for such person in the same manner as required in paragraphs (3)(A), (5), and (6) of subsection (b).

"(4) REPORTING PERIODS.—Reports required to be filed under this subsection shall be filed for the same time periods required for political committees under subsection (a)(4)(B).".

(b) BUILDING FUND EXCEPTION TO THE DEFINITION OF CONTRIBUTION.—

(1) IN GENERAL.—Section 301(8)(B) of the Federal Election Campaign Act of 1971 (2 U.S.C. 431(8)(B)) is amended—

(A) by striking clause (viii); and

(B) by redesignating clauses (ix) through (xv) as clauses (viii) through (xiv), respectively.

(2) NONPREEMPTION OF STATE LAW.—Section 403 of such Act (2 U.S.C. 453) is amended—

(A) by striking "The provisions of this Act" and inserting "(a) IN GENERAL.—Subject to subsection (b), the provisions of this Act"; and

(B) by adding at the end the following:

"(b) STATE AND LOCAL COMMITTEES OF POLITICAL PARTIES.— Notwithstanding any other provision of this Act, a State or local committee of a political party may, subject to State law, use exclusively funds that are not subject to the prohibitions, limitations, and reporting requirements of the Act for the purchase or construction of an office building for such State or local committee.".

TITLE II—NONCANDIDATE CAMPAIGN EXPENDITURES

Subtitle A—Electioneering Communications

SEC. 201. DISCLOSURE OF ELECTIONEERING COMMUNICATIONS.

(a) IN GENERAL.—Section 304 of the Federal Election Campaign Act of 1971 (2 U.S.C. 434), as amended by section 103, is amended by adding at the end the following new subsection:

"(f) DISCLOSURE OF ELECTIONEERING COMMUNICATIONS.—

"(1) STATEMENT REQUIRED.—Every person who makes a disbursement for the direct costs of producing and airing electioneering communications in an aggregate amount in excess of $10,000 during any calendar year shall, within 24 hours of each disclosure date, file with the Commission a statement containing the information described in paragraph (2).

"(2) CONTENTS OF STATEMENT.—Each statement required to be filed under this subsection shall be made under penalty of perjury and shall contain the following information:

"(A) The identification of the person making the disbursement, of any person sharing or exercising direction or control over the activities of such person, and of the custodian of the books and accounts of the person making the disbursement.

"(B) The principal place of business of the person making the disbursement, if not an individual.

"(C) The amount of each disbursement of more than $200 during the period covered by the statement and the identification of the person to whom the disbursement was made.

"(D) The elections to which the electioneering communications pertain and the names (if known) of the candidates identified or to be identified.

"(E) If the disbursements were paid out of a segregated bank account which consists of funds contributed solely by individuals who are United States citizens or nationals or lawfully admitted for permanent residence (as defined in section 101(a)(20) of the Immigration and Nationality Act (8 U.S.C. 1101(a)(20))) directly to this account for electioneering communications, the names and addresses of all contributors who contributed an aggregate amount of $1,000 or more to that account during the period beginning on the first day of the preceding calendar year and

PUBLIC LAW 107–155—MAR. 27, 2002   116 STAT. 89

ending on the disclosure date. Nothing in this subparagraph is to be construed as a prohibition on the use of funds in such a segregated account for a purpose other than electioneering communications.

"(F) If the disbursements were paid out of funds not described in subparagraph (E), the names and addresses of all contributors who contributed an aggregate amount of $1,000 or more to the person making the disbursement during the period beginning on the first day of the preceding calendar year and ending on the disclosure date.

"(3) ELECTIONEERING COMMUNICATION.—For purposes of this subsection—

"(A) IN GENERAL.—(i) The term 'electioneering communication' means any broadcast, cable, or satellite communication which—

"(I) refers to a clearly identified candidate for Federal office;

"(II) is made within—

"(aa) 60 days before a general, special, or run-off election for the office sought by the candidate; or

"(bb) 30 days before a primary or preference election, or a convention or caucus of a political party that has authority to nominate a candidate, for the office sought by the candidate; and

"(III) in the case of a communication which refers to a candidate for an office other than President or Vice President, is targeted to the relevant electorate.

"(ii) If clause (i) is held to be constitutionally insufficient by final judicial decision to support the regulation provided herein, then the term 'electioneering communication' means any broadcast, cable, or satellite communication which promotes or supports a candidate for that office, or attacks or opposes a candidate for that office (regardless of whether the communication expressly advocates a vote for or against a candidate) and which also is suggestive of no plausible meaning other than an exhortation to vote for or against a specific candidate. Nothing in this subparagraph shall be construed to affect the interpretation or application of section 100.22(b) of title 11, Code of Federal Regulations.

"(B) EXCEPTIONS.—The term 'electioneering communication' does not include—

"(i) a communication appearing in a news story, commentary, or editorial distributed through the facilities of any broadcasting station, unless such facilities are owned or controlled by any political party, political committee, or candidate;

"(ii) a communication which constitutes an expenditure or an independent expenditure under this Act;

"(iii) a communication which constitutes a candidate debate or forum conducted pursuant to regulations adopted by the Commission, or which solely promotes such a debate or forum and is made by or on behalf of the person sponsoring the debate or forum; or "(iv) any other communication exempted under such regulations as the Commission may promulgate (consistent with the requirements of this paragraph) to ensure the appropriate implementation of this paragraph, except that under any such regulation a communication may not be exempted if it meets the requirements of this paragraph and is described in section 301(20)(A)(iii).

"(C) TARGETING TO RELEVANT ELECTORATE.—For purposes of this paragraph, a communication which refers to a clearly identified candidate for Federal office is 'targeted to the relevant electorate' if the communication can be received by 50,000 or more persons—

"(i) in the district the candidate seeks to represent, in the case of a candidate for Representative in, or Delegate or Resident Commissioner to, the Congress; or

"(ii) in the State the candidate seeks to represent, in the case of a candidate for Senator.

"(4) DISCLOSURE DATE.—For purposes of this subsection, the term 'disclosure date' means—

"(A) the first date during any calendar year by which a person has made disbursements for the direct costs of producing or airing electioneering communications aggregating in excess of $10,000; and

"(B) any other date during such calendar year by which a person has made disbursements for the direct costs of producing or airing electioneering communications aggregating in excess of $10,000 since the most recent disclosure date for such calendar year.

"(5) CONTRACTS TO DISBURSE.—For purposes of this subsection, a person shall be treated as having made a disbursement if the person has executed a contract to make the disbursement.

"(6) COORDINATION WITH OTHER REQUIREMENTS.—Any requirement to report under this subsection shall be in addition to any other reporting requirement under this Act.

"(7) COORDINATION WITH INTERNAL REVENUE CODE.— Nothing in this subsection may be construed to establish, modify, or otherwise affect the definition of political activities or electioneering activities (including the definition of participating in, intervening in, or influencing or attempting to influence a political campaign on behalf of or in opposition to any candidate for public office) for purposes of the Internal Revenue Code of 1986.".

2 USC 434 note.

(b) RESPONSIBILITIES OF FEDERAL COMMUNICATIONS COMMISSION.—The Federal Communications Commission shall compile and maintain any information the Federal Election Commission may require to carry out section 304(f) of the Federal Election Campaign Act of 1971 (as added by subsection (a)), and shall make such information available to the public on the Federal Communication Commission's website.

SEC. 202. COORDINATED COMMUNICATIONS AS CONTRIBUTIONS.

Section 315(a)(7) of the Federal Election Campaign Act of 1971 (2 U.S.C. 441a(a)(7)) is amended—

(1) by redesignating subparagraph (C) as subparagraph (D); and

(2) by inserting after subparagraph (B) the following:

"(C) if—

"(i) any person makes, or contracts to make, any disbursement for any electioneering communication (within the meaning of section 304(f)(3)); and

"(ii) such disbursement is coordinated with a candidate or an authorized committee of such candidate, a Federal, State, or local political party or committee thereof, or an agent or official of any such candidate, party, or committee; such disbursement or contracting shall be treated as a contribution to the candidate supported by the electioneering communication or that candidate's party and as an expenditure by that candidate or that candidate's party; and".

SEC. 203. PROHIBITION OF CORPORATE AND LABOR DISBURSEMENTS FOR ELECTIONEERING COMMUNICATIONS.

(a) IN GENERAL.—Section 316(b)(2) of the Federal Election Campaign Act of 1971 (2 U.S.C. 441b(b)(2)) is amended by inserting "or for any applicable electioneering communication" before ", but shall not include".

(b) APPLICABLE ELECTIONEERING COMMUNICATION.—Section 316 of such Act is amended by adding at the end the following:

"(c) RULES RELATING TO ELECTIONEERING COMMUNICATIONS.—

"(1) APPLICABLE ELECTIONEERING COMMUNICATION.—For purposes of this section, the term 'applicable electioneering communication' means an electioneering communication (within the meaning of section 304(f)(3)) which is made by any entity described in subsection (a) of this section or by any other person using funds donated by an entity described in subsection (a) of this section.

"(2) EXCEPTION.—Notwithstanding paragraph (1), the term 'applicable electioneering communication' does not include a communication by a section 501(c)(4) organization or a political organization (as defined in section 527(e)(1) of the Internal Revenue Code of 1986) made under section 304(f)(2)(E) or (F) of this Act if the communication is paid for exclusively by funds provided directly by individuals who are United States citizens or nationals or lawfully admitted for permanent residence (as defined in section 101(a)(20) of the Immigration and Nationality Act (8 U.S.C. 1101(a)(20))). For purposes of the preceding sentence, the term 'provided directly by individuals' does not include funds the source of which is an entity described in subsection (a) of this section.

"(3) SPECIAL OPERATING RULES.—

"(A) DEFINITION UNDER PARAGRAPH (1).—An electioneering communication shall be treated as made by an entity described in subsection (a) if an entity described in subsection (a) directly or indirectly disburses any amount for any of the costs of the communication.

"(B) EXCEPTION UNDER PARAGRAPH (2).—A section 501(c)(4) organization that derives amounts from business activities or receives funds from any entity described in subsection (a) shall be considered to have paid for any communication out of such amounts unless such organization paid for the communication out of a segregated account

116 STAT. 92   PUBLIC LAW 107-155—MAR. 27, 2002

to which only individuals can contribute, as described in section 304(f)(2)(E).

"(4) DEFINITIONS AND RULES.—For purposes of this subsection—

"(A) the term 'section 501(c)(4) organization' means—

"(i) an organization described in section 501(c)(4) of the Internal Revenue Code of 1986 and exempt from taxation under section 501(a) of such Code; or

"(ii) an organization which has submitted an application to the Internal Revenue Service for determination of its status as an organization described in clause (i); and

"(B) a person shall be treated as having made a disbursement if the person has executed a contract to make the disbursement.

"(5) COORDINATION WITH INTERNAL REVENUE CODE.— Nothing in this subsection shall be construed to authorize an organization exempt from taxation under section 501(a) of the Internal Revenue Code of 1986 to carry out any activity which is prohibited under such Code.".

SEC. 204. RULES RELATING TO CERTAIN TARGETED ELECTIONEERING COMMUNICATIONS.

Section 316(c) of the Federal Election Campaign Act of 1971 (2 U.S.C. 441b), as added by section 203, is amended by adding at the end the following:

"(6) SPECIAL RULES FOR TARGETED COMMUNICATIONS.—

"(A) EXCEPTION DOES NOT APPLY.—Paragraph (2) shall not apply in the case of a targeted communication that is made by an organization described in such paragraph.

"(B) TARGETED COMMUNICATION.—For purposes of subparagraph (A), the term 'targeted communication' means an electioneering communication (as defined in section 304(f)(3)) that is distributed from a television or radio broadcast station or provider of cable or satellite television service and, in the case of a communication which refers to a candidate for an office other than President or Vice President, is targeted to the relevant electorate.

"(C) DEFINITION.—For purposes of this paragraph, a communication is 'targeted to the relevant electorate' if it meets the requirements described in section 304(f)(3)(C).".

Subtitle B—Independent and Coordinated Expenditures

SEC. 211. DEFINITION OF INDEPENDENT EXPENDITURE.

Section 301 of the Federal Election Campaign Act (2 U.S.C. 431) is amended by striking paragraph (17) and inserting the following:

"(17) INDEPENDENT EXPENDITURE.—The term 'independent expenditure' means an expenditure by a person—

"(A) expressly advocating the election or defeat of a clearly identified candidate; and

"(B) that is not made in concert or cooperation with or at the request or suggestion of such candidate, the

PUBLIC LAW 107-155—MAR. 27, 2002   116 STAT. 93

candidate's authorized political committee, or their agents, or a political party committee or its agents.".

SEC. 212. REPORTING REQUIREMENTS FOR CERTAIN INDEPENDENT EXPENDITURES.

(a) IN GENERAL.—Section 304 of the Federal Election Campaign Act of 1971 (2 U.S.C. 434) (as amended by section 201) is amended—

(1) in subsection (c)(2), by striking the undesignated matter after subparagraph (C); and

(2) by adding at the end the following:

"(g) TIME FOR REPORTING CERTAIN EXPENDITURES.—

"(1) EXPENDITURES AGGREGATING $1,000.—

"(A) INITIAL REPORT.—A person (including a political committee) that makes or contracts to make independent expenditures aggregating $1,000 or more after the 20th day, but more than 24 hours, before the date of an election shall file a report describing the expenditures within 24 hours.

"(B) ADDITIONAL REPORTS.—After a person files a report under subparagraph (A), the person shall file an additional report within 24 hours after each time the person makes or contracts to make independent expenditures aggregating an additional $1,000 with respect to the same election as that to which the initial report relates.

"(2) EXPENDITURES AGGREGATING $10,000.—

"(A) INITIAL REPORT.—A person (including a political committee) that makes or contracts to make independent expenditures aggregating $10,000 or more at any time up to and including the 20th day before the date of an election shall file a report describing the expenditures within 48 hours.

"(B) ADDITIONAL REPORTS.—After a person files a report under subparagraph (A), the person shall file an additional report within 48 hours after each time the person makes or contracts to make independent expenditures aggregating an additional $10,000 with respect to the same election as that to which the initial report relates.

"(3) PLACE OF FILING; CONTENTS.—A report under this subsection—

"(A) shall be filed with the Commission; and

"(B) shall contain the information required by subsection (b)(6)(B)(iii), including the name of each candidate whom an expenditure is intended to support or oppose.".

(b) TIME OF FILING OF CERTAIN STATEMENTS.—

(1) IN GENERAL.—Section 304(g) of such Act, as added by subsection (a), is amended by adding at the end the following:

"(4) TIME OF FILING FOR EXPENDITURES AGGREGATING $1,000.—Notwithstanding subsection (a)(5), the time at which the statement under paragraph (1) is received by the Commission or any other recipient to whom the notification is required to be sent shall be considered the time of filing of the statement with the recipient.".

(2) CONFORMING AMENDMENTS.—(A) Section 304(a)(5) of such Act (2 U.S.C. 434(a)(5)) is amended by striking "the second sentence of subsection (c)(2)" and inserting "subsection (g)(1)".

116 STAT. 94   PUBLIC LAW 107–155—MAR. 27, 2002

(B) Section 304(d)(1) of such Act (2 U.S.C. 434(d)(1)) is amended by inserting "or (g)" after "subsection (c)".

~~SEC. 213. INDEPENDENT VERSUS COORDINATED EXPENDITURES BY PARTY.~~

Section 315(d) of the Federal Election Campaign Act of 1971 (2 U.S.C. 441a(d)) is amended—

(1) in paragraph (1), by striking "and (3)" and inserting ", (3), and (4)"; and

(2) by adding at the end the following:

"(4) INDEPENDENT VERSUS COORDINATED EXPENDITURES BY PARTY.—

"(A) IN GENERAL.—On or after the date on which a political party nominates a candidate, no committee of the political party may make—

"(i) any coordinated expenditure under this subsection with respect to the candidate during the election cycle at any time after it makes any independent expenditure (as defined in section 301(17)) with respect to the candidate during the election cycle; or

"(ii) any independent expenditure (as defined in section 301(17)) with respect to the candidate during the election cycle at any time after it makes any coordinated expenditure under this subsection with respect to the candidate during the election cycle.

"(B) APPLICATION.—For purposes of this paragraph, all political committees established and maintained by a national political party (including all congressional campaign committees) and all political committees established and maintained by a State political party (including any subordinate committee of a State committee) shall be considered to be a single political committee.

"(C) TRANSFERS.—A committee of a political party that makes coordinated expenditures under this subsection with respect to a candidate shall not, during an election cycle, transfer any funds to, assign authority to make coordinated expenditures under this subsection to, or receive a transfer of funds from, a committee of the political party that has made or intends to make an independent expenditure with respect to the candidate.".

SEC. 214. COORDINATION WITH CANDIDATES OR POLITICAL PARTIES.

(a) IN GENERAL.—Section 315(a)(7)(B) of the Federal Election Campaign Act of 1971 (2 U.S.C. 441a(a)(7)(B)) is amended—

(1) by redesignating clause (ii) as clause (iii); and

(2) by inserting after clause (i) the following new clause:

"(ii) expenditures made by any person (other than a candidate or candidate's authorized committee) in cooperation, consultation, or concert with, or at the request or suggestion of, a national, State, or local committee of a political party, shall be considered to be contributions made to such party committee; and".

(b) REPEAL OF CURRENT REGULATIONS.—The regulations on coordinated communications paid for by persons other than candidates, authorized committees of candidates, and party committees adopted by the Federal Election Commission and published in the Federal Register at page 76138 of volume 65, Federal Register, on December 6, 2000, are repealed as of the date by which the

PUBLIC LAW 107–155—MAR. 27, 2002   116 STAT. 95

Commission is required to promulgate new regulations under subsection (c) (as described in section 402(c)(1)).

(c) REGULATIONS BY THE FEDERAL ELECTION COMMISSION.—   2 USC 441a note.
The Federal Election Commission shall promulgate new regulations on coordinated communications paid for by persons other than candidates, authorized committees of candidates, and party committees. The regulations shall not require agreement or formal collaboration to establish coordination. In addition to any subject determined by the Commission, the regulations shall address—

    (1) payments for the republication of campaign materials;

    (2) payments for the use of a common vendor;

    (3) payments for communications directed or made by persons who previously served as an employee of a candidate or a political party; and

    (4) payments for communications made by a person after substantial discussion about the communication with a candidate or a political party.

(d) MEANING OF CONTRIBUTION OR EXPENDITURE FOR THE PURPOSES OF SECTION 316.—Section 316(b)(2) of the Federal Election Campaign Act of 1971 (2 U.S.C. 441b(b)(2)) is amended by striking "shall include" and inserting "includes a contribution or expenditure, as those terms are defined in section 301, and also includes".

TITLE III—MISCELLANEOUS

SEC. 301. USE OF CONTRIBUTED AMOUNTS FOR CERTAIN PURPOSES.

Title III of the Federal Election Campaign Act of 1971 (2 U.S.C. 431 et seq.) is amended by striking section 313 and inserting the following:

"SEC. 313. USE OF CONTRIBUTED AMOUNTS FOR CERTAIN PURPOSES.   2 USC 439a.

"(a) PERMITTED USES.—A contribution accepted by a candidate, and any other donation received by an individual as support for activities of the individual as a holder of Federal office, may be used by the candidate or individual—

    "(1) for otherwise authorized expenditures in connection with the campaign for Federal office of the candidate or individual;

    "(2) for ordinary and necessary expenses incurred in connection with duties of the individual as a holder of Federal office;

    "(3) for contributions to an organization described in section 170(c) of the Internal Revenue Code of 1986; or

    "(4) for transfers, without limitation, to a national, State, or local committee of a political party.

"(b) PROHIBITED USE.—

    "(1) IN GENERAL.—A contribution or donation described in subsection (a) shall not be converted by any person to personal use.

    "(2) CONVERSION.—For the purposes of paragraph (1), a contribution or donation shall be considered to be converted to personal use if the contribution or amount is used to fulfill any commitment, obligation, or expense of a person that would exist irrespective of the candidate's election campaign or individual's duties as a holder of Federal office, including—

        "(A) a home mortgage, rent, or utility payment;

        "(B) a clothing purchase;

PUBLIC LAW 107–155—MAR. 27, 2002

"(C) a noncampaign-related automobile expense;

"(D) a country club membership;

"(E) a vacation or other noncampaign-related trip;

"(F) a household food item;

"(G) a tuition payment;

"(H) admission to a sporting event, concert, theater, or other form of entertainment not associated with an election campaign; and

"(I) dues, fees, and other payments to a health club or recreational facility.".

SEC. 302. PROHIBITION OF FUNDRAISING ON FEDERAL PROPERTY.

Section 607 of title 18, United States Code, is amended—

(1) by striking subsection (a) and inserting the following:

"(a) PROHIBITION.—

"(1) IN GENERAL.—It shall be unlawful for any person to solicit or receive a donation of money or other thing of value in connection with a Federal, State, or local election from a person who is located in a room or building occupied in the discharge of official duties by an officer or employee of the United States. It shall be unlawful for an individual who is an officer or employee of the Federal Government, including the President, Vice President, and Members of Congress, to solicit or receive a donation of money or other thing of value in connection with a Federal, State, or local election, while in any room or building occupied in the discharge of official duties by an officer or employee of the United States, from any person.

"(2) PENALTY.—A person who violates this section shall be fined not more than $5,000, imprisoned not more than 3 years, or both."; and

(2) in subsection (b), by inserting "or Executive Office of the President" after "Congress".

SEC. 303. STRENGTHENING FOREIGN MONEY BAN.

Section 319 of the Federal Election Campaign Act of 1971 (2 U.S.C. 441e) is amended—

(1) by striking the heading and inserting the following: "CONTRIBUTIONS AND DONATIONS BY FOREIGN NATIONALS"; and

(2) by striking subsection (a) and inserting the following:

"(a) PROHIBITION.—It shall be unlawful for—

"(1) a foreign national, directly or indirectly, to make—

"(A) a contribution or donation of money or other thing of value, or to make an express or implied promise to make a contribution or donation, in connection with a Federal, State, or local election;

"(B) a contribution or donation to a committee of a political party; or

"(C) an expenditure, independent expenditure, or disbursement for an electioneering communication (within the meaning of section 304(f)(3)); or

"(2) a person to solicit, accept, or receive a contribution or donation described in subparagraph (A) or (B) of paragraph (1) from a foreign national.".

SEC. 304. MODIFICATION OF INDIVIDUAL CONTRIBUTION LIMITS IN RESPONSE TO EXPENDITURES FROM PERSONAL FUNDS.

(a) INCREASED LIMITS FOR INDIVIDUALS.—Section 315 of the Federal Election Campaign Act of 1971 (2 U.S.C. 441a) is amended—

    (1) in subsection (a)(1), by striking "No person" and inserting "Except as provided in subsection (i), no person"; and

    (2) by adding at the end the following:

"(i) INCREASED LIMIT TO ALLOW RESPONSE TO EXPENDITURES FROM PERSONAL FUNDS.—

    "(1) INCREASE.—

        "(A) IN GENERAL.—Subject to paragraph (2), if the opposition personal funds amount with respect to a candidate for election to the office of Senator exceeds the threshold amount, the limit under subsection (a)(1)(A) (in this subsection referred to as the 'applicable limit') with respect to that candidate shall be the increased limit.

        "(B) THRESHOLD AMOUNT.—

            "(i) STATE-BY-STATE COMPETITIVE AND FAIR CAMPAIGN FORMULA.—In this subsection, the threshold amount with respect to an election cycle of a candidate described in subparagraph (A) is an amount equal to the sum of—

                "(I) $150,000; and

                "(II) $0.04 multiplied by the voting age population.

            "(ii) VOTING AGE POPULATION.—In this subparagraph, the term 'voting age population' means in the case of a candidate for the office of Senator, the voting age population of the State of the candidate (as certified under section 315(e)).

        "(C) INCREASED LIMIT.—Except as provided in clause (ii), for purposes of subparagraph (A), if the opposition personal funds amount is over—

            "(i) 2 times the threshold amount, but not over 4 times that amount—

                "(I) the increased limit shall be 3 times the applicable limit; and

                "(II) the limit under subsection (a)(3) shall not apply with respect to any contribution made with respect to a candidate if such contribution is made under the increased limit of subparagraph (A) during a period in which the candidate may accept such a contribution;

            "(ii) 4 times the threshold amount, but not over 10 times that amount—

                "(I) the increased limit shall be 6 times the applicable limit; and

                "(II) the limit under subsection (a)(3) shall not apply with respect to any contribution made with respect to a candidate if such contribution is made under the increased limit of subparagraph (A) during a period in which the candidate may accept such a contribution; and

            "(iii) 10 times the threshold amount—

"(I) the increased limit shall be 6 times the applicable limit;

"(II) the limit under subsection (a)(3) shall not apply with respect to any contribution made with respect to a candidate if such contribution is made under the increased limit of subparagraph (A) during a period in which the candidate may accept such a contribution; and

"(III) the limits under subsection (d) with respect to any expenditure by a State or national committee of a political party shall not apply.

"(D) OPPOSITION PERSONAL FUNDS AMOUNT.—The opposition personal funds amount is an amount equal to the excess (if any) of—

"(i) the greatest aggregate amount of expenditures from personal funds (as defined in section 304(a)(6)(B)) that an opposing candidate in the same election makes; over

"(ii) the aggregate amount of expenditures from personal funds made by the candidate with respect to the election.

"(2) TIME TO ACCEPT CONTRIBUTIONS UNDER INCREASED LIMIT.—

"(A) IN GENERAL.—Subject to subparagraph (B), a candidate and the candidate's authorized committee shall not accept any contribution, and a party committee shall not make any expenditure, under the increased limit under paragraph (1)—

"(i) until the candidate has received notification of the opposition personal funds amount under section 304(a)(6)(B); and

"(ii) to the extent that such contribution, when added to the aggregate amount of contributions previously accepted and party expenditures previously made under the increased limits under this subsection for the election cycle, exceeds 110 percent of the opposition personal funds amount.

"(B) EFFECT OF WITHDRAWAL OF AN OPPOSING CANDIDATE.—A candidate and a candidate's authorized committee shall not accept any contribution and a party shall not make any expenditure under the increased limit after the date on which an opposing candidate ceases to be a candidate to the extent that the amount of such increased limit is attributable to such an opposing candidate.

"(3) DISPOSAL OF EXCESS CONTRIBUTIONS.—

Deadline.

"(A) IN GENERAL.—The aggregate amount of contributions accepted by a candidate or a candidate's authorized committee under the increased limit under paragraph (1) and not otherwise expended in connection with the election with respect to which such contributions relate shall, not later than 50 days after the date of such election, be used in the manner described in subparagraph (B).

"(B) RETURN TO CONTRIBUTORS.—A candidate or a candidate's authorized committee shall return the excess contribution to the person who made the contribution.

"(j) LIMITATION ON REPAYMENT OF PERSONAL LOANS.—Any candidate who incurs personal loans made after the effective date of the Bipartisan Campaign Reform Act of 2002 in connection with the candidate's campaign for election shall not repay (directly or indirectly), to the extent such loans exceed $250,000, such loans from any contributions made to such candidate or any authorized committee of such candidate after the date of such election.".

(b) NOTIFICATION OF EXPENDITURES FROM PERSONAL FUNDS.— Section 304(a)(6) of the Federal Election Campaign Act of 1971 (2 U.S.C. 434(a)(6)) is amended—

(1) by redesignating subparagraph (B) as subparagraph (E); and

(2) by inserting after subparagraph (A) the following:

"(B) NOTIFICATION OF EXPENDITURE FROM PERSONAL FUNDS.—

"(i) DEFINITION OF EXPENDITURE FROM PERSONAL FUNDS.— In this subparagraph, the term 'expenditure from personal funds' means—

"(I) an expenditure made by a candidate using personal funds; and

"(II) a contribution or loan made by a candidate using personal funds or a loan secured using such funds to the candidate's authorized committee.

"(ii) DECLARATION OF INTENT.—Not later than the date that is 15 days after the date on which an individual becomes a candidate for the office of Senator, the candidate shall file a declaration stating the total amount of expenditures from personal funds that the candidate intends to make, or to obligate to make, with respect to the election that will exceed the State-by-State competitive and fair campaign formula with— *Deadline.*

"(I) the Commission; and

"(II) each candidate in the same election.

"(iii) INITIAL NOTIFICATION.—Not later than 24 hours after a candidate described in clause (ii) makes or obligates to make an aggregate amount of expenditures from personal funds in excess of 2 times the threshold amount in connection with any election, the candidate shall file a notification with— *Deadline.*

"(I) the Commission; and

"(II) each candidate in the same election.

"(iv) ADDITIONAL NOTIFICATION.—After a candidate files an initial notification under clause (iii), the candidate shall file an additional notification each time expenditures from personal funds are made or obligated to be made in an aggregate amount that exceed $10,000 with—

"(I) the Commission; and

"(II) each candidate in the same election.

Such notification shall be filed not later than 24 hours after the expenditure is made. *Deadline.*

"(v) CONTENTS.—A notification under clause (iii) or (iv) shall include—

"(I) the name of the candidate and the office sought by the candidate;

"(II) the date and amount of each expenditure; and

"(III) the total amount of expenditures from personal funds that the candidate has made, or obligated to make, with respect to an election as of the date of the expenditure that is the subject of the notification.

"(C) NOTIFICATION OF DISPOSAL OF EXCESS CONTRIBUTIONS.— In the next regularly scheduled report after the date of the election

116 STAT. 100   PUBLIC LAW 107–155—MAR. 27, 2002

for which a candidate seeks nomination for election to, or election to, Federal office, the candidate or the candidate's authorized committee shall submit to the Commission a report indicating the source and amount of any excess contributions (as determined under paragraph (1) of section 315(i)) and the manner in which the candidate or the candidate's authorized committee used such funds.

"(D) ENFORCEMENT.—For provisions providing for the enforcement of the reporting requirements under this paragraph, see section 309.".

(c) DEFINITIONS.—Section 301 of the Federal Election Campaign Act of 1971 (2 U.S.C. 431), as amended by section 101(b), is further amended by adding at the end the following:

"(25) ELECTION CYCLE.—For purposes of sections 315(i) and 315A and paragraph (26), the term 'election cycle' means the period beginning on the day after the date of the most recent election for the specific office or seat that a candidate is seeking and ending on the date of the next election for that office or seat. For purposes of the preceding sentence, a primary election and a general election shall be considered to be separate elections.

"(26) PERSONAL FUNDS.—The term 'personal funds' means an amount that is derived from—

"(A) any asset that, under applicable State law, at the time the individual became a candidate, the candidate had legal right of access to or control over, and with respect to which the candidate had—

"(i) legal and rightful title; or
"(ii) an equitable interest;

"(B) income received during the current election cycle of the candidate, including—

"(i) a salary and other earned income from bona fide employment;
"(ii) dividends and proceeds from the sale of the candidate's stocks or other investments;
"(iii) bequests to the candidate;
"(iv) income from trusts established before the beginning of the election cycle;
"(v) income from trusts established by bequest after the beginning of the election cycle of which the candidate is the beneficiary;
"(vi) gifts of a personal nature that had been customarily received by the candidate prior to the beginning of the election cycle; and
"(vii) proceeds from lotteries and similar legal games of chance; and

"(C) a portion of assets that are jointly owned by the candidate and the candidate's spouse equal to the candidate's share of the asset under the instrument of conveyance or ownership, but if no specific share is indicated by an instrument of conveyance or ownership, the value of ½ of the property.".

SEC. 305. LIMITATION ON AVAILABILITY OF LOWEST UNIT CHARGE FOR FEDERAL CANDIDATES ATTACKING OPPOSITION.

(a) IN GENERAL.—Section 315(b) of the Communications Act of 1934 (47 U.S.C. 315(b)) is amended—

(1) by striking "(b) The charges" and inserting the following:

"(b) CHARGES.—

"(1) IN GENERAL.—The charges";

(2) by redesignating paragraphs (1) and (2) as subparagraphs (A) and (B), respectively; and

(3) by adding at the end the following:

"(2) CONTENT OF BROADCASTS.—

"(A) IN GENERAL.—In the case of a candidate for Federal office, such candidate shall not be entitled to receive the rate under paragraph (1)(A) for the use of any broadcasting station unless the candidate provides written certification to the broadcast station that the candidate (and any authorized committee of the candidate) shall not make any direct reference to another candidate for the same office, in any broadcast using the rights and conditions of access under this Act, unless such reference meets the requirements of subparagraph (C) or (D).

"(B) LIMITATION ON CHARGES.—If a candidate for Federal office (or any authorized committee of such candidate) makes a reference described in subparagraph (A) in any broadcast that does not meet the requirements of subparagraph (C) or (D), such candidate shall not be entitled to receive the rate under paragraph (1)(A) for such broadcast or any other broadcast during any portion of the 45-day and 60-day periods described in paragraph (1)(A), that occur on or after the date of such broadcast, for election to such office.

"(C) TELEVISION BROADCASTS.—A candidate meets the requirements of this subparagraph if, in the case of a television broadcast, at the end of such broadcast there appears simultaneously, for a period no less than 4 seconds—

"(i) a clearly identifiable photographic or similar image of the candidate; and

"(ii) a clearly readable printed statement, identifying the candidate and stating that the candidate has approved the broadcast and that the candidate's authorized committee paid for the broadcast.

"(D) RADIO BROADCASTS.—A candidate meets the requirements of this subparagraph if, in the case of a radio broadcast, the broadcast includes a personal audio statement by the candidate that identifies the candidate, the office the candidate is seeking, and indicates that the candidate has approved the broadcast.

"(E) CERTIFICATION.—Certifications under this section shall be provided and certified as accurate by the candidate (or any authorized committee of the candidate) at the time of purchase.

"(F) DEFINITIONS.—For purposes of this paragraph, the terms 'authorized committee' and 'Federal office' have the meanings given such terms by section 301 of the Federal Election Campaign Act of 1971 (2 U.S.C. 431).".

(b) CONFORMING AMENDMENT.—Section 315(b)(1)(A) of the Communications Act of 1934 (47 U.S.C. 315(b)(1)(A)), as amended by this Act, is amended by inserting "subject to paragraph (2)," before "during the forty-five days".

47 USC 315 note. (c) EFFECTIVE DATE.—The amendments made by this section shall apply to broadcasts made after the effective date of this Act.

SEC. 306. SOFTWARE FOR FILING REPORTS AND PROMPT DISCLOSURE OF CONTRIBUTIONS.

Section 304(a) of the Federal Election Campaign Act of 1971 (2 U.S.C. 434(a)) is amended by adding at the end the following:

"(12) SOFTWARE FOR FILING OF REPORTS.—

"(A) IN GENERAL.—The Commission shall—

"(i) promulgate standards to be used by vendors to develop software that—

"(I) permits candidates to easily record information concerning receipts and disbursements required to be reported under this Act at the time of the receipt or disbursement;

"(II) allows the information recorded under subclause (I) to be transmitted immediately to the Commission; and

"(III) allows the Commission to post the information on the Internet immediately upon receipt; and

"(ii) make a copy of software that meets the standards promulgated under clause (i) available to each person required to file a designation, statement, or report in electronic form under this Act.

"(B) ADDITIONAL INFORMATION.—To the extent feasible, the Commission shall require vendors to include in the software developed under the standards under subparagraph (A) the ability for any person to file any designation, statement, or report required under this Act in electronic form.

"(C) REQUIRED USE.—Notwithstanding any provision of this Act relating to times for filing reports, each candidate for Federal office (or that candidate's authorized committee) shall use software that meets the standards promulgated under this paragraph once such software is made available to such candidate.

"(D) REQUIRED POSTING.—The Commission shall, as soon as practicable, post on the Internet any information received under this paragraph.".

SEC. 307. MODIFICATION OF CONTRIBUTION LIMITS.

(a) INCREASE IN INDIVIDUAL LIMITS FOR CERTAIN CONTRIBUTIONS.—Section 315(a)(1) of the Federal Election Campaign Act of 1971 (2 U.S.C. 441a(a)(1)) is amended—

(1) in subparagraph (A), by striking "$1,000" and inserting "$2,000"; and

(2) in subparagraph (B), by striking "$20,000" and inserting "$25,000".

(b) INCREASE IN ANNUAL AGGREGATE LIMIT ON INDIVIDUAL CONTRIBUTIONS.—Section 315(a)(3) of the Federal Election Campaign Act of 1971 (2 U.S.C. 441a(a)(3)) is amended to read as follows:

"(3) During the period which begins on January 1 of an odd-numbered year and ends on December 31 of the next even-numbered year, no individual may make contributions aggregating more than—

"(A) $37,500, in the case of contributions to candidates and the authorized committees of candidates;

"(B) $57,500, in the case of any other contributions, of which not more than $37,500 may be attributable to contributions to political committees which are not political committees of national political parties.".

(c) INCREASE IN SENATORIAL CAMPAIGN COMMITTEE LIMIT.— Section 315(h) of the Federal Election Campaign Act of 1971 (2 U.S.C. 441a(h)) is amended by striking "$17,500" and inserting "$35,000".

(d) INDEXING OF CONTRIBUTION LIMITS.—Section 315(c) of the Federal Election Campaign Act of 1971 (2 U.S.C. 441a(c)) is amended—

(1) in paragraph (1)—

(A) by striking the second and third sentences;

(B) by inserting "(A)" before "At the beginning"; and

(C) by adding at the end the following:

"(B) Except as provided in subparagraph (C), in any calendar year after 2002—

"(i) a limitation established by subsections (a)(1)(A), (a)(1)(B), (a)(3), (b), (d), or (h) shall be increased by the percent difference determined under subparagraph (A);

"(ii) each amount so increased shall remain in effect for the calendar year; and

"(iii) if any amount after adjustment under clause (i) is not a multiple of $100, such amount shall be rounded to the nearest multiple of $100.

"(C) In the case of limitations under subsections (a)(1)(A), (a)(1)(B), (a)(3), and (h), increases shall only be made in odd-numbered years and such increases shall remain in effect for the 2-year period beginning on the first day following the date of the last general election in the year preceding the year in which the amount is increased and ending on the date of the next general election."; and

(2) in paragraph (2)(B), by striking "means the calendar year 1974" and inserting "means—

"(i) for purposes of subsections (b) and (d), calendar year 1974; and

"(ii) for purposes of subsections (a)(1)(A), (a)(1)(B), (a)(3), and (h), calendar year 2001".

(e) EFFECTIVE DATE.—The amendments made by this section shall apply with respect to contributions made on or after January 1, 2003.

2 USC 441a note.

SEC. 308. DONATIONS TO PRESIDENTIAL INAUGURAL COMMITTEE.

(a) IN GENERAL.—Chapter 5 of title 36, United States Code, is amended by—

(1) redesignating section 510 as section 511; and

(2) inserting after section 509 the following:

"§ 510. Disclosure of and prohibition on certain donations

"(a) IN GENERAL.—A committee shall not be considered to be the Inaugural Committee for purposes of this chapter unless the committee agrees to, and meets, the requirements of subsections (b) and (c).

"(b) DISCLOSURE.—

PUBLIC LAW 107–155—MAR. 27, 2002

Deadline.
Reports.

"(1) IN GENERAL.—Not later than the date that is 90 days after the date of the Presidential inaugural ceremony, the committee shall file a report with the Federal Election Commission disclosing any donation of money or anything of value made to the committee in an aggregate amount equal to or greater than $200.

"(2) CONTENTS OF REPORT.—A report filed under paragraph (1) shall contain—

"(A) the amount of the donation;

"(B) the date the donation is received; and

"(C) the name and address of the person making the donation.

"(c) LIMITATION.—The committee shall not accept any donation from a foreign national (as defined in section 319(b) of the Federal Election Campaign Act of 1971 (2 U.S.C. 441e(b))).".

(b) REPORTS MADE AVAILABLE BY FEC.—Section 304 of the Federal Election Campaign Act of 1971 (2 U.S.C. 434), as amended by sections 103, 201, and 212 is amended by adding at the end the following:

"(h) REPORTS FROM INAUGURAL COMMITTEES.—The Federal Election Commission shall make any report filed by an Inaugural Committee under section 510 of title 36, United States Code, accessible to the public at the offices of the Commission and on the Internet not later than 48 hours after the report is received by the Commission.".

SEC. 309. PROHIBITION ON FRAUDULENT SOLICITATION OF FUNDS.

Section 322 of the Federal Election Campaign Act of 1971 (2 U.S.C. 441h) is amended—

(1) by inserting "(a) IN GENERAL.—" before "No person"; and

(2) by adding at the end the following:

"(b) FRAUDULENT SOLICITATION OF FUNDS.—No person shall—

"(1) fraudulently misrepresent the person as speaking, writing, or otherwise acting for or on behalf of any candidate or political party or employee or agent thereof for the purpose of soliciting contributions or donations; or

"(2) willfully and knowingly participate in or conspire to participate in any plan, scheme, or design to violate paragraph (1).".

2 USC 431 note.

SEC. 310. STUDY AND REPORT ON CLEAN MONEY CLEAN ELECTIONS LAWS.

(a) CLEAN MONEY CLEAN ELECTIONS DEFINED.—In this section, the term "clean money clean elections" means funds received under State laws that provide in whole or in part for the public financing of election campaigns.

(b) STUDY.—

(1) IN GENERAL.—The Comptroller General shall conduct a study of the clean money clean elections of Arizona and Maine.

(2) MATTERS STUDIED.—

(A) STATISTICS ON CLEAN MONEY CLEAN ELECTIONS CANDIDATES.—The Comptroller General shall determine—

(i) the number of candidates who have chosen to run for public office with clean money clean elections including—

(I) the office for which they were candidates;

PUBLIC LAW 107–155—MAR. 27, 2002   116 STAT. 105

(II) whether the candidate was an incumbent or a challenger; and
(III) whether the candidate was successful in the candidate's bid for public office; and
(ii) the number of races in which at least one candidate ran an election with clean money clean elections.
(B) EFFECTS OF CLEAN MONEY CLEAN ELECTIONS.—The Comptroller General of the United States shall describe the effects of public financing under the clean money clean elections laws on the 2000 elections in Arizona and Maine.   *Arizona.*
Maine.

(c) REPORT.—Not later than 1 year after the date of enactment of this Act, the Comptroller General of the United States shall submit a report to the Congress detailing the results of the study conducted under subsection (b).   *Deadline.*

SEC. 311. CLARITY STANDARDS FOR IDENTIFICATION OF SPONSORS OF ELECTION-RELATED ADVERTISING.

Section 318 of the Federal Election Campaign Act of 1971 (2 U.S.C. 441d) is amended—
(1) in subsection (a)—
(A) in the matter preceding paragraph (1)—
(i) by striking "Whenever" and inserting "Whenever a political committee makes a disbursement for the purpose of financing any communication through any broadcasting station, newspaper, magazine, outdoor advertising facility, mailing, or any other type of general public political advertising, or whenever";
(ii) by striking "an expenditure" and inserting "a disbursement";
(iii) by striking "direct"; and
(iv) by inserting "or makes a disbursement for an electioneering communication (as defined in section 304(f)(3))" after "public political advertising"; and
(B) in paragraph (3), by inserting "and permanent street address, telephone number, or World Wide Web address" after "name"; and
(2) by adding at the end the following:
"(c) SPECIFICATION.—Any printed communication described in subsection (a) shall—
"(1) be of sufficient type size to be clearly readable by the recipient of the communication;
"(2) be contained in a printed box set apart from the other contents of the communication; and
"(3) be printed with a reasonable degree of color contrast between the background and the printed statement.
"(d) ADDITIONAL REQUIREMENTS.—
"(1) COMMUNICATIONS BY CANDIDATES OR AUTHORIZED PERSONS.—
"(A) BY RADIO.—Any communication described in paragraph (1) or (2) of subsection (a) which is transmitted through radio shall include, in addition to the requirements of that paragraph, an audio statement by the candidate that identifies the candidate and states that the candidate has approved the communication.
"(B) BY TELEVISION.—Any communication described in paragraph (1) or (2) of subsection (a) which is transmitted

through television shall include, in addition to the requirements of that paragraph, a statement that identifies the candidate and states that the candidate has approved the communication. Such statement—

"(i) shall be conveyed by—

"(I) an unobscured, full-screen view of the candidate making the statement, or

"(II) the candidate in voice-over, accompanied by a clearly identifiable photographic or similar image of the candidate; and

"(ii) shall also appear in writing at the end of the communication in a clearly readable manner with a reasonable degree of color contrast between the background and the printed statement, for a period of at least 4 seconds.

"(2) COMMUNICATIONS BY OTHERS.—Any communication described in paragraph (3) of subsection (a) which is transmitted through radio or television shall include, in addition to the requirements of that paragraph, in a clearly spoken manner, the following audio statement: '_____ is responsible for the content of this advertising.' (with the blank to be filled in with the name of the political committee or other person paying for the communication and the name of any connected organization of the payor). If transmitted through television, the statement shall be conveyed by an unobscured, full-screen view of a representative of the political committee or other person making the statement, or by a representative of such political committee or other person in voice-over, and shall also appear in a clearly readable manner with a reasonable degree of color contrast between the background and the printed statement, for a period of at least 4 seconds.".

SEC. 312. INCREASE IN PENALTIES.

(a) IN GENERAL.—Subparagraph (A) of section 309(d)(1) of the Federal Election Campaign Act of 1971 (2 U.S.C. 437g(d)(1)(A)) is amended to read as follows:

"(A) Any person who knowingly and willfully commits a violation of any provision of this Act which involves the making, receiving, or reporting of any contribution, donation, or expenditure—

"(i) aggregating $25,000 or more during a calendar year shall be fined under title 18, United States Code, or imprisoned for not more than 5 years, or both; or

"(ii) aggregating $2,000 or more (but less than $25,000) during a calendar year shall be fined under such title, or imprisoned for not more than 1 year, or both.".

2 USC 437g note.   (b) EFFECTIVE DATE.—The amendment made by this section shall apply to violations occurring on or after the effective date of this Act.

SEC. 313. STATUTE OF LIMITATIONS.

(a) IN GENERAL.—Section 406(a) of the Federal Election Campaign Act of 1971 (2 U.S.C. 455(a)) is amended by striking "3" and inserting "5".

2 USC 455 note.   (b) EFFECTIVE DATE.—The amendment made by this section shall apply to violations occurring on or after the effective date of this Act.

SEC. 314. SENTENCING GUIDELINES.

28 USC 994 note.

(a) IN GENERAL.—The United States Sentencing Commission shall—

(1) promulgate a guideline, or amend an existing guideline under section 994 of title 28, United States Code, in accordance with paragraph (2), for penalties for violations of the Federal Election Campaign Act of 1971 and related election laws; and

(2) submit to Congress an explanation of any guidelines promulgated under paragraph (1) and any legislative or administrative recommendations regarding enforcement of the Federal Election Campaign Act of 1971 and related election laws.

(b) CONSIDERATIONS.—The Commission shall provide guidelines under subsection (a) taking into account the following considerations:

(1) Ensure that the sentencing guidelines and policy statements reflect the serious nature of such violations and the need for aggressive and appropriate law enforcement action to prevent such violations.

(2) Provide a sentencing enhancement for any person convicted of such violation if such violation involves—

(A) a contribution, donation, or expenditure from a foreign source;

(B) a large number of illegal transactions;

(C) a large aggregate amount of illegal contributions, donations, or expenditures;

(D) the receipt or disbursement of governmental funds; and

(E) an intent to achieve a benefit from the Federal Government.

(3) Assure reasonable consistency with other relevant directives and guidelines of the Commission.

(4) Account for aggravating or mitigating circumstances that might justify exceptions, including circumstances for which the sentencing guidelines currently provide sentencing enhancements.

(5) Assure the guidelines adequately meet the purposes of sentencing under section 3553(a)(2) of title 18, United States Code.

(c) EFFECTIVE DATE; EMERGENCY AUTHORITY TO PROMULGATE GUIDELINES.—

(1) EFFECTIVE DATE.—Notwithstanding section 402, the United States Sentencing Commission shall promulgate guidelines under this section not later than the later of—

(A) 90 days after the effective date of this Act; or

(B) 90 days after the date on which at least a majority of the members of the Commission are appointed and holding office.

(2) EMERGENCY AUTHORITY TO PROMULGATE GUIDELINES.—The Commission shall promulgate guidelines under this section in accordance with the procedures set forth in section 21(a) of the Sentencing Reform Act of 1987, as though the authority under such Act has not expired.

116 STAT. 108   PUBLIC LAW 107–155—MAR. 27, 2002

SEC. 315. INCREASE IN PENALTIES IMPOSED FOR VIOLATIONS OF CONDUIT CONTRIBUTION BAN.

(a) INCREASE IN CIVIL MONEY PENALTY FOR KNOWING AND WILLFUL VIOLATIONS.—Section 309(a) of the Federal Election Campaign Act of 1971 (2 U.S.C. 437g(a)) is amended—

(1) in paragraph (5)(B), by inserting before the period at the end the following: "(or, in the case of a violation of section 320, which is not less than 300 percent of the amount involved in the violation and is not more than the greater of $50,000 or 1,000 percent of the amount involved in the violation)"; and

(2) in paragraph (6)(C), by inserting before the period at the end the following: "(or, in the case of a violation of section 320, which is not less than 300 percent of the amount involved in the violation and is not more than the greater of $50,000 or 1,000 percent of the amount involved in the violation)".

(b) INCREASE IN CRIMINAL PENALTY.—Section 309(d)(1) of such Act (2 U.S.C. 437g(d)(1)) is amended by adding at the end the following new subparagraph:

"(D) Any person who knowingly and willfully commits a violation of section 320 involving an amount aggregating more than $10,000 during a calendar year shall be—

"(i) imprisoned for not more than 2 years if the amount is less than $25,000 (and subject to imprisonment under subparagraph (A) if the amount is $25,000 or more);

"(ii) fined not less than 300 percent of the amount involved in the violation and not more than the greater of—

"(I) $50,000; or

"(II) 1,000 percent of the amount involved in the violation; or

"(iii) both imprisoned under clause (i) and fined under clause (ii).".

2 USC 437g note.   (c) EFFECTIVE DATE.—The amendments made by this section shall apply with respect to violations occurring on or after the effective date of this Act.

SEC. 316. RESTRICTION ON INCREASED CONTRIBUTION LIMITS BY TAKING INTO ACCOUNT CANDIDATE'S AVAILABLE FUNDS.

Section 315(i)(1) of the Federal Election Campaign Act of 1971 (2 U.S.C. 441a(i)(1)), as added by this Act, is amended by adding at the end the following:

"(E) SPECIAL RULE FOR CANDIDATE'S CAMPAIGN FUNDS.—

"(i) IN GENERAL.—For purposes of determining the aggregate amount of expenditures from personal funds under subparagraph (D)(ii), such amount shall include the gross receipts advantage of the candidate's authorized committee.

"(ii) GROSS RECEIPTS ADVANTAGE.—For purposes of clause (i), the term 'gross receipts advantage' means the excess, if any, of—

"(I) the aggregate amount of 50 percent of gross receipts of a candidate's authorized committee during any election cycle (not including contributions from personal funds of the candidate)

PUBLIC LAW 107–155—MAR. 27, 2002   116 STAT. 109

that may be expended in connection with the election, as determined on June 30 and December 31 of the year preceding the year in which a general election is held, over

"(II) the aggregate amount of 50 percent of gross receipts of the opposing candidate's authorized committee during any election cycle (not including contributions from personal funds of the candidate) that may be expended in connection with the election, as determined on June 30 and December 31 of the year preceding the year in which a general election is held.".

SEC. 317. CLARIFICATION OF RIGHT OF NATIONALS OF THE UNITED STATES TO MAKE POLITICAL CONTRIBUTIONS.

Section 319(b)(2) of the Federal Election Campaign Act of 1971 (2 U.S.C. 441e(b)(2)) is amended by inserting after "United States" the following: "or a national of the United States (as defined in section 101(a)(22) of the Immigration and Nationality Act)".

SEC. 318. PROHIBITION OF CONTRIBUTIONS BY MINORS.

Title III of the Federal Election Campaign Act of 1971 (2 U.S.C. 431 et seq.), as amended by section 101, is further amended by adding at the end the following new section:

"PROHIBITION OF CONTRIBUTIONS BY MINORS

"SEC. 324. An individual who is 17 years old or younger shall not make a contribution to a candidate or a contribution or donation to a committee of a political party.".

2 USC 441k.

SEC. 319. MODIFICATION OF INDIVIDUAL CONTRIBUTION LIMITS FOR HOUSE CANDIDATES IN RESPONSE TO EXPENDITURES FROM PERSONAL FUNDS.

(a) INCREASED LIMITS.—Title III of the Federal Election Campaign Act of 1971 (2 U.S.C. 431 et seq.) is amended by inserting after section 315 the following new section:

"MODIFICATION OF CERTAIN LIMITS FOR HOUSE CANDIDATES IN RESPONSE TO PERSONAL FUND EXPENDITURES OF OPPONENTS

"SEC. 315A. (a) AVAILABILITY OF INCREASED LIMIT.—

"(1) IN GENERAL.—Subject to paragraph (3), if the opposition personal funds amount with respect to a candidate for election to the office of Representative in, or Delegate or Resident Commissioner to, the Congress exceeds $350,000—

"(A) the limit under subsection (a)(1)(A) with respect to the candidate shall be tripled;

"(B) the limit under subsection (a)(3) shall not apply with respect to any contribution made with respect to the candidate if the contribution is made under the increased limit allowed under subparagraph (A) during a period in which the candidate may accept such a contribution; and

"(C) the limits under subsection (d) with respect to any expenditure by a State or national committee of a political party on behalf of the candidate shall not apply.

"(2) DETERMINATION OF OPPOSITION PERSONAL FUNDS AMOUNT.—

2 USC 441a–1.

"(A) IN GENERAL.—The opposition personal funds amount is an amount equal to the excess (if any) of—

"(i) the greatest aggregate amount of expenditures from personal funds (as defined in subsection (b)(1)) that an opposing candidate in the same election makes; over

"(ii) the aggregate amount of expenditures from personal funds made by the candidate with respect to the election.

"(B) SPECIAL RULE FOR CANDIDATE'S CAMPAIGN FUNDS.—

"(i) IN GENERAL.—For purposes of determining the aggregate amount of expenditures from personal funds under subparagraph (A), such amount shall include the gross receipts advantage of the candidate's authorized committee.

"(ii) GROSS RECEIPTS ADVANTAGE.—For purposes of clause (i), the term 'gross receipts advantage' means the excess, if any, of—

"(I) the aggregate amount of 50 percent of gross receipts of a candidate's authorized committee during any election cycle (not including contributions from personal funds of the candidate) that may be expended in connection with the election, as determined on June 30 and December 31 of the year preceding the year in which a general election is held, over

"(II) the aggregate amount of 50 percent of gross receipts of the opposing candidate's authorized committee during any election cycle (not including contributions from personal funds of the candidate) that may be expended in connection with the election, as determined on June 30 and December 31 of the year preceding the year in which a general election is held.

"(3) TIME TO ACCEPT CONTRIBUTIONS UNDER INCREASED LIMIT.—

"(A) IN GENERAL.—Subject to subparagraph (B), a candidate and the candidate's authorized committee shall not accept any contribution, and a party committee shall not make any expenditure, under the increased limit under paragraph (1)—

"(i) until the candidate has received notification of the opposition personal funds amount under subsection (b)(1); and

"(ii) to the extent that such contribution, when added to the aggregate amount of contributions previously accepted and party expenditures previously made under the increased limits under this subsection for the election cycle, exceeds 100 percent of the opposition personal funds amount.

"(B) EFFECT OF WITHDRAWAL OF AN OPPOSING CANDIDATE.—A candidate and a candidate's authorized committee shall not accept any contribution and a party shall not make any expenditure under the increased limit after the date on which an opposing candidate ceases to be a candidate to the extent that the amount of such increased limit is attributable to such an opposing candidate.

"(4) DISPOSAL OF EXCESS CONTRIBUTIONS.—

"(A) IN GENERAL.—The aggregate amount of contributions accepted by a candidate or a candidate's authorized committee under the increased limit under paragraph (1) and not otherwise expended in connection with the election with respect to which such contributions relate shall, not later than 50 days after the date of such election, be used in the manner described in subparagraph (B).

"(B) RETURN TO CONTRIBUTORS.—A candidate or a candidate's authorized committee shall return the excess contribution to the person who made the contribution.

"(b) NOTIFICATION OF EXPENDITURES FROM PERSONAL FUNDS.—

"(1) IN GENERAL.—

"(A) DEFINITION OF EXPENDITURE FROM PERSONAL FUNDS.—In this paragraph, the term 'expenditure from personal funds' means—

"(i) an expenditure made by a candidate using personal funds; and

"(ii) a contribution or loan made by a candidate using personal funds or a loan secured using such funds to the candidate's authorized committee.

"(B) DECLARATION OF INTENT.—Not later than the date that is 15 days after the date on which an individual becomes a candidate for the office of Representative in, or Delegate or Resident Commissioner to, the Congress, the candidate shall file a declaration stating the total amount of expenditures from personal funds that the candidate intends to make, or to obligate to make, with respect to the election that will exceed $350,000. [Deadline.]

"(C) INITIAL NOTIFICATION.—Not later than 24 hours after a candidate described in subparagraph (B) makes or obligates to make an aggregate amount of expenditures from personal funds in excess of $350,000 in connection with any election, the candidate shall file a notification. [Deadline.]

"(D) ADDITIONAL NOTIFICATION.—After a candidate files an initial notification under subparagraph (C), the candidate shall file an additional notification each time expenditures from personal funds are made or obligated to be made in an aggregate amount that exceeds $10,000. Such notification shall be filed not later than 24 hours after the expenditure is made. [Deadline.]

"(E) CONTENTS.—A notification under subparagraph (C) or (D) shall include—

"(i) the name of the candidate and the office sought by the candidate;

"(ii) the date and amount of each expenditure; and

"(iii) the total amount of expenditures from personal funds that the candidate has made, or obligated to make, with respect to an election as of the date of the expenditure that is the subject of the notification.

"(F) PLACE OF FILING.—Each declaration or notification required to be filed by a candidate under subparagraph (C), (D), or (E) shall be filed with—

"(i) the Commission; and

116 STAT. 112   PUBLIC LAW 107–155—MAR. 27, 2002

"(ii) each candidate in the same election and the national party of each such candidate.

"(2) NOTIFICATION OF DISPOSAL OF EXCESS CONTRIBUTIONS.—In the next regularly scheduled report after the date of the election for which a candidate seeks nomination for election to, or election to, Federal office, the candidate or the candidate's authorized committee shall submit to the Commission a report indicating the source and amount of any excess contributions (as determined under subsection (a)) and the manner in which the candidate or the candidate's authorized committee used such funds.

"(3) ENFORCEMENT.—For provisions providing for the enforcement of the reporting requirements under this subsection, see section 309.".

(b) CONFORMING AMENDMENT.—Section 315(a)(1) of the Federal Election Campaign Act of 1971 (2 U.S.C. 441a), as amended by section 304(a), is amended by striking "subsection (i)," and inserting "subsection (i) and section 315A,".

TITLE IV—SEVERABILITY; EFFECTIVE DATE

2 USC 454 note.   **SEC. 401. SEVERABILITY.**

If any provision of this Act or amendment made by this Act, or the application of a provision or amendment to any person or circumstance, is held to be unconstitutional, the remainder of this Act and amendments made by this Act, and the application of the provisions and amendment to any person or circumstance, shall not be affected by the holding.

2 USC 431 note.   **SEC. 402. EFFECTIVE DATES AND REGULATIONS.**

(a) GENERAL EFFECTIVE DATE.—

(1) IN GENERAL.—Except as provided in the succeeding provisions of this section, the effective date of this Act, and the amendments made by this Act, is November 6, 2002.

(2) MODIFICATION OF CONTRIBUTION LIMITS.—The amendments made by—

(A) section 102 shall apply with respect to contributions made on or after January 1, 2003; and

(B) section 307 shall take effect as provided in subsection (e) of such section.

(3) SEVERABILITY; EFFECTIVE DATES AND REGULATIONS; JUDICIAL REVIEW.—Title IV shall take effect on the date of enactment of this Act.

(4) PROVISIONS NOT TO APPLY TO RUNOFF ELECTIONS.—Section 323(b) of the Federal Election Campaign Act of 1971 (as added by section 101(a)), section 103(a), title II, sections 304 (including section 315(j) of Federal Election Campaign Act of 1971, as added by section 304(a)(2)), 305 (notwithstanding subsection (c) of such section), 311, 316, 318, and 319, and title V (and the amendments made by such sections and titles) shall take effect on November 6, 2002, but shall not apply with respect to runoff elections, recounts, or election contests resulting from elections held prior to such date.

(b) SOFT MONEY OF NATIONAL POLITICAL PARTIES.—

PUBLIC LAW 107–155—MAR. 27, 2002   116 STAT. 113

(1) IN GENERAL.—Except for subsection (b) of such section, section 323 of the Federal Election Campaign Act of 1971 (as added by section 101(a)) shall take effect on November 6, 2002.

(2) TRANSITIONAL RULES FOR THE SPENDING OF SOFT MONEY OF NATIONAL POLITICAL PARTIES.—

(A) IN GENERAL.—Notwithstanding section 323(a) of the Federal Election Campaign Act of 1971 (as added by section 101(a)), if a national committee of a political party described in such section (including any person who is subject to such section under paragraph (2) of such section), has received funds described in such section prior to November 6, 2002, the rules described in subparagraph (B) shall apply with respect to the spending of the amount of such funds in the possession of such committee as of such date.

(B) USE OF EXCESS SOFT MONEY FUNDS.—

(i) IN GENERAL.—Subject to clauses (ii) and (iii), the national committee of a political party may use the amount described in subparagraph (A) prior to January 1, 2003, solely for the purpose of—

(I) retiring outstanding debts or obligations that were incurred solely in connection with an election held prior to November 6, 2002; or

(II) paying expenses or retiring outstanding debts or paying for obligations that were incurred solely in connection with any runoff election, recount, or election contest resulting from an election held prior to November 6, 2002.

(ii) PROHIBITION ON USING SOFT MONEY FOR HARD MONEY EXPENSES, DEBTS, AND OBLIGATIONS.—A national committee of a political party may not use the amount described in subparagraph (A) for any expenditure (as defined in section 301(9) of the Federal Election Campaign Act of 1971 (2 U.S.C. 431(9))) or for retiring outstanding debts or obligations that were incurred for such an expenditure.

(iii) PROHIBITION OF BUILDING FUND USES.—A national committee of a political party may not use the amount described in subparagraph (A) for activities to defray the costs of the construction or purchase of any office building or facility.

(c) REGULATIONS.—

(1) IN GENERAL.—Except as provided in paragraph (2), the Federal Election Commission shall promulgate regulations to carry out this Act and the amendments made by this Act that are under the Commission's jurisdiction not later than 270 days after the date of enactment of this Act.   Deadline.

(2) SOFT MONEY OF POLITICAL PARTIES.—Not later than 90 days after the date of enactment of this Act, the Federal Election Commission shall promulgate regulations to carry out title I of this Act and the amendments made by such title.   Deadline.

SEC. 403. JUDICIAL REVIEW.   2 USC 437h note.

(a) SPECIAL RULES FOR ACTIONS BROUGHT ON CONSTITUTIONAL GROUNDS.—If any action is brought for declaratory or injunctive relief to challenge the constitutionality of any provision of this

116 STAT. 114   PUBLIC LAW 107–155—MAR. 27, 2002

Act or any amendment made by this Act, the following rules shall apply:

(1) The action shall be filed in the United States District Court for the District of Columbia and shall be heard by a 3-judge court convened pursuant to section 2284 of title 28, United States Code.

(2) A copy of the complaint shall be delivered promptly to the Clerk of the House of Representatives and the Secretary of the Senate.

(3) A final decision in the action shall be reviewable only by appeal directly to the Supreme Court of the United States. Such appeal shall be taken by the filing of a notice of appeal within 10 days, and the filing of a jurisdictional statement within 30 days, of the entry of the final decision.

(4) It shall be the duty of the United States District Court for the District of Columbia and the Supreme Court of the United States to advance on the docket and to expedite to the greatest possible extent the disposition of the action and appeal.

(b) INTERVENTION BY MEMBERS OF CONGRESS.—In any action in which the constitutionality of any provision of this Act or any amendment made by this Act is raised (including but not limited to an action described in subsection (a)), any member of the House of Representatives (including a Delegate or Resident Commissioner to the Congress) or Senate shall have the right to intervene either in support of or opposition to the position of a party to the case regarding the constitutionality of the provision or amendment. To avoid duplication of efforts and reduce the burdens placed on the parties to the action, the court in any such action may make such orders as it considers necessary, including orders to require intervenors taking similar positions to file joint papers or to be represented by a single attorney at oral argument.

(c) CHALLENGE BY MEMBERS OF CONGRESS.—Any Member of Congress may bring an action, subject to the special rules described in subsection (a), for declaratory or injunctive relief to challenge the constitutionality of any provision of this Act or any amendment made by this Act.

(d) APPLICABILITY.—

(1) INITIAL CLAIMS.—With respect to any action initially filed on or before December 31, 2006, the provisions of subsection (a) shall apply with respect to each action described in such section.

(2) SUBSEQUENT ACTIONS.—With respect to any action initially filed after December 31, 2006, the provisions of subsection (a) shall not apply to any action described in such section unless the person filing such action elects such provisions to apply to the action.

TITLE V—ADDITIONAL DISCLOSURE PROVISIONS

SEC. 501. INTERNET ACCESS TO RECORDS.

Section 304(a)(11)(B) of the Federal Election Campaign Act of 1971 (2 U.S.C. 434(a)(11)(B)) is amended to read as follows:

Deadline.

"(B) The Commission shall make a designation, statement, report, or notification that is filed with the Commission under

PUBLIC LAW 107-155—MAR. 27, 2002   116 STAT. 115

this Act available for inspection by the public in the offices of the Commission and accessible to the public on the Internet not later than 48 hours (or not later than 24 hours in the case of a designation, statement, report, or notification filed electronically) after receipt by the Commission.".

SEC. 502. MAINTENANCE OF WEBSITE OF ELECTION REPORTS.   2 USC 438a.

(a) IN GENERAL.—The Federal Election Commission shall maintain a central site on the Internet to make accessible to the public all publicly available election-related reports and information.

(b) ELECTION-RELATED REPORT.—In this section, the term "election-related report" means any report, designation, or statement required to be filed under the Federal Election Campaign Act of 1971.

(c) COORDINATION WITH OTHER AGENCIES.—Any Federal executive agency receiving election-related information which that agency is required by law to publicly disclose shall cooperate and coordinate with the Federal Election Commission to make such report available through, or for posting on, the site of the Federal Election Commission in a timely manner.

SEC. 503. ADDITIONAL DISCLOSURE REPORTS.   2 USC 434.

(a) PRINCIPAL CAMPAIGN COMMITTEES.—Section 304(a)(2)(B) of   Deadlines.
the Federal Election Campaign Act of 1971 is amended by striking "the following reports" and all that follows through the period and inserting "the treasurer shall file quarterly reports, which shall be filed not later than the 15th day after the last day of each calendar quarter, and which shall be complete as of the last day of each calendar quarter, except that the report for the quarter ending December 31 shall be filed not later than January 31 of the following calendar year.".

(b) NATIONAL COMMITTEE OF A POLITICAL PARTY.—Section 304(a)(4) of such Act (2 U.S.C. 434(a)(4)) is amended by adding at the end the following flush sentence: "Notwithstanding the preceding sentence, a national committee of a political party shall file the reports required under subparagraph (B).".

SEC. 504. PUBLIC ACCESS TO BROADCASTING RECORDS.

Section 315 of the Communications Act of 1934 (47 U.S.C. 315), as amended by this Act, is amended by redesignating subsections (e) and (f) as subsections (f) and (g), respectively, and inserting after subsection (d) the following:

"(e) POLITICAL RECORD.—

"(1) IN GENERAL.—A licensee shall maintain, and make available for public inspection, a complete record of a request to purchase broadcast time that—

"(A) is made by or on behalf of a legally qualified candidate for public office; or

"(B) communicates a message relating to any political matter of national importance, including—

"(i) a legally qualified candidate;

"(ii) any election to Federal office; or

"(iii) a national legislative issue of public importance.

"(2) CONTENTS OF RECORD.—A record maintained under paragraph (1) shall contain information regarding—

"(A) whether the request to purchase broadcast time is accepted or rejected by the licensee;

116 STAT. 116   PUBLIC LAW 107–155—MAR. 27, 2002

"(B) the rate charged for the broadcast time;
"(C) the date and time on which the communication is aired;
"(D) the class of time that is purchased;
"(E) the name of the candidate to which the communication refers and the office to which the candidate is seeking election, the election to which the communication refers, or the issue to which the communication refers (as applicable);
"(F) in the case of a request made by, or on behalf of, a candidate, the name of the candidate, the authorized committee of the candidate, and the treasurer of such committee; and
"(G) in the case of any other request, the name of the person purchasing the time, the name, address, and phone number of a contact person for such person, and a list of the chief executive officers or members of the executive committee or of the board of directors of such person.

"(3) TIME TO MAINTAIN FILE.—The information required under this subsection shall be placed in a political file as soon as possible and shall be retained by the licensee for a period of not less than 2 years.".

Approved March 27, 2002.

LEGISLATIVE HISTORY—H.R. 2356 (S. 27):

HOUSE REPORTS: No. 107–131, Pt. 1 (Comm. on House Administration).
CONGRESSIONAL RECORD, Vol. 148 (2002):
    Feb. 13, considered and passed House.
    Mar. 18–20, considered and passed Senate.
WEEKLY COMPILATION OF PRESIDENTIAL DOCUMENTS, Vol. 38 (2002):
    Mar. 27, Presidential statement.

○

Selected Regulations

Code of Federal Regulations

11

Revised as of February 3, 2003

Federal Elections

Containing a codification of documents of general applicability and future effect

As of February 3, 2003

With Ancillaries

Published by
Office of the Federal Register
National Archives and Records
Administration

A Special Edition of the Federal Register

person, or by other individualized means to assist them in registering to vote. Voter registration activity includes, but is not limited to, printing and distributing registration and voting information, providing individuals with voter registration forms, and assisting individuals in the completion and filing of such forms.

(3) *Get-out-the-vote activity* means contacting registered voters by telephone, in person, or by other individualized means, to assist them in engaging in the act of voting. Get-out-the-vote activity shall not include any communication by an association or similar group of candidates for State or local office or of individuals holding State or local office if such communication refers only to one or more State or local candidates. Get-out-the-vote activity includes, but is not limited to:

(i) Providing to individual voters, within 72 hours of an election, information such as the date of the election, the times when polling places are open, and the location of particular polling places; and

(ii) Offering to transport or actually transporting voters to the polls.

(4) *Voter identification* means creating or enhancing voter lists by verifying or adding information about the voters' likelihood of voting in an upcoming election or their likelihood of voting for specific candidates. This paragraph shall not apply to an association or similar group of candidates for State or local office or of individuals holding State or local office if the association or group engages in voter identification that refers only to one or more State or local candidates.

(b) As used in part 300 of this chapter, *Federal election activity* means any of the activities described in paragraphs (b)(1) through (b)(4) of this section.

(1) Voter registration activity during the period that begins on the date that is 120 calendar days before the date that a regularly scheduled Federal election is held and ends on the date of the election. For purposes of voter registration activity, the term "election" does not include any special election.

(2) The following activities conducted in connection with an election in which

§ 100.24 Federal election activity (2 U.S.C. 431(20)).

(a) As used in this section, and in part 300 of this chapter,

(1) *In connection with an election in which a candidate for Federal office appears on the ballot* means:

(i) The period of time beginning on the date of the earliest filing deadline for access to the primary election ballot for Federal candidates as determined by State law, or in those States that do not conduct primaries, on January 1 of each even-numbered year and ending on the date of the general election, up to and including the date of any general runoff.

(ii) In an odd-numbered year, the period beginning on the date on which the date of a special election in which a candidate for Federal office appears on the ballot is set and ending on the date of the special election.

(2) *Voter registration activity* means contacting individuals by telephone, in

one or more candidates for Federal office appears on the ballot (regardless of whether one or more candidates for State or local office also appears on the ballot):

(i) Voter identification.

(ii) Generic campaign activity, as defined in 11 CFR 100.25.

(iii) Get-out-the-vote activity.

(3) A public communication that refers to a clearly identified candidate for Federal office, regardless of whether a candidate for State or local election is also mentioned or identified, and that promotes or supports, or attacks or opposes any candidate for Federal office. This paragraph applies whether or not the communication expressly advocates a vote for or against a Federal candidate.

(4) Services provided during any month by an employee of a State, district, or local committee of a political party who spends more than 25 percent of that individual's compensated time during that month on activities in connection with a Federal election.

(c) *Exceptions. Federal election activity* does not include any amount expended or disbursed by a State, district, or local committee of a political party for any of the following activities:

(1) A public communication that refers solely to one or more clearly identified candidates for State or local office and that does not promote or support, or attack or oppose a clearly identified candidate for Federal office; provided, however, that such a public communication shall be considered a Federal election activity if it constitutes voter registration activity, generic campaign activity, get-out-the-vote activity, or voter identification.

(2) A contribution to a candidate for State or local office, provided the contribution is not designated to pay for voter registration activity, voter identification, generic campaign activity, get-out-the-vote activity, a public communication, or employee services as set forth in paragraphs (a)(1) through (4) of this section.

(3) The costs of a State, district, or local political convention, meeting or conference.

(4) The costs of grassroots campaign materials, including buttons, bumper stickers, handbills, brochures, posters,

and yard signs, that name or depict only candidates for State or local office.

[67 FR 49110, July 29, 2002]

§ 100.25   Generic campaign activity (2 U.S.C. 431(21)).

Generic campaign activity means a public communication that promotes or opposes a political party and does not promote or oppose a clearly identified Federal candidate or a non-Federal candidate.

[67 FR 49110, July 29, 2002]

§ 100.26   Public communication (2 U.S.C. 431(22)).

Public communication means a communication by means of any broadcast, cable or satellite communication, newspaper, magazine, outdoor advertising facility, mass mailing or telephone bank to the general public, or any other form of general public political advertising. The term public communication shall not include communications over the Internet.

[67 FR 49110, July 29, 2002]

§ 100.27   Mass mailing (2 U.S.C. 431(23)).

Mass mailing means a mailing by United States mail or facsimile of more than 500 pieces of mail matter of an identical or substantially similar nature within any 30-day period. A mass mailing does not include electronic mail or Internet communications. For purposes of this section, *substantially similar* includes communications that include substantially the same template or language, but vary in non-material respects such as communications customized by the recipient's name, occupation, or geographic location.

[67 FR 49110, July 29, 2002]

§ 100.28   Telephone bank (2 U.S.C. 431(24)).

Telephone bank means more than 500 telephone calls of an identical or substantially similar nature within any 30-day period. A telephone bank does not include electronic mail or Internet communications transmitted over telephone lines. For purposes of this section, *substantially similar* includes communications that include substantially the same template or language, but vary in non-material respects such as communications customized by the recipient's name, occupation, or geographic location.

[67 FR 49110, July 29, 2002]

§ 100.29 Electioneering communication (2 U.S.C. 434(f)(3)).

(a) *Electioneering communication* means any broadcast, cable, or satellite communication that:

(1) Refers to a clearly identified candidate for Federal office;

(2) Is publicly distributed within 60 days before a general election for the office sought by the candidate; or within 30 days before a primary or preference election, or a convention or caucus of a political party that has authority to nominate a candidate, for the office sought by the candidate, and the candidate referenced is seeking the nomination of that political party; and

(3) Is targeted to the relevant electorate, in the case of a candidate for Senate or the House of Representatives.

(b) For purposes of this section—(1) *Broadcast, cable, or satellite communication* means a communication that is publicly distributed by a television station, radio station, cable television system, or satellite system.

(2) *Refers to a clearly identified candidate* means that the candidate's name, nickname, photograph, or drawing appears, or the identity of the candidate is otherwise apparent through an unambiguous reference such as "the President," "your Congressman," or "the incumbent," or through an unambiguous reference to his or her status as a candidate such as "the Democratic presidential nominee" or "the Republican candidate for Senate in the State of Georgia."

(3)(i) *Publicly distributed* means aired, broadcast, cablecast or otherwise disseminated for a fee through the facilities of a television station, radio station, cable television system, or satellite system.

(ii) In the case of a candidate for nomination for President or Vice President, *publicly distributed* means the requirements of paragraph (b)(3)(i) of this section are met and the communication:

(A) Can be received by 50,000 or more persons in a State where a primary election, as defined in 11 CFR 9032.7, is being held within 30 days; or

(B) Can be received by 50,000 or more persons anywhere in the United States within the period between 30 days before the first day of the national nominating convention and the conclusion of the convention.

(4) *A special election* or a *runoff election* is a primary election if held to nominate a candidate. A *special election* or a *runoff election* is a general election if held to elect a candidate.

(5) *Targeted to the relevant electorate* means the communication can be received by 50,000 or more persons—

(i) In the district the candidate seeks to represent, in the case of a candidate for Representative in or Delegate or Resident Commissioner to, the Congress; or

(ii) In the State the candidate seeks to represent, in the case of a candidate for Senator.

(6)(i) Information on the number of persons in a Congressional district or State that can receive a communication publicly distributed by a television station, radio station, a cable television system, or satellite system, shall be available on the Federal Communications Commission's Web site, *http://www.fcc.gov.* A link to that site is available on the Federal Election Commission's Web site, *http://www.fec.gov.* If the Federal Communications Commission's Web site indicates that a communication cannot be received by 50,000 or more persons in the specified Congressional district or State, then such information shall be a complete defense against any charge that such communication constitutes an electioneering communication, so long as such information is posted on the Federal Communications Commission's Web site on or before the date the communication is publicly distributed.

(ii) If the Federal Communications Commission's Web site does not indicate whether a communication can be received by 50,000 or more persons in the specified Congressional district or

State, it shall be a complete defense against any charge that a communication reached 50,000 or more persons when the maker of a communication:

(A) Reasonably relies on written documentation obtained from the broadcast station, radio station, cable system, or satellite system that states that the communication cannot be received by 50,000 or more persons in the specified Congressional district (for U.S. House of Representatives candidates) or State (for U.S. Senate candidates or presidential primary candidates);

(B) Does not publicly distribute the communication on a broadcast station, radio station, or cable system, located in any Metropolitan Area in the specified Congressional district (for U.S. House of Representatives candidates) or State (for U.S. Senate candidates or presidential primary candidates); or

(C) Reasonably believes that the communication cannot be received by 50,000 or more persons in the specified Congressional district (for U.S. House of Representatives candidates) or State (for U.S. Senate candidates or presidential primary candidates).

(7)(i) *Can be received by 50,000 or more persons* means—

(A) In the case of a communication transmitted by an FM radio broadcast station or network, where the Congressional district or State lies entirely within the station's or network's protected or primary service contour, that the population of the Congressional district or State is 50,000 or more; or

(B) In the case of a communication transmitted by an FM radio broadcast station or network, where a portion of the Congressional district or State lies outside of the protected or primary service contour, that the population of the part of the Congressional district or State lying within the station's or network's protected or primary service contour is 50,000 or more; or

(C) In the case of a communication transmitted by an AM radio broadcast station or network, where the Congressional district or State lies entirely within the station's or network's most outward service area, that the population of the Congressional district or State is 50,000 or more; or

(D) In the case of a communication transmitted by an AM radio broadcast station or network, where a portion of the Congressional district or State lies outside of the station's or network's most outward service area, that the population of the part of the Congressional district or State lying within the station's or network's most outward service area is 50,000 or more; or

(E) In the case of a communication appearing on a television broadcast station or network, where the Congressional district or State lies entirely within the station's or network's Grade B broadcast contour, that the population of the Congressional district or State is 50,000 or more; or

(F) In the case of a communication appearing on a television broadcast station or network, where a portion of the Congressional district or State lies outside of the Grade B broadcast contour—

(1) That the population of the part of the Congressional district or State lying within the station's or network's Grade B broadcast contour is 50,000 or more; or

(2) That the population of the part of the Congressional district or State lying within the station's or network's broadcast contour, when combined with the viewership of that television station or network by cable and satellite subscribers within the Congressional district or State lying outside the broadcast contour, is 50,000 or more; or

(G) In the case of a communication appearing exclusively on a cable or satellite television system, but not on a broadcast station or network, that the viewership of the cable system or satellite system lying within a Congressional district or State is 50,000 or more; or

(H) In the case of a communication appearing on a cable television network, that the total cable and satellite viewership within a Congressional district or State is 50,000 or more.

(ii) Cable or satellite television viewership is determined by multiplying the number of subscribers within a Congressional district or State, or a part thereof, as appropriate, by the current national average household size, as determined by the Bureau of the Census.

(iii) A determination that a communication can be received by 50,000 or more persons based on the application of the formula at paragraph (b)(7)(i)(G) or (H) of this section shall create a rebuttable presumption that may be overcome by demonstrating that—

(A) One or more cable or satellite systems did not carry the network on which the communication was publicly distributed at the time the communication was publicly distributed; and

(B) Applying the formula to the remaining cable and satellite systems results in a determination that the cable network or systems upon which the communication was publicly distributed could not be received by 50,000 persons or more.

(c) *Electioneering communication* does not include any communication that:

(1) Is publicly disseminated through a means of communication other than a broadcast, cable, or satellite television or radio station. For example, electioneering communication does not include communications appearing in print media, including a newspaper or magazine, handbill, brochure, bumper sticker, yard sign, poster, billboard, and other written materials, including mailings; communications over the Internet, including electronic mail; or telephone communications;

(2) Appears in a news story, commentary, or editorial distributed through the facilities of any broadcast, cable, or satellite television or radio station, unless such facilities are owned or controlled by any political party, political committee, or candidate. A news story distributed through a broadcast, cable, or satellite television or radio station owned or controlled by any political party, political committee, or candidate is nevertheless exempt if the news story meets the requirements described in 11 CFR 100.132(a) and (b);

(3) Constitutes an expenditure or independent expenditure provided that the expenditure or independent expenditure is required to be reported under the Act or Commission regulations;

(4) Constitutes a candidate debate or forum conducted pursuant to 11 CFR 110.13, or that solely promotes such a debate or forum and is made by or on behalf of the person sponsoring the debate or forum;

(5) Is not described in 2 U.S.C. 431(20)(A)(iii) and is paid for by a candidate for State or local office in connection with an election to State or local office; or

(6) Is paid for by any organization operating under section 501(c)(3) of the Internal Revenue Code of 1986. Nothing in this section shall be deemed to supersede the requirements of the Internal Revenue Code for securing or maintaining 501(c)(3) status.

[67 FR 65210, 65217, Oct. 23, 2002]

§§100.30–100.32 [Reserved]

§100.33 Personal funds.

Personal funds of a candidate means the sum of all of the following:

(a) *Assets.* Amounts derived from any asset that, under applicable State law, at the time the individual became a candidate, the candidate had legal right of access to or control over, and with respect to which the candidate had—

(1) Legal and rightful title; or

(2) An equitable interest;

(b) *Income.* Income received during the current election cycle, as defined in 11 CFR 400.2, of the candidate, including:

(1) A salary and other earned income that the candidate earns from bona fide employment;

(2) Income from the candidate's stocks or other investments including interest, dividends, or proceeds from the sale or liquidation of such stocks or investments;

(3) Bequests to the candidate;

(4) Income from trusts established before the beginning of the election cycle as defined in 11 CFR 400.2;

(5) Income from trusts established by bequest after the beginning of the election cycle of which the candidate is the beneficiary;

(6) Gifts of a personal nature that had been customarily received by the candidate prior to the beginning of the election cycle, as defined in 11 CFR 400.2; and

(7) Proceeds from lotteries and similar legal games of chance; and

(c) *Jointly owned assets.* Amounts derived from a portion of assets that are owned jointly by the candidate and the candidate's spouse as follows:

(1) The portion of assets that is equal to the candidate's share of the asset under the instrument of conveyance or ownership; provided, however,

(2) If no specific share is indicated by an instrument of conveyance or ownership, the value of one-half of the property.

[68 FR 3995, Jan. 27, 2003]

EFFECTIVE DATE NOTE: At 68 FR 3995, Jan. 27, 2003, § 100.33 was added, effective Feb. 26, 2003.

when added to other contributions from that individual to that candidate or committee, shall not exceed the contribution limitations set forth at 11 CFR part 110. A loan, to the extent it is repaid, is no longer a contribution.

(3) Except as provided in paragraph (b)(4) of this section, a loan is a contribution by each endorser or guarantor. Each endorser or guarantor shall be deemed to have contributed that portion of the total amount of the

§ 100.56

§ 100.56 Office building or facility for national party committees.

A gift, subscription, loan, advance, or deposit of money or anything of value to a national party committee for the purchase or construction of an office building or facility is a contribution.

§ 100.84

§ 100.84 Office building for State, local, or district party committees or organizations.

A donation made to a non-Federal account of a State, local, or district party committee or organization in accordance with 11 CFR 300.35 for the purchase or construction of an office building is not a contribution. A donation includes a gift, subscription, loan, advance, or deposit of money or anything of value.

§ 100.144 **Office building for State, local, or district party committees or organizations.**

A payment, distribution, loan, advance, or deposit of money or anything of value, made by, or on behalf of, a State, local, or district party committee or organization for the purchase or construction of an office building in accordance with 11 CFR 300.35 is not an expenditure.

§ 104.20 **Reporting electioneering communications (2 U.S.C. 434(f)).**

(a) *Definitions.*

(1) *Disclosure date* means:

(i) The first date on which an electioneering communication is publicly distributed provided that the person making the electioneering communication has made one or more disbursements, or has executed one or more contracts to make disbursements, for the direct costs of producing or airing one or more electioneering communications aggregating in excess of $10,000; or

(ii) Any other date during the same calendar year on which an electioneering communication is publicly distributed provided that the person making the electioneering communication has made one or more disbursements, or has executed one or more contracts to make disbursements, for the direct costs of producing or airing one or more electioneering communications aggregating in excess of $10,000 since the most recent disclosure date during such calendar year.

(2) *Direct costs of producing or airing electioneering communications* means the following:

(i) Costs charged by a vendor, such as studio rental time, staff salaries, costs of video or audio recording media, and talent; or

(ii) The cost of airtime on broadcast, cable or satellite radio and television stations, studio time, material costs, and the charges for a broker to purchase the airtime.

(3) *Persons sharing or exercising direction or control* means officers, directors, executive directors or their equivalent, partners, and in the case of unincorporated organizations, owners, of the entity or person making the disbursement for the electioneering communication.

(4) *Identification* has the same meaning as in 11 CFR 100.12.

(5) *Publicly distributed* has the same meaning as in 11 CFR 100.29(b)(3).

(b) *Who must report and when.* Every person who has made an electioneering communication, as defined in 11 CFR 100.29, aggregating in excess of $10,000 during any calendar year shall file a statement with the Commission by 11:59 p.m. Eastern Standard/Daylight Time on the day following the disclosure date. The statement shall be filed under penalty of perjury, shall contain the information set forth in paragraph (c) of this section, and shall be filed on FEC Form 9. Political committees that make communications that are described in 11 CFR 100.29(a) must report such communications as expenditures or independent expenditures under 11 CFR 104.3 and 104.4, and not under this section.

(c) *Contents of statement.* Statements of electioneering communications filed under paragraph (b) of this section shall disclose the following information:

(1) The identification of the person who made the disbursement, or who executed a contract to make a disbursement, and, if the person is not an individual, the person's principal place of business;

(2) The identification of any person sharing or exercising direction or control over the activities of the person who made the disbursement or who executed a contract to make a disbursement;

(3) The identification of the custodian of the books and accounts from which the disbursements were made;

(4) The amount of each disbursement, or amount obligated, of more than $200 during the period covered by the statement, the date the disbursement was made, or the contract was executed, and the identification of the person to whom that disbursement was made;

(5) All clearly identified candidates referred to in the electioneering communication and the elections in which they are candidates;

(6) The disclosure date, as defined in paragraph (a) of this section;

(7) If the disbursements were paid exclusively from a segregated bank account consisting of funds provided solely by individuals who are United States citizens, United States nationals, or who are lawfully admitted for permanent residence under 8 U.S.C. 1101(a)(20), the name and address of each donor who donated an amount aggregating $1,000 or more to the segregated bank account, aggregating since the first day of the preceding calendar year; and

(8) If the disbursements were not paid exclusively from a segregated bank account described in paragraph (c)(7) of this section, the name and address of each donor who donated an amount aggregating $1,000 or more to the person making the disbursement, aggregating since the first day of the preceding calendar year.

(d) *Recordkeeping.* All persons who make electioneering communications or who accept donations for the purpose of making electioneering communications must maintain records in accordance with 11 CFR 104.14.

(e) *State waivers.* Statements of electioneering communications that must be filed with the Commission must also be filed with the Secretary of State of the appropriate State if the State has not obtained a waiver under 11 CFR 108.1(b).

[68 FR 419, Jan. 3, 2003; 68 FR 5075, Jan. 31, 2003]

§ 106.7 **Allocation of expenses between Federal and non-Federal accounts by party committees, other than for Federal election activities.**

(a) National party committees are prohibited from raising or spending non-Federal funds. Therefore, these committees shall not allocate expenditures and disbursements between Federal and non-Federal accounts. All disbursements by a national party committee must be made from a Federal account.

(b) State, district, and local party committees that make expenditures and disbursements in connection with both Federal and non-Federal elections for activities that are not Federal election activities pursuant to 11 CFR 100.24 may use only funds subject to the prohibitions and limitations of the Act, or they may allocate such expenditures and disbursements between their Federal and their non-Federal accounts. State, district, and local party committees that are political committees that have established separate Federal and non-Federal accounts under 11 CFR 102.5(a)(1)(i) shall allocate expenses between those accounts according to paragraphs (c) and (d) of this section. Party organizations that are not political committees but have established separate Federal and non-Federal accounts, or that make Federal and non-Federal disbursements from a single

Federal Election Commission §106.7

account, shall also allocate their Federal and non-Federal expenses according to paragraphs (c) and (d) of this section. In lieu of establishing separate accounts, party organizations that are not political committees may choose to use a reasonable accounting method approved by the Commission (including any method embedded in software provided or approved by the Commission) pursuant to 11 CFR 102.5 and 300.30.

(c) *Costs allocable by State, district, and local party committees between Federal and non-Federal accounts.* (1) *Salaries and wages.* State, district, and local party committees must pay salaries and wages from funds that comply with State law for employees who spend 25% or less of their time in any given month on Federal election activity or activity in connection with a Federal election. *See* 11 CFR 300.33(c)(2).

(2) *Administrative costs.* State, district, and local party committees may either pay administrative costs, including rent, utilities, office equipment, office supplies, postage for other than mass mailings, and routine building maintenance, upkeep and repair, from their Federal account, or allocate such expenses between their Federal and non-Federal accounts, except that any such expenses directly attributable to a clearly identified Federal candidate must be paid only from the Federal account.

(3) *Exempt party activities that are not Federal election activities.* State, district, and local party committees may pay expenses for party activities that are exempt from the definitions of contribution and expenditure under 11 CFR 100.80, 100.87 or 100.89, and 100.140, 100.147 or 100.149, that are conducted in conjunction with non-Federal activity, and that are not Federal election activities pursuant to 11 CFR 100.24, from their Federal accounts, or may allocate these expenses between their Federal and non-Federal accounts.

(4) *Certain fundraising costs.* State, district, and local party committees may allocate the direct costs of certain fundraising programs or events between their Federal and non-Federal accounts provided that none of the proceeds from the activities or events will ever be used for Federal election activities. The proceeds of fundraising al-

located pursuant to this paragraph must be segregated in bank accounts that are never used for Federal election activity. Direct costs of fundraising include disbursements for the planning and administration of specific fundraising events or programs.

(5) *Voter-drive activities that do not qualify as Federal election activities and that are not party exempt activities.* Other than for salaries and wages as described in paragraph (c)(1) of this section, expenses for voter identification, voter registration, and get-out-the-vote drives, and any other activities that urge the general public to register or vote, or that promote or oppose a political party, without promoting or opposing a candidate or non-Federal candidate, that do not qualify as Federal election activities and that are not exempt party activities, must be paid with Federal funds or may be allocated between the committee's Federal and non-Federal accounts.

(d) *Allocation percentages, ratios, and record-keeping.* (1) *Salaries and wages.* Committees must keep a monthly log of the percentage of time each employee spends in connection with a Federal election. Allocations of salaries and wages shall be undertaken as follows:

(i) Salaries and wages paid for employees who spend 25% or less of their compensated time in a given month on Federal election activities or on activities in connection with a Federal election shall be paid from funds that comply with State law.

(ii) Salaries and wages paid for employees who spend more than 25% of their compensated time in a given month on Federal election activities or on activities in connection with a Federal election must be paid only from a Federal account. *See* 11 CFR 300.33(c)(2), and paragraph (e)(2) of this section.

(2) *Administrative costs.* State, district, and local party committees that choose to allocate administrative expenses may do so subject to the following requirements:

(i) *Presidential election years.* In any even year in which a Presidential candidate, but no Senate candidate appears on the ballot, and in the preceding year, State, district, and local party committees must allocate at least 28% of administrative expenses to their Federal accounts.

(ii) *Presidential and Senate election year.* In any even year in which a Presidential candidate and a Senate candidate appear on the ballot, and in the preceding year, State, district, and local party committees must allocate at least 36% of administrative expenses to their Federal accounts.

(iii) *Senate election year.* In any even year in which a Senate candidate, but no Presidential candidate, appears on the ballot, and in the preceding year, State, district, and local party committees must allocate at least 21% of administrative expenses to their Federal account.

(iv) *Non-Presidential and non-Senate year.* In any even year in which neither a Presidential nor a Senate candidate appears on the ballot, and in the preceding year, State, district, and local party committees must allocate at least 15% of administrative expenses to their Federal account.

(3) *Exempt party activities and voter drive activities that are not Federal election activities.* State, district, and local party committees that choose to allocate expenses for exempt activities conducted in conjunction with non-Federal activities and voter drive activities, that are not Federal election activities, must do so subject to the following requirements:

(i) *Presidential election years.* In any even year in which a Presidential candidate, but no Senate candidate appears on the ballot, and in the preceding year, State, district, and local party committees must allocate at least 28% of these expenses to their Federal accounts.

(ii) *Presidential and Senate election year.* In any even year in which a Presidential candidate and a Senate candidate appear on the ballot, and in the preceding year, State, district, and local party committees must allocate at least 36% of these expenses to their Federal accounts.

(iii) *Senate election year.* In any even year in which a Senate candidate, but no Presidential candidate, appears on the ballot, and in the preceding year, State, district, and local party committees must allocate at least 21% of

these expenses to their Federal account.

(iv) *Non-Presidential and non-Senate year.* In any even year in which neither a Presidential nor a Senate candidate appears on the ballot, and in the preceding year, State, district, and local party committee must allocate at least 15% of these expenses to their Federal account.

(4) *Fundraising for Federal and non-Federal accounts.* If Federal and non-Federal funds are collected by a State, district, or local party committee through a joint fundraising activity, that committee must allocate its direct fundraising costs using the funds received method and according to the following procedures:

(i) The committee must allocate its fundraising costs based on the ratio of funds received into its Federal account to its total receipts from each fundraising program or event. This ratio shall be estimated prior to each such program or event based upon the committee's reasonable prediction of its Federal and non-Federal revenue from that program or event, and must be noted in the committee's report for the period in which the first disbursement for such program or event occurred, submitted pursuant to 11 CFR 104.5. Any disbursements for fundraising costs made prior to the actual program or event must be allocated according to this estimated ratio.

(ii) No later than the date 60 days after each fundraising program or event from which both Federal and non-Federal funds are collected, the committee shall adjust the allocation ratio for that program or event to reflect the actual ratio of funds received. If the non-Federal account has paid more than its allocable share, the committee shall transfer funds from its Federal to its non-Federal account, as necessary, to reflect the adjusted allocation ratio. If the Federal account has paid more than its allocable share, the committee shall make any transfers of funds from its non-Federal to its Federal account to reflect the adjusted allocation ratio within the 60-day time period established by this paragraph. The committee shall make note of any such adjustments and transfers in its

Federal Election Commission

report for any period in which a transfer was made, and shall also report the date of the fundraising program or event that serves as the basis for the transfer. In the case of a telemarketing or direct mail campaign, the date for purposes of this paragraph is the last day of the telemarketing campaign, or the day on which the final direct mail solicitations are mailed.

(e) *Costs not allocable by State, district, and local party committees between Federal and non-Federal accounts.* The following costs incurred by State, district, and local party committees shall be paid only with Federal funds:

(1) Disbursements for State, district, and local party committees for activities that refer only to one or more candidates for Federal office must not be allocated. All such disbursements must be made from a Federal account.

(2) *Salaries and wages.* Salaries and wages for employees who spend more than 25% of their compensated time in a given month on activities in connection with a Federal election must not be allocated. All such disbursements must be made from a Federal account. *See* 11 CFR 300.33(c)(2).

(3) *Federal election activities.* Activities that are Federal election activities pursuant to 11 CFR 100.24 must not be allocated between Federal and non-Federal accounts. Only Federal funds, or a mixture of Federal funds and Levin funds, as provided in 11 CFR 300.33, may be used.

(4) *Fundraising Costs.* Expenses incurred by State, district, and local party committees directly related to programs or events undertaken to raise funds to be used, in whole or in part, for activities in connection with Federal and non-Federal elections that are Federal election activities pursuant to 11 CFR 100.24 must not be allocated between Federal and non-Federal accounts. Except as provided in 11 CFR 300.32(a)(4), all such disbursements must be made from a Federal account.

(f) *Transfers between accounts to cover allocable expenses.* State, district, and local party committees may transfer funds from their non-Federal to their Federal accounts or to an allocation account solely to meet allocable expenses under this section and only pursuant to the following requirements:

(1) *Payments from Federal accounts or from allocation accounts.* (i) State, district, and local party committees must pay the entire amount of an allocable expense from their Federal accounts and transfer funds from their non-Federal account to the Federal account solely to cover the non-Federal share of that allocable expense; or

(ii) State, district, or local party committees may establish a separate allocation account into which funds from its Federal and non-Federal accounts may be deposited solely for the purpose of paying the allocable expenses of joint Federal and non-Federal activities.

(2) *Timing.* (i) If a Federal or allocation account is used to make allocable expenditures and disbursements, State, district, and local party committees must transfer funds from their non-Federal to their Federal or allocation account to meet allocable expenses no more than 10 days before and no more than 60 days after the payments for which they are designated are made from a Federal or allocation account, except that transfers may be made more than 10 days before a payment is made from the Federal or allocation account if advance payment is required by the vendor(s) and if such payment is based on a reasonable estimate of the activity's final costs as determined by the committee and the vendor(s) involved.

(ii) Any portion of a transfer from a committee's non-Federal account to its Federal or allocation account that does not meet the requirement of paragraph (f)(2)(i) of this section shall be presumed to be a loan or contribution from the non-Federal account to the Federal or allocation account, in violation of the Act.

[67 FR 49118, July 29, 2002, as amended at 67 FR 78681, Dec. 26, 2002]

PART 109—COORDINATED AND INDEPENDENT EXPENDITURES (2 U.S.C. 431(17), 441a(a) and (d), AND PUB. L. 107–155 SEC. 214(c))

Sec.

Federal Election Commission

109.35 What are the restrictions on a political party making both independent expenditures and coordinated party expenditures in connection with the general election of a candidate?

109.36 Are there additional circumstances under which a political party committee is prohibited from making independent expenditures?

109.37 What is a "party coordinated communication"?

AUTHORITY: 2 U.S.C. 431(17), 434(c), 438(a)(8), 441a, 441d; Sec. 214(c) of Pub. L. 107-155, 116 Stat. 81.

SOURCE: 68 FR 451, Jan. 3, 2003, unless otherwise noted.

Subpart A—Scope and Definitions

§ 109.1 When will this part apply?

This part applies to expenditures that are made independently from a candidate, an authorized committee, a political party committee, or their agents, and to those payments that are made in coordination with a candidate, an authorized committee, a political party committee, or their agents. The rules in this part explain how these types of payments must be reported and how they must be treated by candidates, authorized committees, and political party committees. In addition, subpart D of part 109 describes procedures and limits that apply only to payments, transfers, and assignments made by political party committees.

§ 109.2 [Reserved]

§ 109.3 Definitions.

For the purposes of 11 CFR part 109 only, agent means any person who has actual authority, either express or implied, to engage in any of the following activities on behalf of the specified persons:

(a) In the case of a national, State, district, or local committee of a political party, any one or more of the activities listed in paragraphs (a)(1) through (a)(5) of this section:

(1) To request or suggest that a communication be created, produced, or distributed.

(2) To make or authorize a communication that meets one or more of the content standards set forth in 11 CFR 109.21(c).

(3) To create, produce, or distribute any communication at the request or suggestion of a candidate.

(4) To be materially involved in decisions regarding:

(i) The content of the communication;

(ii) The intended audience for the communication;

(iii) The means or mode of the communication;

(iv) The specific media outlet used for the communication;

(v) The timing or frequency of the communication; or,

(vi) The size or prominence of a printed communication, or duration of a communication by means of broadcast, cable, or satellite.

(5) To make or direct a communication that is created, produced, or distributed with the use of material or information derived from a substantial discussion about the communication with a candidate.

(b) In the case of an individual who is a Federal candidate or an individual holding Federal office, any one or more of the activities listed in paragraphs (b)(1) through (b)(6) of this section:

(1) To request or suggest that a communication be created, produced, or distributed.

(2) To make or authorize a communication that meets one or more of the content standards set forth in 11 CFR 109.21(c).

(3) To request or suggest that any other person create, produce, or distribute any communication.

(4) To be materially involved in decisions regarding:

(i) The content of the communication;

(ii) The intended audience for the communication;

(iii) The means or mode of the communication;

(iv) The specific media outlet used for the communication;

(v) The timing or frequency of the communication;

(vi) The size or prominence of a printed communication, or duration of a communication by means of broadcast, cable, or satellite.

(5) To provide material or information to assist another person in the

§ 109.10

creation, production, or distribution of any communication.

(6) To make or direct a communication that is created, produced, or distributed with the use of material or information derived from a substantial discussion about the communication with a different candidate.

Subpart B—Independent Expenditures

§ 109.10 How do political committees and other persons report independent expenditures?

(a) Political committees, including political party committees, must report independent expenditures under 11 CFR 104.4.

(b) Every person that is not a political committee and that makes independent expenditures aggregating in excess of $250 with respect to a given election in a calendar year shall file a verified statement or report on FEC Form 5 in accordance with 11 CFR 104.4(e) containing the information required by paragraph (e) of this section. Every person filing a report or statement under this section shall do so in accordance with the quarterly reporting schedule specified in 11 CFR 104.5(a)(1)(i) and (ii) and shall file a report or statement for any quarterly period during which any such independent expenditures that aggregate in excess of $250 are made and in any quarterly reporting period thereafter in which additional independent expenditures are made.

(c) Every person that is not a political committee and that makes independent expenditures aggregating $10,000 or more with respect to a given election any time during the calendar year up to and including the 20th day before an election, must report the independent expenditures on FEC Form 5, or by signed statement if the person is not otherwise required to file electronically under 11 CFR 104.18. (See 11 CFR 104.4(f) for aggregation.) The person making the independent expenditures aggregating $10,000 or more must ensure that the Commission receives the report or statement by 11:59 p.m. Eastern Standard/Daylight Time on the second day following the date on which a communication is publicly dis-

tributed or otherwise publicly disseminated. Each time subsequent independent expenditures relating to the same election aggregate an additional $10,000 or more, the person making the independent expenditures must ensure that the Commission receives a new 48-hour report of the subsequent independent expenditures. Each 48-hour report must contain the information required by paragraph (e)(1) of this section.

(d) Every person making, after the 20th day, but more than 24 hours before 12:01 a.m. of the day of an election, independent expenditures aggregating $1,000 or more with respect to a given election must report those independent expenditures and ensure that the Commission receives the report or signed statement by 11:59 p.m. Eastern Standard/Daylight Time on the day following the date on which a communication is publicly distributed or otherwise publicly disseminated. Each time subsequent independent expenditures relating to the same election aggregate $1,000 or more, the person making the independent expenditures must ensure that the Commission receives a new 24-hour report of the subsequent independent expenditures. (See 11 CFR 104.4(f) for aggregation.) Such report or statement shall contain the information required by paragraph (e) of this section.

(e) Content of verified reports and statements and verification of reports and statements.

(1) *Contents of verified reports and statement.* If a signed report or statement is submitted, the report or statement shall include:

(i) The reporting person's name, mailing address, occupation, and the name of his or her employer, if any;

(ii) The identification (name and mailing address) of the person to whom the expenditure was made;

(iii) The amount, date, and purpose of each expenditure;

(iv) A statement that indicates whether such expenditure was in support of, or in opposition to a candidate, together with the candidate's name and office sought;

(v) A verified certification under penalty of perjury as to whether such expenditure was made in cooperation, consultation, or concert with, or at the request or suggestion of a candidate, a candidate's authorized committee, or their agents, or a political party committee or its agents; and

(vi) The identification of each person who made a contribution in excess of $200 to the person filing such report, which contribution was made for the purpose of furthering the reported independent expenditure.

(2) *Verification of independent expenditure statements and reports.* Every person shall verify reports and statements of independent expenditures filed pursuant to the requirements of this section by one of the methods stated in paragraph (e)(2)(i) or (ii) of this section. Any report or statement verified under either of these methods shall be treated for all purposes (including penalties for perjury) in the same manner as a document verified by signature.

(i) For reports or statements filed on paper (*e.g.*, by hand-delivery, U.S. Mail, or facsimile machine), the person who made the independent expenditure shall certify, under penalty of perjury, the independence of the expenditure by handwritten signature immediately following the certification required by paragraph (e)(1)(v) of this section.

(ii) For reports or statements filed by electronic mail, the person who made the independent expenditure shall certify, under penalty of perjury, the independence of the expenditure by typing the treasurer's name immediately following the certification required by paragraph (e)(1)(v) of this section.

§ 109.11 When is a "non-authorization notice" (disclaimer) required?

Whenever any person makes an independent expenditure for the purpose of financing communications expressly advocating the election or defeat of a clearly identified candidate, such person shall comply with the requirements of 11 CFR 110.11.

Subpart C—Coordination

§ 109.20 What does "coordinated" mean?

(a) *Coordinated* means made in cooperation, consultation or concert with, or at the request or suggestion of, a candidate, a candidate's authorized

committee, or their agents, or a political party committee or its agents.

(b) Any expenditure that is coordinated within the meaning of paragraph (a) of this section, but that is not made for a coordinated communication under 11 CFR 109.21 or a party coordinated communication under 11 CFR 109.37, is either an in-kind contribution to, or a coordinated party expenditure with respect to, the candidate or political party committee with whom or with which it was coordinated and must be reported as an expenditure made by that candidate or political party committee, unless otherwise exempted under 11 CFR part 100, subparts C or E.

§ 109.21 What is a "coordinated communication"?

(a) *Definition.* A communication is coordinated with a candidate, an authorized committee, a political party committee, or an agent of any of the foregoing when the communication:

(1) Is paid for by a person other than that candidate, authorized committee, political party committee, or agent of any of the foregoing;

(2) Satisfies at least one of the content standards in paragraph (c) of this section; and

(3) Satisfies at least one of the conduct standards in paragraph (d) of this section.

(b) *Treatment as an in-kind contribution and expenditure; Reporting*—(1) *General rule.* A payment for a coordinated communication is made for the purpose of influencing a Federal election, and is an in-kind contribution under 11 CFR 100.52(d) to the candidate, authorized committee, or political party committee with whom or which it is coordinated, unless excepted under 11 CFR part 100, subpart C, and must be reported as an expenditure made by that candidate, authorized committee, or political party committee under 11 CFR 104.13, unless excepted under 11 CFR part 100, subpart E.

(2) *In-kind contributions resulting from conduct described in paragraphs (d)(4) or (d)(5) of this section.* Notwithstanding paragraph (b)(1) of this section, the candidate, authorized committee, or political party committee with whom or which a communication is coordinated does not receive or accept an in-

kind contribution, and is not required to report an expenditure, that results from conduct described in paragraphs (d)(4) or (d)(5) of this section, unless the candidate, authorized committee, or political party committee, or an agent of any of the foregoing, engages in conduct described in paragraphs (d)(1) through (d)(3) of this section.

(3) *Reporting of coordinated communications.* A political committee, other than a political party committee, that makes a coordinated communication must report the payment for the communication as a contribution made to the candidate or political party committee with whom or which it was coordinated and as an expenditure in accordance with 11 CFR 104.3(b)(1)(v). A candidate, authorized committee, or political party committee with whom or which a communication paid for by another person is coordinated must report the usual and normal value of the communication as an in-kind contribution in accordance with 11 CFR 104.13, meaning that it must report the amount of the payment as a receipt under 11 CFR 104.3(a) and as an expenditure under 11 CFR 104.3(b).

(c) *Content standards.* Each of the types of content described in paragraphs (c)(1) through (c)(4) satisfies the content standard of this section.

(1) A communication that is an electioneering communication under 11 CFR 100.29.

(2) A public communication that disseminates, distributes, or republishes, in whole or in part, campaign materials prepared by a candidate, the candidate's authorized committee, or an agent of any of the foregoing, unless the dissemination, distribution, or republication is excepted under 11 CFR 109.23(b). For a communication that satisfies this content standard, see paragraph (d)(6) of this section.

(3) A public communication that expressly advocates the election or defeat of a clearly identified candidate for Federal office.

(4) A communication that is a public communication, as defined in 11 CFR 100.26, and about which each of the following statements in paragraphs (c)(4)(i), (ii), and (iii) of this section are true.

(i) The communication refers to a political party or to a clearly identified candidate for Federal office;

(ii) The public communication is publicly distributed or otherwise publicly disseminated 120 days or fewer before a general, special, or runoff election, or 120 days or fewer before a primary or preference election, or a convention or caucus of a political party that has authority to nominate a candidate; and

(iii) The public communication is directed to voters in the jurisdiction of the clearly identified candidate or to voters in a jurisdiction in which one or more candidates of the political party appear on the ballot.

(d) *Conduct standards.* Any one of the following types of conduct satisfies the conduct standard of this section whether or not there is agreement or formal collaboration, as defined in paragraph (e) of this section:

(1) *Request or suggestion.*

(i) The communication is created, produced, or distributed at the request or suggestion of a candidate or an authorized committee, political party committee, or agent of any of the foregoing; or

(ii) The communication is created, produced, or distributed at the suggestion of a person paying for the communication and the candidate, authorized committee, political party committee, or agent of any of the foregoing, assents to the suggestion.

(2) *Material involvement.* A candidate, an authorized committee, a political party committee, or an agent of any of the foregoing, is materially involved in decisions regarding:

(i) The content of the communication;

(ii) The intended audience for the communication;

(iii) The means or mode of the communication;

(iv) The specific media outlet used for the communication;

(v) The timing or frequency of the communication; or

(vi) The size or prominence of a printed communication, or duration of a communication by means of broadcast, cable, or satellite.

(3) *Substantial discussion.* The communication is created, produced, or distributed after one or more substantial

Federal Election Commission §109.21

discussions about the communication between the person paying for the communication, or the employees or agents of the person paying for the communication, and the candidate who is clearly identified in the communication, or his or her authorized committee, or his or her opponent or the opponent's authorized committee, or a political party committee, or an agent of any of the foregoing. A discussion is substantial within the meaning of this paragraph if information about the candidate's or political party committee's campaign plans, projects, activities, or needs is conveyed to a person paying for the communication, and that information is material to the creation, production, or distribution of the communication.

(4) *Common vendor.* All of the following statements in paragraphs (d)(4)(i) through (d)(4)(iii) of this section are true:

(i) The person paying for the communication, or an agent of such person, contracts with or employs a commercial vendor, as defined in 11 CFR 116.1(c), to create, produce, or distribute the communication;

(ii) That commercial vendor, including any owner, officer, or employee of the commercial vendor, has provided any of the following services to the candidate who is clearly identified in the communication, or his or her authorized committee, or his or her opponent or the opponent's authorized committee, or a political party committee, or an agent of any of the foregoing, in the current election cycle:

(A) Development of media strategy, including the selection or purchasing of advertising slots;

(B) Selection of audiences;

(C) Polling;

(D) Fundraising;

(E) Developing the content of a public communication;

(F) Producing a public communication;

(G) Identifying voters or developing voter lists, mailing lists, or donor lists;

(H) Selecting personnel, contractors, or subcontractors; or

(I) Consulting or otherwise providing political or media advice; and

(iii) That commercial vendor uses or conveys to the person paying for the communication:

(A) Information about the clearly identified candidate's campaign plans, projects, activities, or needs, or his or her opponent's campaign plans, projects, activities, or needs, or a political party committee's campaign plans, projects, activities, or needs and that information is material to the creation, production, or distribution of the communication; or

(B) Information used previously by the commercial vendor in providing services to the candidate who is clearly identified in the communication, or his or her authorized committee, or his or her opponent or the opponent's authorized committee, or a political party committee, or an agent of any of the foregoing, and that information is material to the creation, production, or distribution of the communication.

(5) *Former employee or independent contractor.* Both of the following statements in paragraph (d)(5)(i) and (d)(5)(ii) of this section are true:

(i) The communication is paid for by a person, or by the employer of a person, who was an employee or independent contractor of the candidate who is clearly identified in the communication, or his or her authorized committee, or his or her opponent or the opponent's authorized committee, or a political party committee, or an agent of any of the foregoing, during the current election cycle; and

(ii) That former employee or independent contractor uses or conveys to the person paying for the communication:

(A) Information about the clearly identified candidate's campaign plans, projects, activities, or needs, or his or her opponent's campaign plans, projects, activities, or needs, or a political party committee's campaign plans, projects, activities, or needs, and that information is material to the creation, production, or distribution of the communication; or

(B) Information used by the former employee or independent contractor in providing services to the candidate who is clearly identified in the communication, or his or her authorized committee, or his or her opponent or the opponent's authorized committee, or a political party committee, or an agent of any of the foregoing, and that information is material to the creation, production, or distribution of the communication.

(6) *Dissemination, distribution, or republication of campaign material.* A communication that satisfies the content standard of paragraph (c)(2) of this section or 11 CFR 109.37(a)(2)(i) shall only satisfy the conduct standards of paragraphs (d)(1) through (d)(3) of this section on the basis of conduct by the candidate, the candidate's authorized committee, or the agents of any of the foregoing, that occurs after the original preparation of the campaign materials that are disseminated, distributed, or republished. The conduct standards of paragraphs (d)(4) and (d)(5) of this section may also apply to such communications as provided in those paragraphs.

(e) *Agreement or formal collaboration.* Agreement or formal collaboration between the person paying for the communication and the candidate clearly identified in the communication, his or her authorized committee, his or her opponent, or the opponent's authorized committee, a political party committee, or an agent of any of the foregoing, is not required for a communication to be a coordinated communication. *Agreement* means a mutual understanding or meeting of the minds on all or any part of the material aspects of the communication or its dissemination. *Formal collaboration* means planned, or systematically organized, work on the communication.

(f) *Safe harbor for responses to inquiries about legislative or policy issues.* A candidate's or a political party committee's response to an inquiry about that candidate's or political party committee's positions on legislative or policy issues, but not including a discussion of campaign plans, projects, activities, or needs, does not satisfy any of the conduct standards in paragraph (d) of this section.

§ 109.22 **Who is prohibited from making coordinated communications?**

Any person who is otherwise prohibited from making contributions or expenditures under any part of the Act or Commission regulations is prohibited from paying for a coordinated communication.

§ 109.23 **Dissemination, distribution, or republication of candidate campaign materials.**

(a) *General rule.* The financing of the dissemination, distribution, or republication, in whole or in part, of any broadcast or any written, graphic, or other form of campaign materials prepared by the candidate, the candidate's authorized committee, or an agent of either of the foregoing shall be considered a contribution for the purposes of contribution limitations and reporting responsibilities of the person making the expenditure. The candidate who prepared the campaign material does not receive or accept an in-kind contribution, and is not required to report an expenditure, unless the dissemination, distribution, or republication of campaign materials is a coordinated communication under 11 CFR 109.21 or a party coordinated communication under 11 CFR 109.37.

(b) *Exceptions.* The following uses of campaign materials do not constitute a contribution to the candidate who originally prepared the materials:

(1) The campaign material is disseminated, distributed, or republished by the candidate, the candidate's authorized committee, or an agent of either of the foregoing who prepared that material;

(2) The campaign material is incorporated into a communication that advocates the defeat of the candidate or party that prepared the material;

(3) The campaign material is disseminated, distributed, or republished in a news story, commentary, or editorial exempted under 11 CFR 100.73 or 11 CFR 100.132;

(4) The campaign material used consists of a brief quote of materials that demonstrate a candidate's position as part of a person's expression of its own views; or

(5) A national political party committee or a State or subordinate political party committee pays for such dissemination, distribution, or republication of campaign materials using coordinated party expenditure authority under 11 CFR 109.32.

Federal Election Commission

Subpart D—Special Provisions for Political Party Committees

§ 109.30 How are political party committees treated for purposes of coordinated and independent expenditures?

Political party committees may make independent expenditures subject to the provisions in this subpart. See 11 CFR 109.35 and 109.36. Political party committees may also make coordinated party expenditures in connection with the general election campaign of a candidate, subject to the limits and other provisions in this subpart. See 11 CFR 109.32 through 11 CFR 109.35.

§ 109.31 [Reserved]

§ 109.32 What are the coordinated party expenditure limits?

(a) *Coordinated party expenditures in Presidential elections.* (1) The national committee of a political party may make coordinated party expenditures in connection with the general election campaign of any candidate for President of the United States affiliated with the party.

(2) The coordinated party expenditures shall not exceed an amount equal to two cents multiplied by the voting age population of the United States. See 11 CFR 110.18. This limitation shall be increased in accordance with 11 CFR 110.17.

(3) Any coordinated party expenditure under paragraph (a) of this section shall be in addition to—

(i) Any expenditure by a national committee of a political party serving as the principal campaign committee of a candidate for President of the United States; and

(ii) Any contribution by the national committee to the candidate permissible under 11 CFR 110.1 or 110.2.

(4) Any coordinated party expenditures made by the national committee of a political party pursuant to paragraph (a) of this section, or made by any other party committee under authority assigned by a national committee of a political party under 11 CFR 109.33, on behalf of that party's Presidential candidate shall not count against the candidate's expenditure limitations under 11 CFR 110.8.

(b) *Coordinated party expenditures in other Federal elections.* (1) The national committee of a political party, and a State committee of a political party, including any subordinate committee of a State committee, may each make coordinated party expenditures in connection with the general election campaign of a candidate for Federal office in that State who is affiliated with the party.

(2) The coordinated party expenditures shall not exceed:

(i) In the case of a candidate for election to the office of Senator, or of Representative from a State which is entitled to only one Representative, the greater of—

(A) Two cents multiplied by the voting age population of the State (see 11 CFR 110.18); or

(B) Twenty thousand dollars.

(ii) In the case of a candidate for election to the office of Representative, Delegate, or Resident Commissioner in any other State, $10,000.

(3) The limitations in paragraph (b)(2) of this section shall be increased in accordance with 11 CFR 110.17.

(4) Any coordinated party expenditure under paragraph (b) of this section shall be in addition to any contribution by a political party committee to the candidate permissible under 11 CFR 110.1 or 110.2.

§ 109.33 May a political party committee assign its coordinated party expenditure authority to another political party committee?

(a) *Assignment.* Except as provided in 11 CFR 109.35(c), the national committee of a political party and a State committee of a political party, including any subordinate committee of a State committee, may assign its authority to make coordinated party expenditures authorized by 11 CFR 109.32 to another political party committee. Such an assignment must be made in writing, must state the amount of the authority assigned, and must be received by the assignee committee before any coordinated party expenditure is made pursuant to the assignment.

(b) *Compliance.* For purposes of the coordinated party expenditure limits, *State committee* includes a subordinate committee of a State committee and includes a district or local committee to which coordinated party expenditure authority has been assigned. State committees and subordinate State committees and such district or local committees combined shall not exceed the coordinated party expenditure limits set forth in 11 CFR 109.32. The State committee shall administer the limitation in one of the following ways:

(1) The State committee shall be responsible for insuring that the coordinated party expenditures of the entire party organization are within the coordinated party expenditure limits, including receiving reports from any subordinate committee of a State committee or district or local committee making coordinated party expenditures under 11 CFR 109.32, and filing consolidated reports showing all coordinated party expenditures in the State with the Commission; or

(2) Any other method, submitted in advance and approved by the Commission, that permits control over coordinated party expenditures.

(c) *Recordkeeping.* (1) A political party committee that assigns its authority to make coordinated party expenditures under this section must maintain the written assignment for at least three years in accordance with 11 CFR 104.14.

(2) A political party committee that is assigned authority to make coordinated party expenditures under this section must maintain the written assignment for at least three years in accordance with 11 CFR 104.14.

§ 109.34 When may a political party committee make coordinated party expenditures?

A political party committee authorized to make coordinated party expenditures may make such expenditures in connection with the general election campaign before or after its candidate has been nominated. All pre-nomination coordinated party expenditures shall be subject to the coordinated party expenditure limitations of this subpart, whether or not the candidate on whose behalf they are made receives the party's nomination.

§ 109.36 Are there additional circumstances under which a political party committee is prohibited from making independent expenditures?

The national committee of a political party must not make independent expenditures in connection with the general election campaign of a candidate for President of the United States if the national committee of that political party is designated as the authorized committee of its Presidential candidate pursuant to 11 CFR 9002.1(c).

§ 109.37 What is a "party coordinated communication"?

(a) *Definition.* A political party communication is coordinated with a candidate, a candidate's authorized committee, or agent of any of the foregoing, when the communication satisfies the conditions set forth in paragraphs (a)(1), (a)(2), and (a)(3) of this section.

(1) The communication is paid for by a political party committee or its agent.

(2) The communication satisfies at least one of the content standards described in paragraphs (a)(2)(i) through (a)(2)(iii) of this section.

(i) A public communication that disseminates, distributes, or republishes, in whole or in part, campaign materials prepared by a candidate, the candidate's authorized committee, or an agent of any of the foregoing, unless the dissemination, distribution, or republication is excepted under 11 CFR 109.23(b). For a communication that satisfies this content standard, see 11 CFR 109.21(d)(6).

(ii) A public communication that expressly advocates the election or defeat of a clearly identified candidate for Federal office.

(iii) A communication that is a public communication, as defined in 11 CFR 100.26, and about which each of the following statements in paragraphs (a)(2)(iii)(A) through (a)(2)(iii)(C) of this section are true.

(A) The communication refers to a clearly identified candidate for Federal office;

(B) The public communication is publicly distributed or otherwise publicly disseminated 120 days or fewer before a general, special, or runoff election, or 120 days or fewer before a primary or preference election, or a convention or caucus of a political party that has authority to nominate a candidate; and

(C) The public communication is directed to voters in the jurisdiction of the clearly identified candidate.

(3) The communication satisfies at least one of the conduct standards in 11 CFR 109.21(d)(1) through (d)(6), subject to the provisions of 11 CFR 109.21(e). A candidate's response to an inquiry about that candidate's positions on legislative or policy issues, but not including a discussion of campaign plans, projects, activities, or needs, does not satisfy any of the conduct standards in 11 CFR 109.21(d)(1) through (d)(6). Notwithstanding paragraph (b)(1) of this section, the candidate with whom a party coordinated communication is coordinated does not receive or accept an in-kind contribution, and is not required to report an expenditure, that results from conduct described in 11 CFR 109.21(d)(4) or (d)(5), unless the candidate, authorized committee, or an agent of any of the foregoing, engages in conduct described in 11 CFR 109.21(d)(1) through (d)(3).

(b) *Treatment of a party coordinated communication.* A payment by a political party committee for a communication that is coordinated with a candidate, and that is not otherwise exempted under 11 CFR part 100, subpart C or E, must be treated by the political party committee making the payment as either:

(1) An in-kind contribution for the purpose of influencing a Federal election under 11 CFR 100.52(d) to the candidate with whom it was coordinated, which must be reported under 11 CFR part 104; or

(2) A coordinated party expenditure pursuant to coordinated party expenditure authority under 11 CFR 109.32 in connection with the general election campaign of the candidate with whom it was coordinated, which must be reported under 11 CFR part 104.

Federal Election Commission

§ **110.5 Aggregate bi-annual contribution limitation for individuals (2 U.S.C. 441a(a)(3)).**

(a) *Scope.* This section applies to all contributions made by any individual, except individuals prohibited from making contributions under 11 CFR 110.19 and 110.20 and 11 CFR part 115.

(b) *Bi-annual limitations.* (1) In the two-year period beginning on January 1 of an odd-numbered year and ending on December 31 of the next even-numbered year, no individual shall make contributions aggregating more than $95,000, including no more than:

(i) $37,500 in the case of contributions to candidates and the authorized committees of candidates; and

(ii) $57,500 in the case of any other contributions, of which not more than $37,500 may be attributable to contributions to political committees that are not political committees of any national political parties.

(2) Contributions to candidates made under the increased contribution limitations under 11 CFR part 400, during periods in which such candidates may accept contributions, are not subject to the contribution limitations of paragraph (b)(1) of this section.

(3) The contribution limitations in paragraph (b)(1) of this section shall be increased by the percent difference in the price index in accordance with 11 CFR 110.17. The increased contribution limitations shall be in effect for the two calendar years starting on January 1 of the year in which the contribution limitations are increased.

(4) In every odd-numbered year, the Commission will publish in the FEDERAL REGISTER the amount of the contribution limitations in effect and place such information on the Commission's Web site.

§ **110.11 Communications; advertising; disclaimers (2 U.S.C 441d).**

(a) *Scope.* This section applies only to public communications, defined for this section to include the communications at 11 CFR 100.26 plus unsolicited electronic mail of more than 500 substantially similar communications and Internet websites of political committees available to the general public, and electioneering communications as defined in 11 CFR 100.29. The following types of such communications must include disclaimers, as specified in this section:

(1) All public communications for which a political committee makes a disbursement.

(2) All public communications by any person that expressly advocate the election or defeat of a clearly identified candidate.

(3) All public communications by any person that solicit any contribution.

(4) All electioneering communications by any person.

(b) *General content requirements.* A disclaimer required by paragraph (a) of this section must contain the following information:

(1) If the communication, including any solicitation, is paid for and authorized by a candidate, an authorized committee of a candidate, or an agent of either of the foregoing, the disclaimer must clearly state that the communication has been paid for by the authorized political committee;

(2) If the communication, including any solicitation, is authorized by a candidate, an authorized committee of a candidate, or an agent of either of the foregoing, but is paid for by any other person, the disclaimer must clearly state that the communication is paid for by such other person and is authorized by such candidate, authorized committee, or agent; or

(3) If the communication, including any solicitation, is not authorized by a candidate, authorized committee of a candidate, or an agent of either of the foregoing, the disclaimer must clearly state the full name and permanent street address, telephone number, or World Wide Web address of the person

who paid for the communication, and that the communication is not authorized by any candidate or candidate's committee.

(c) *Disclaimer specifications*—(1) *Specifications for all disclaimers.* A disclaimer required by paragraph (a) of this section must be presented in a clear and conspicuous manner, to give the reader, observer, or listener adequate notice of the identity of the person or political committee that paid for and, where required, that authorized the communication. A disclaimer is not clear and conspicuous if it is difficult to read or hear, or if the placement is easily overlooked.

(2) *Specific requirements for printed communications.* In addition to the general requirement of paragraphs (b) and (c)(1) of this section, a disclaimer required by paragraph (a) of this section that appears on any printed public communication must comply with all of the following:

(i) The disclaimer must be of sufficient type size to be clearly readable by the recipient of the communication. A disclaimer in twelve (12)-point type size satisfies the size requirement of this paragraph (c)(2)(i) when it is used for signs, posters, flyers, newspapers, magazines, or other printed material that measure no more than twenty-four (24) inches by thirty-six (36) inches.

(ii) The disclaimer must be contained in a printed box set apart from the other contents of the communication.

(iii) The disclaimer must be printed with a reasonable degree of color contrast between the background and the printed statement. A disclaimer satisfies the color contrast requirement of this paragraph (c)(2)(iii) if it is printed in black text on a white background or if the degree of color contrast between the background and the text of the disclaimer is no less than the color contrast between the background and the largest text used in the communication.

(iv) The disclaimer need not appear on the front or cover page of the communication as long as it appears within the communication, except on communications, such as billboards, that contain only a front face.

(v) A communication that would require a disclaimer if distributed separately, that is included in a package of materials, must contain the required disclaimer.

(3) *Specific requirements for radio and television communications authorized by candidates.* In addition to the general requirements of paragraphs (b) and (c)(1) of this section, a communication that is authorized or paid for by a candidate or the authorized committee of a candidate (*see* paragraph (b)(1) or (b)(2) of this section) that is transmitted through radio or television, or through any broadcast, cable, or satellite transmission, must comply with the following:

(i) A communication transmitted through radio must include an audio statement by the candidate that identifies the candidate and states that he or she has approved the communication; or

(ii) A communication transmitted through television or through any broadcast, cable, or satellite transmission, must include a statement that identifies the candidate and states that he or she has approved the communication. The candidate shall convey the statement either:

(A) Through an unobscured, full-screen view of himself or herself making the statement, or

(B) Through a voice-over by himself or herself, accompanied by a clearly identifiable photographic or similar image of the candidate. A photographic or similar image of the candidate shall be considered clearly identified if it is at least eighty (80) percent of the vertical screen height.

(iii) A communication transmitted through television or through any broadcast, cable, or satellite transmission, must also include a similar statement that must appear in clearly readable writing at the end of the television communication. To be clearly readable, this statement must meet all of the following three requirements:

(A) The statement must appear in letters equal to or greater than four (4) percent of the vertical picture height;

(B) The statement must be visible for a period of at least four (4) seconds; and

(C) The statement must appear with a reasonable degree of color contrast between the background and the text of the statement. A statement satisfies the color contrast requirement of this paragraph (c)(3)(iii)(C) if it is printed in black text on a white background or if the degree of color contrast between the background and the text of the statement is no less than the color contrast between the background and the largest type size used in the communication.

(iv) The following are examples of acceptable statements that satisfy the spoken statement requirements of paragraph (c)(3) of this section with respect to a radio, television, or other broadcast, cable, or satellite communication, but they are not the only allowable statements:

(A) "I am [insert name of candidate], a candidate for [insert Federal office sought], and I approved this advertisement."

(B) "My name is [insert name of candidate]. I am running for [insert Federal office sought], and I approved this message."

(4) *Specific requirements for radio and television communications paid for by other persons and not authorized by a candidate.* In addition to the general requirements of paragraphs (b) and (c)(1) of this section, a communication not authorized by a candidate or a candidate's authorized committee that is transmitted through radio or television or through any broadcast, cable, or satellite transmission, must comply with the following:

(i) A communication transmitted through radio or television or through any broadcast, cable, or satellite transmission, must include the following audio statement, "XXX is responsible for the content of this advertising," spoken clearly, with the blank to be filled in with the name of the political committee or other person paying for the communication, and the name of the connected organization, if any, of the payor unless the name of the connected organization is already provided in the "XXX is responsible" statement; and

(ii) A communication transmitted through television, or through any broadcast, cable, or satellite transmission, must include the audio statement required by paragraph (c)(4)(i) of

this section. That statement must be conveyed by an unobscured full-screen view of a representative of the political committee or other person making the statement, or by a representative of such political committee or other person in voice-over.

(iii) A communication transmitted through television or through any broadcast, cable, or satellite transmission, must also include a similar statement that must appear in clearly readable writing at the end of the communication. To be clearly readable, the statement must meet all of the following three requirements:

(A) The statement must appear in letters equal to or greater than four (4) percent of the vertical picture height;

(B) The statement must be visible for a period of at least four (4) seconds; and

(C) The statement must appear with a reasonable degree of color contrast between the background and the disclaimer statement. A disclaimer satisfies the color contrast requirement of this paragraph (c)(4)(iii)(C) if it is printed in black text on a white background or if the degree of color contrast between the background and the text of the disclaimer is no less than the color contrast between the background and the largest type size used in the communication.

(d) *Coordinated party expenditures and independent expenditures by political party committees.*

(1)(i) For a communication paid for by a political party committee pursuant to 2 U.S.C. 441a(d), the disclaimer required by paragraph (a) of this section must identify the political party committee that makes the expenditure as the person who paid for the communication, regardless of whether the political party committee was acting in its own capacity or as the designated agent of another political party committee.

(ii) A communication made by a political party committee pursuant to 2 U.S.C. 441a(d) and distributed prior to the date the party's candidate is nominated shall satisfy the requirements of this section if it clearly states who paid for the communication.

(2) For purposes of this section, a communication paid for by a political

party committee, other than a communication covered by paragraph (d)(1)(ii) of this section, that is being treated as a coordinated expenditure under 2 U.S.C. 441a(d) and that was made with the approval of a candidate, a candidate's authorized committee, or the agent of either shall identify the political party that paid for the communication and shall state that the communication is authorized by the candidate or candidate's authorized committee.

(3) For a communication paid for by a political party committee that constitutes an independent expenditure under 11 CFR 100.16, the disclaimer required by this section must identify the political party committee that paid for the communication, and must state that the communication is not authorized by any candidate or candidate's authorized committee.

(e) *Exempt activities.* A public communication authorized by a candidate, authorized committee, or political party committee, that qualifies as an exempt activity under 11 CFR 100.140, 100.147, 100.148, or 100.149, must comply with the disclaimer requirements of paragraphs (a), (b), (c)(1), and (c)(2) of this section, unless excepted under paragraph (f)(1) of this section, but the disclaimer does not need to state whether the communication is authorized by a candidate, or any authorized committee or agent of any candidate.

(f) *Exceptions.* (1) The requirements of paragraphs (a) through (e) of this section do not apply to the following:

(i) Bumper stickers, pins, buttons, pens, and similar small items upon which the disclaimer cannot be conveniently printed;

(ii) Skywriting, water towers, wearing apparel, or other means of displaying an advertisement of such a nature that the inclusion of a disclaimer would be impracticable; or

(iii) Checks, receipts, and similar items of minimal value that are used for purely administrative purposes and do not contain a political message.

(2) For purposes of this section, whenever a separate segregated fund or its connected organization solicits contributions to the fund from those persons it may solicit under the applicable provisions of 11 CFR part 114, or makes

a communication to those persons, such communication shall not be considered a type of public communication and need not contain the disclaimer required by paragraphs (a) through (c) of this section.

(g) *Comparable rate for campaign purposes.* (1) No person who sells space in a newspaper or magazine to a candidate, an authorized committee of a candidate, or an agent of the candidate, for use in connection with the candidate's campaign for nomination or for election, shall charge an amount for the space which exceeds the comparable rate for the space for non-campaign purposes.

(2) For purposed of this section, comparable rate means the rate charged to a national or general rate advertiser, and shall include discount privileges usually and normally available to a national or general rate advertiser.

[67 FR 76975, Dec. 13, 2002]

Federal Election Commission

(2) Willfully and knowingly participate in or conspire to participate in any plan, scheme, or design to violate paragraph (a)(1) of this section.

(b) *Fraudulent solicitation of funds.* No person shall—

(1) Fraudulently misrepresent the person as speaking, writing, or otherwise acting for or on behalf of any candidate or political party or employee or agent thereof for the purpose of soliciting contributions or donations; or

(2) Willfully and knowingly participate in or conspire to participate in any plan, scheme, or design to violate paragraph (b)(1) of this section.

[67 FR 76977, Dec. 13, 2002]

§ 114.10 Nonprofit corporations exempt from the prohibitions on making independent expenditures and electioneering communications.

(a) *Scope.* This section describes those nonprofit corporations that qualify for an exemption in 11 CFR 114.2. It sets out the procedures for demonstrating qualified nonprofit corporation status, for reporting independent expenditures and electioneering communications, and for disclosing the potential use of donations for political purposes.

(b) *Definitions.* For the purposes of this section—

(1) *The promotion of political ideas* includes issue advocacy, election influencing activity, and research, training or educational activity that is expressly tied to the organization's political goals.

(2) A corporation's *express purpose* includes:

(i) The corporation's purpose as stated in its charter, articles of incorporation, or bylaws, except that a statement such as "any lawful purpose," "any lawful activity," or other comparable statement will not preclude a

§ 110.16 Prohibitions on fraudulent misrepresentations.

(a) *In general.* No person who is a candidate for Federal office or an employee or agent of such a candidate shall—

(1) Fraudulently misrepresent the person or any committee or organization under the person's control as speaking or writing or otherwise acting for or on behalf of any other candidate or political party or employee or agent thereof in a matter which is damaging to such other candidate or political party or employee or agent thereof; or

Federal Election Commission

finding under paragraph (c) of this section that the corporation's only express purpose is the promotion of political ideas;

(ii) The corporation's purpose as publicly stated by the corporation or its agents; and

(iii) Purposes evidenced by activities in which the corporation actually engages.

(3)(i) The term *business activities* includes but is not limited to:

(A) Any provision of goods or services that results in income to the corporation; and

(B) Advertising or promotional activity which results in income to the corporation, other than in the form of membership dues or donations.

(ii) The term *business activities* does not include fundraising activities that are expressly described as requests for donations that may be used for political purposes, such as supporting or opposing candidates.

(4) The term *shareholder* has the same meaning as the term *stockholder*, as defined in 11 CFR 114.1(h).

(c) *Qualified nonprofit corporations.* For the purposes of this section, a qualified nonprofit corporation is a corporation that has all the characteristics set forth in paragraphs (c)(1) through (c)(5) of this section:

(1) Its only express purpose is the promotion of political ideas, as defined in paragraph (b)(1) of this section;

(2) It cannot engage in business activities;

(3) It has:

(i) No shareholders or other persons, other than employees and creditors with no ownership interest, affiliated in any way that could allow them to make a claim on the organization's assets or earnings; and

(ii) No persons who are offered or who receive any benefit that is a disincentive for them to disassociate themselves with the corporation on the basis of the corporation's position on a political issue. Such benefits include but are not limited to:

(A) Credit cards, insurance policies or savings plans; and

(B) Training, education, or business information, other than that which is necessary to enable recipients to engage in the promotion of the group's political ideas.

(4) It:

(i) Was not established by a business corporation or labor organization;

(ii) Does not directly or indirectly accept donations of anything of value from business corporations, or labor organizations; and

(iii) If unable, for good cause, to demonstrate through accounting records that paragraph (c)(4)(ii) of this section is satisfied, has a written policy against accepting donations from business corporations or labor organizations; and

(5) It is described in 26 U.S.C. 501(c)(4).

(d) *Permitted corporate independent expenditures and electioneering communications.* (1) A qualified nonprofit corporation may make independent expenditures, as defined in 11 CFR 100.16, without violating the prohibitions against corporate expenditures contained in 11 CFR part 114.

(2) A qualified nonprofit corporation may make electioneering communications, as defined in 11 CFR 100.29, without violating the prohibitions against corporate expenditures contained in 11 CFR part 114.

(3) Except as provided in paragraphs (d)(1) and (d)(2) of this section, qualified nonprofit corporations remain subject to the requirements and limitations of 11 CFR part 114, including those provisions prohibiting corporate contributions, whether monetary or in-kind.

(e) *Qualified nonprofit corporations; reporting requirements*—(1) *Procedures for demonstrating qualified nonprofit corporation status.* (i) If a corporation makes independent expenditures under paragraph (d)(1) of this section that aggregate in excess of $250 in a calendar year, the corporation shall certify, in accordance with paragraph (e)(1)(i)(B) of this section, that it is eligible for an exemption from the prohibitions against corporate expenditures contained in 11 CFR part 114.

(A) This certification is due no later than the due date of the first independent expenditure report required under paragraph (e)(2)(i) of this section.

SUBCHAPTER C—BIPARTISAN CAMPAIGN REFORM ACT OF 2002—(BCRA) REGULATIONS

PART 300—NON-FEDERAL FUNDS

Sec.
300.1 Scope, effective date, and organization.
300.2 Definitions.

Subpart A—National Party Committees

300.10 General prohibitions on raising and spending non-Federal funds (2 U.S.C. 441; (a) and (c)).
300.11 Prohibition on fundraising for and donating to certain tax-exempt organizations (2 U.S.C. 441; (d)).
300.12 Transition rules.
300.13 Reporting (2 U.S.C. 431 note and 434 (e)).

Subpart B—State, District, and Local Party Committees and Organizations

300.30 Accounts.
300.31 Receipt of Levin funds.
300.32 Expenditures and disbursements.
300.33 Allocation of costs of Federal election activity.
300.34 Transfers.
300.35 Office buildings.
300.36 Reporting Federal election activity; recordkeeping.
300.37 Prohibitions on fundraising for and donating to certain tax-exempt organizations (2 U.S.C. 441i (d)).

Subpart C—Tax-Exempt Organizations

300.50 Prohibited fundraising by national party committees (2 U.S.C. 441i(d)).
300.51 Prohibited fundraising by State, district, and local party committees (2 U.S.C. 441i(d)).
300.52 Fundraising by Federal candidates and Federal officeholders (2 U.S.C. 441i(e)(4)).

Subpart D—Federal Candidates and Officeholders

300.60 Scope (2 U.S.C. 441i (e)(1)).
300.61 Federal elections (2 U.S.C. 441i (e)(1)(A)).
300.62 Non-Federal elections (2 U.S.C. 441i (e)(1)(B)).
300.63 Exception for State party candidates (2 U.S.C. 441i (e)(2)).
300.64 Exemption for attending, speaking, or appearing as a featured guest at fundraising events (2 U.S.C. 441i (e)(3)).
300.65 Exceptions for certain tax-exempt organizations (2 U.S.C. 441i (e)(1) and (4)).

Subpart E—State and Local Candidates

300.70 Scope (2 U.S.C. 441i (f)(1)).
300.71 Federal funds required for certain public communications (2 U.S.C. 441i(f)(1)).
300.72 Federal funds not required for certain communications (2 U.S.C. 441i(f)(2)).

AUTHORITY: 2 U.S.C. 434(e), 438(a)(8), 441a(a), 441i, 453.

SOURCE: 67 FR 49120, July 29, 2002, unless otherwise noted.

§ 300.1 Scope and effective date, and organization.

(a) *Introduction.* This part implements changes to the Federal Election Campaign Act of 1971, as amended ("FECA" or the "Act"), enacted by Title I of the Bipartisan Campaign Finance Reform Act of 2002 ("BCRA"). Public Law 107–155. Unless expressly stated to the contrary, nothing in this part alters the definitions, restrictions, liabilities, and obligations imposed by sections 431 to 455 of Title 2, United States Code, or regulations prescribed thereunder (11 CFR parts 100 to 116).

(b) *Effective dates.* (1) Except as otherwise specifically provided in this part, this part shall take effect on November 6, 2002. However, subpart B of this part shall not apply with respect to runoff elections, recounts, or election contests resulting from elections held prior to such date. *See* 11 CFR 300.12 for transition rules applicable to subpart A of this part.

(2) The increase in individual contribution limits to State committees of political parties, as described in 11 CFR 110.1(c)(5), shall apply to contributions made on or after January 1, 2003.

(c) *Organization of part.* Part 300, which generally addresses non-Federal funds and closely related topics, is organized into five subparts. Each subpart is oriented to the perspective of a category of persons facing issues related to non-Federal funds.

(1) Subpart A of this part prescribes rules pertaining to national party committees, including general non-Federal

funds prohibitions, fundraising, and donation prohibitions with regard to certain tax-exempt organizations, transition rules as BCRA takes effect, and reporting.

(2) Subpart B of this part pertains to State, district, and local political party committees and organizations. Subpart B of this part focuses on "Levin Amendment" to BCRA; office buildings; and fundraising and donation prohibitions with regard to certain tax-exempt organizations.

(3) Subpart C of this part addresses non-Federal funds from the perspective of tax-exempt organizations, setting out rules about prohibited fundraising for certain tax-exempt organizations by national party committees, State, district, and local party committees, and Federal candidates and officeholders.

(4) Subpart D of this part includes regulations pertaining to soliciting non-Federal funds from the perspective of Federal candidates and officeholders in Federal and non-Federal elections; including exceptions for those who are also State candidates and exemptions for those attending, speaking, and appearing as featured guests at fundraising events, or who solicit for certain tax-exempt organizations.

(5) Subpart E of this part focuses on State and local candidates, including regulations about using Federal funds for certain public communications, and exceptions for entirely non-Federal communications.

(6) For rules pertaining to convention and host committees, see 11 CFR part 9008.

§ 300.2 Definitions.

(a) *501(c) organization that makes expenditures or disbursements in connection with a Federal election.* A 501(c) organization *that makes expenditures or disbursements in connection with a Federal election* as that term is used in 11 CFR 300.11, 300.37, 300.50, and 300.51 includes an organization that, within the current election cycle, plans to:

(1) Make expenditures or disbursements in connection with an election for Federal office including for Federal election activity; or

(2) Pay a debt incurred from the making of expenditures or disburse-

ments in connection with an election for Federal office (including for Federal election activity) in a prior election cycle.

(b) *Agent.* For the purposes of part 300 of chapter I, agent means any person who has actual authority, either express or implied, to engage in any of the following activities on behalf of the specified persons:

(1) In the case of a national committee of a political party:

(i) To solicit, direct, or receive any contribution, donation, or transfer of funds; or,

(ii) To solicit any funds for, or make or direct any donations to, an organization that is described in 26 U.S.C 501(c) and exempt from taxation under 26 U.S.C. 501(a) (or has submitted an application for determination of tax exempt status under 26 U.S.C. 501(a)), or an organization described in 26 U.S.C. 527 (other than a political committee, a State, district, or local committee of a political party, or the authorized campaign committee of a candidate for State or local office).

(2) In the case of a State, district, or local committee of a political party:

(i) To expend or disburse any funds for Federal election activity; or

(ii) To transfer, or accept a transfer of, funds to make expenditures or disbursements for Federal election activity; or

(iii) To engage in joint fundraising activities with any person if any part of the funds raised are used, in whole or in part, to pay for Federal election activity; or

(iv) To solicit any funds for, or make or direct any donations to, an organization that is described in 26 U.S.C. 501(c) and exempt from taxation under 26 U.S.C. 501(a) (or has submitted an application for determination of tax exempt status under 26 U.S.C. 501(a)), or an organization described in 26 U.S.C. 527 (other than a political committee, a State, district, or local committee of a political party, or the authorized campaign committee of a candidate for State or local office).

(3) In the case of an individual who is a Federal candidate or an individual holding Federal office, to solicit, receive, direct, transfer, or spend funds in connection with any election.

Federal Election Commission §300.2

(4) In the case of an individual who is a candidate for State or local office, to spend funds for a public communication (*see* 11 CFR 100.26).

(c) *Directly or indirectly establish, finance, maintain, or control.* (1) This paragraph (c) applies to national, State, district, and local committees of a political party, candidates, and holders of Federal office, including an officer, employee, or agent of any of the foregoing persons, which shall be referred to as "sponsors" in this section.

(2) To determine whether a sponsor directly or indirectly established, finances, maintains, or controls an entity, the factors described in paragraphs (c)(2)(i) through (x) of this section must be examined in the context of the overall relationship between sponsor and the entity to determine whether the presence of any factor or factors is evidence that the sponsor directly or indirectly established, finances, maintains, or controls the entity. Such factors include, but are not limited to:

(i) Whether a sponsor, directly or through its agent, owns controlling interest in the voting stock or securities of the entity;

(ii) Whether a sponsor, directly or through its agent, has the authority or ability to direct or participate in the governance of the entity through provisions of constitutions, bylaws, contracts, or other rules, or through formal or informal practices or procedures;

(iii) Whether a sponsor, directly or through its agent, has the authority or ability to hire, appoint, demote, or otherwise control the officers, or other decision-making employees or members of the entity;

(iv) Whether a sponsor has a common or overlapping membership with the entity that indicates a formal or ongoing relationship between the sponsor and the entity;

(v) Whether a sponsor has common or overlapping officers or employees with the entity that indicates a formal or ongoing relationship between the sponsor and the entity;

(vi) Whether a sponsor has any members, officers, or employees who were members, officers or employees of the entity that indicates a formal or ongoing relationship between the sponsor and the entity, or that indicates the creation of a successor entity;

(vii) Whether a sponsor, directly or through its agent, provides funds or goods in a significant amount or on an ongoing basis to the entity, such as through direct or indirect payments for administrative, fundraising, or other costs, but not including the transfer to a committee of its allocated share of proceeds jointly raised pursuant to 11 CFR 102.17, and otherwise lawfully;

(viii) Whether a sponsor, directly or through its agent, causes or arranges for funds in a significant amount or on an ongoing basis to be provided to the entity, but not including the transfer to a committee of its allocated share of proceeds jointly raised pursuant to 11 CFR 102.17, and otherwise lawfully;

(ix) Whether a sponsor, directly or through its agent, had an active or significant role in the formation of the entity; and

(x) Whether the sponsor and the entity have similar patterns of receipts or disbursements that indicate a formal or ongoing relationship between the sponsor and the entity.

(3) *Safe harbor.* On or after November 6, 2002, an entity shall not be deemed to be directly or indirectly established, maintained, or controlled by another entity unless, based on the entities' actions and activities solely after November 6, 2002, they satisfy the requirements of this section. If an entity receives funds from another entity prior to November 6, 2002, and the recipient entity disposes of the funds prior to November 6, 2002, the receipt of such funds prior to November 6, 2002 shall have no bearing on determining whether the recipient entity is financed by the sponsoring entity within the meaning of this section.

(4) *Determinations by the Commission.* (i) A sponsor or entity may request an advisory opinion of the Commission to determine whether the sponsor is no longer directly or indirectly financing, maintaining, or controlling the entity for purposes of this part. The request for such an advisory opinion must meet the requirements of 11 CFR part 112 and must demonstrate that the entity is not directly or indirectly financed, maintained, or controlled by the sponsor.

(ii) Notwithstanding the fact that a sponsor may have established an entity within the meaning of paragraph (c)(2) of this section, the sponsor or the entity may request an advisory opinion of the Commission determining that the relationship between the sponsor and the entity has been severed. The request for such an advisory opinion must meet the requirements of 11 CFR part 112, and must demonstrate that all material connections between the sponsor and the entity have been severed for two years.

(iii) Nothing in this section shall require entities that are separate organizations on November 6, 2002 to obtain an advisory opinion to operate separately from each other.

(d) *Disbursement. Disbursement* means any purchase or payment made by:

(1) A political committee; or

(2) Any other person, including an organization that is not a political committee, that is subject to the Act.

(e) *Donation.* For purposes of part 300, *donation* means a payment, gift, subscription, loan, advance, deposit, or anything of value given to a person, but does not include contributions.

(f) *Federal account. Federal account* means an account at a campaign depository that contains funds to be used in connection with a Federal election.

(g) *Federal Funds. Federal funds* mean funds that comply with the limitations, prohibitions, and reporting requirements of the Act.

(h) *Levin account. Levin account* means an account at a campaign depository established by a State, district, or local committee of a political party pursuant to 11 CFR 300.30, for purposes of making expenditures or disbursements for Federal election activity or non-Federal activity (subject to State law) under 11 CFR 300.32.

(i) *Levin funds* mean funds that are raised pursuant to 11 CFR 300.31 and are or will be disbursed pursuant to 11 CFR 300.32.

(j) *Non-Federal account* means an account that contains funds to be used in connection with a State or local election or allocable expenses under 11 CFR 106.7, 300.30, or 300.33.

(k) *Non-Federal funds* mean funds that are not subject to the limitations and prohibitions of the Act.

(l) [Reserved]

(m) *To solicit.* For the purposes of part 300, *to solicit* means to ask that another person make a contribution, donation, transfer of funds, or otherwise provide anything of value, whether the contribution, donation, transfer of funds, or thing of value, is to be made or provided directly, or through a conduit or intermediary. A solicitation does not include merely providing information or guidance as to the requirement of particular law.

(n) *To direct.* For the purposes of part 300, *to direct* means to ask a person who has expressed an intent to make a contribution, donation, or transfer of funds, or to provide anything of value, to make that contribution, donation, or transfer of funds, or to provide that thing of value, including through a conduit or intermediary. Direction does not include merely providing information or guidance as to the requirement of particular law.

(o) *Individual holding Federal office. Individual holding Federal office* means an individual elected to or serving in the office of President or Vice President of the United States; or a Senator or a Representative in, or Delegate or Resident Commissioner to, the Congress of the United States.

[67 FR 49120, July 29, 2002, as amended at 67 FR 78682, Dec. 26, 2002]

Subpart A—National Party Committees

§ 300.10 General prohibitions on raising and spending non-Federal funds (2 U.S.C. 441i(a) and (c)).

(a) *Prohibitions.* A national committee of a political party, including a national congressional campaign committee, must not:

(1) Solicit, receive, or direct to another person a contribution, donation, or transfer of funds, or any other thing of value that is not subject to the prohibitions, limitations and reporting requirements of the Act;

(2) Spend any funds that are not subject to the prohibitions, limitations, and reporting requirements of the Act; or

(3) Solicit, receive, direct, or transfer to another person, or spend, Levin funds.

Federal Election Commission

(b) *Fundraising costs.* A national committee of a political party, including a national congressional campaign committee, must use only Federal funds to raise funds that are used, in whole or in part, for expenditures and disbursements for Federal election activity.

(c) *Application.* This section also applies to:

(1) An officer or agent acting on behalf of a national party committee or a national congressional campaign committee; and

(2) An entity that is directly or indirectly established, financed, maintained, or controlled by a national party committee or a national congressional campaign committee.

§ 300.11 **Prohibitions on fundraising for and donating to certain tax-exempt organizations (2 U.S.C 441i(d)).**

(a) *Prohibitions.* A national committee of a political party, including a national congressional campaign committee, must not solicit any funds for, or make or direct any donations to the following organizations:

(1) An organization that is described in 26 U.S.C. 501(c) and exempt from taxation under section 26 U.S.C. 501(a) and that makes expenditures or disbursements in connection with an election for Federal office, including expenditures or disbursements for Federal election activity;

(2) An organization that has submitted an application for tax-exempt status under 26 U.S.C. 501(c) and that makes expenditures or disbursements in connection with an election for Federal office, including expenditures or disbursements for Federal election activity; or

(3) An organization described in 26 U.S.C. 527, unless the organization is:

(i) A political committee under 11 CFR 100.5;

(ii) A State, district, or local committee of a political party; or

(iii) The authorized campaign committee of a State or local candidate;

(b) *Application.* This section also applies to:

(1) An officer or agent acting on behalf of a national party committee, including a national congressional campaign committee;

(2) An entity that is directly or indirectly established, financed, maintained, or controlled by a national party committee, including a national congressional campaign committee, or an officer or agent acting on behalf of such an entity; or

(3) An entity that is directly or indirectly established, financed, maintained, or controlled by an agent of a national, State, district, or local committee of a political party, including a national congressional campaign committee.

(c) *Determining whether a section 501(c) organization makes expenditures or disbursements in connection with Federal elections.* In determining whether a section 501(c) organization is one that makes expenditures or disbursements in connection with a Federal election, including expenditures or disbursements for Federal election activity, pursuant to paragraphs (a)(1) and (2) of this section, a national committee of a political party, including a national congressional campaign committee, or any other person described in paragraph (b) of this section, may obtain and rely upon a certification from the organization that satisfies the criteria described in paragraph (d) of this section.

(d) *Certification.* A national committee of a political party, including a national congressional campaign committee, or any person described in paragraph (b) of this section, may rely upon a certification that meets all of the following criteria:

(1) The certification is a signed written statement by an officer or other authorized representative of the organization with knowledge of the organization's activities;

(2) The certification states that within the current election cycle, the organization has not made, and does not intend to make, expenditures or disbursements in connection with an election for Federal office (including for Federal election activity); and

(3) The certification states that the organization does not intend to pay debts incurred from the making of expenditures or disbursements in connection with an election for Federal office (including for Federal election activity) in a prior election cycle.

(e) If a national committee of a political party or any person described in paragraph (b) of this section has actual knowledge that the certification is false, the certification may not be relied upon.

(f) It is not prohibited for a national party or its agent to respond to a request for information about a tax-exempt group that shares the party's political or philosophical goals.

§ 300.12 Transition rules.

(a) *Permissible uses of excess non-Federal funds.* Non-Federal funds received before November 6, 2002, by a national committee of a political party, including a national congressional campaign committee, and in its possession on that date, must be used before January 1, 2003. Subject to the restrictions in paragraph (b) of this section, such funds may be used solely as follows:

(1) To retire outstanding debts or obligations that were incurred solely in connection with an election held prior to November 6, 2002; or

(2) To pay expenses, retire outstanding debts, or pay for obligations incurred solely in connection with any run-off election, recount, or election contest resulting from an election held prior to November 6, 2002.

(b) *Prohibited uses of non-Federal funds.* Non-Federal funds received by a national committee of a political party, including a national congressional campaign committee, before November 6, 2002, and in its possession on that date, may not be used for the following purposes:

(1) To pay any expenditure as defined in 2 U.S.C. 431(9);

(2) To retire outstanding debts or obligations that were incurred for any expenditure; or

(3) To defray the costs of the construction or purchase of any office building or facility.

(c) Any non-Federal funds remaining after payment of debts and obligations permitted in paragraph (a) of this section must be either disgorged to the United States Treasury, or returned by check to the donors, no later than December 31, 2002. Any refund checks not cashed by February 28, 2003 must be disgorged to the United States Treasury by March 31, 2003.

(d) *National party committee office building or facility accounts.* Before November 6, 2002, a national committee of a political party, including a national congressional campaign committee, may accept funds into its party office building or facility account, established pursuant to repealed 2 U.S.C. 431(8)(B)(viii), and may use the funds in the account only for the construction or purchase of an office building or facility. After November 5, 2002, the national party committees may no longer accept funds into such an account and must not use such funds for the purchase or construction of any office building or facility. Funds on deposit in any party office building or facility account on November 6, 2002, must be either disgorged to the United States Treasury or returned by check to the donors no later than December 31, 2002. Any refund checks not cashed by February 28, 2003 must be disgorged to the United States Treasury by March 31, 2003.

(e) *Application.* This section also applies to:

(1) An officer or agent acting on behalf of a national party committee or a national congressional campaign committee; and

(2) An entity that is directly or indirectly established, financed, maintained, or controlled by a national party committee or a national congressional campaign committee.

(f) *Treatment of Federal and non-Federal accounts during transition period.* The following provisions applicable to the allocation of, and payment for, expenses between Federal and non-Federal accounts of national party committees shall remain in effect between November 6 and December 31, 2002: 11 CFR 106.5(a),(b), (c), (f) and (g).

§ 300.13 Reporting (2 U.S.C. 431 note and 434(e)).

(a) *In general.* The national committee of a political party, any national congressional campaign committee of a political party, and any subordinate committee of either, shall report all receipts and disbursements during the reporting period.

(b) *Termination report for non-Federal accounts.* Unless a committee described in paragraph (a) of this section issues refund checks to donors as permitted by 11 CFR 300.12(c), each committee described in paragraph (a) of this section must file a termination report disclosing the disposition of funds in all non-Federal accounts and building fund accounts by January 31, 2003. Each committee that issues refund checks to donors must file a termination report covering the period ending March 31, 2003 disclosing the disposition of any refund checks not cashed by February 28, 2003, as required by 11 CFR 300.12(c) and (d).

(c) *Transitional reporting rules.* (1) The reporting requirements covering receipts in 11 CFR 104.8(e) and (f) and disbursements in 11 CFR 104.9(e) for national party committee non-Federal accounts and building fund accounts shall remain in effect for the reports covering activity between November 6 and December 31, 2002.

(2) The reporting requirements covering disbursements in 11 CFR 104.9 (c) and (d) for national party committee non-Federal accounts and building fund accounts shall remain in effect for the reports covering activity between November 6, 2002 and March 31, 2003.

Subpart B—State, District, and Local Party Committees and Organizations

§ 300.30 Accounts.

(a) *Scope and introduction.* This section applies to State, district, or local committees or organizations of a political party, whether or not the committee is a political committee under 11 CFR 100.5, that have receipts or make disbursements for Federal election activity. Paragraph (b) of this section describes and explains the types of accounts available to a political party committee or organization covered by this section. Paragraph (c) of this section sets out the account structure that must be maintained by a political party committee or organization covered by this section.

(b) *Types of accounts.* Each State, district, and local party organization or committee that has receipts or makes disbursements for Federal election activity must establish one or more of the following types of accounts, pursuant to paragraph (c) of this section.

(1) *Non-Federal accounts.* The funds deposited into this account are governed by State law. Disbursements, contributions, and expenditures made wholly or in part in connection with Federal elections must not be made from any non-Federal account, except as permitted by paragraph (c)(3)(ii) of this section, 11 CFR 102.5(a)(4), 11 CFR 106.7(d)(1)(i), 11 CFR 300.33 and 11 CFR 300.34.

(2) *Levin account.* The funds deposited into this account must comply with 11 CFR 300.31. Such funds may be used for the categories of activities described at 11 CFR 300.32(b).

(3) *Federal account.* Federal accounts may be used for the deposit of contributions and the making of expenditures pursuant to the following conditions:

(i) Only contributions that are permissible pursuant to the limitations and prohibitions of the Act may be deposited into any Federal account, regardless of whether such contributions are for use in connection with Federal or non-Federal elections. *See* 11 CFR 103.3 regarding impermissible funds.

(ii) Only contributions solicited and received pursuant to the following conditions may be deposited in a Federal account:

(A) Contributions must be designated by the contributors for the Federal account;

(B) The solicitation must expressly state that contributions may be used wholly or in part in connection with a Federal election; or

(C) The contributor must be informed that all contributions are subject to the limitations and prohibitions of the Act.

(iii) All disbursements, contributions, and expenditures made wholly or in part by any State, district, or local party organization or committee in connection with a Federal election must be made from either:

(A) A Federal account, except as permitted by 11 CFR 300.32; or

(B) A separate allocation account (*see* paragraph (b)(4) of this section).

(iv) If all payments in connection with a Federal election, including payments for Federal election activities, are to be made from a Federal account, expenditures and disbursements for costs that are allocable pursuant to 11 CFR 106.7 or 11 CFR 300.33 must be made from the Federal account in their entirety, with the shares of a non-Federal account or of a Levin account being transferred to the Federal account pursuant to 11 CFR 106.7 and 11 CFR 300.33.

(v) No transfers may be made to a Federal account from any other account(s) maintained by a State, district, or local party committee or organization from any other party organization or committee at any level for the purpose of financing activity in connection with Federal elections, except as provided by paragraph (b)(3)(iv) of this section or 11 CFR 300.33 and 300.34.

(4) *Allocation accounts.* At the discretion of the party committee or organization, separate allocation accounts may be established for purposes of making allocable expenditures and disbursements.

(i) Only funds from the party organization's or committee's Federal and non-Federal accounts may be deposited into an allocation account used to make allocable expenditures and disbursements for activities in connection with Federal and non-Federal elections.

(ii) Only funds from the party organization's or committee's Federal account and Levin funds from its non-Federal or Levin account(s) may be deposited into an allocation account used to make allocable expenditures and disbursements for activities undertaken pursuant to 11 CFR 300.32(b).

(iii) Once a party organization or committee has established a separate allocation account for activities in connection with Federal and non-Federal elections and a separate account for activities undertaken pursuant to 11 CFR 300.32(b), all allocable expenses must be paid from the appropriate allocation account for as long as that account is maintained.

(iv) The party organization or committee must transfer to the appropriate allocation account funds from its Federal and non-Federal or Levin accounts in amounts proportionate to the Federal, non-Federal and Levin shares of each allocable expense pursuant to 11 CFR 106.7 and 11 CFR 300.33.

The transfers must be made pursuant to 11 CFR 300.33 and 300.34.

(v) No funds contained in an allocation account may be transferred to any other account maintained by the party committee or organization.

(vi) For reporting purposes, all allocation accounts must be treated as Federal accounts.

(c) *Required account or accounts.* Each State, district, and local party organization or committee that has receipts or makes disbursements for Federal election activity must establish its accounts in accordance with paragraphs (c)(1), or (c)(2), or (c)(3) of this section.

(1) One or more Federal accounts in a campaign depository, in accordance with 11 CFR part 103, which must be treated as a separate political committee and be required to comply with the requirements of the Act including the registration and reporting requirements of 11 CFR part 102 and part 104. State, district, and local party organizations or committees may choose to make non-Federal disbursements, subject to State law, and disbursements for Federal election activity from a Federal account provided that such disbursements are reported pursuant to 11 CFR 104.17 and 11 CFR 300.36, and provided that contributors of the Federal funds so used were notified that their contributions were subject to the limitations and prohibitions of the Act.

(2) Establish at least three separate accounts in depositories as follows—

(i) One or more Federal accounts;

(ii) One or more Levin accounts; and

(iii) One or more Non-Federal accounts.

(3) Establish two separate accounts in depositories as follows:

(i) One or more Federal accounts, and;

(ii) An account that must function as both a Non-Federal account and a Levin account. If such an account is used, the State, district, and local party must demonstrate through a reasonable accounting method approved by the Commission (including any method embedded in software provided or approved by the Commission) that whenever such organization makes a disbursement for activities undertaken pursuant to 11 CFR 300.32(b), that organization had received sufficient contributions or Levin funds to make such disbursement.

(d) *Recordkeeping.* All party organizations or committees must keep records of deposits into and disbursements from such accounts, and, upon request, must make such records available for examination by the Commission.

§ 300.31 Receipt of Levin funds.

(a) *General rule.* Levin funds expended or disbursed by any State, district, or local committee must be raised solely by the committee that expends or disburses them.

(b) *Compliance with State law.* Each donation of Levin funds solicited or accepted by a State, district, or local committee of a political party must be lawful under the laws of the State in which the committee is organized.

(c) *Donations from sources permitted by State law but prohibited by the Act.* If the laws of the State in which a State, district, or local committee of a political party is organized permit donations to the committee from a source prohibited by the Act and this chapter, other than 2 U.S.C. 441e, the committee may solicit and accept donations of Levin funds from that source, subject to paragraph (d) of this section.

(d) *Donation amount limitation.* (1) *General rule.* A State, district, or local committee of a political party must not solicit or accept from any person (including any entity established, financed, maintained, or controlled by such person) one or more donations of Levin funds aggregating more than $10,000 in a calendar year.

(2) *Effect of different State limitations.* If the laws of the State in which a State, district, or local committee of a political party is organized limit donations to that committee to less than the amount specified in paragraph (d)(1) of this section, then the State law amount limitations shall control. If the laws of the State in which a State, district, or local committee of a political party is organized permit donations to that committee in amounts greater than the amount specified in paragraph (d)(1) of this section, then the amount limitations in paragraph (d)(1) of this section shall control.

(3) *No affiliation of committees for purposes of this paragraph.* For purposes of determining compliance with paragraph (d) of this section only, State, district, and local committees of the same political party shall not be considered affiliated. Subject to the amount limitations specified in paragraphs (d)(1) and (d)(2) of this section, a person (including any entity directly or indirectly established, financed, maintained, or controlled by such person) may donate without additional limitation to each and every State, district, and local committee of a political party.

(e) *No Levin funds from a national party committee or a Federal candidate or officeholder.* A State, district, or local committee of a political party disbursing Levin funds pursuant to 11 CFR 300.32 must not accept or use for such purposes any donations or other funds that are solicited, received, directed, transferred, or spent by or in the name of any of the following persons:

(1) A national committee of a political party (including a national congressional campaign committee of a political party), any officer or agent acting on behalf of such a national party committee, or any entity that is directly or indirectly established, financed, maintained, or controlled by such a national party committee. Notwithstanding 11 CFR 102.17, a State, district or local committee of a political party must not raise Levin funds by means of joint fundraising with a national committee of a political party, any officer or agent acting on behalf of such a national party committee, or any entity that is directly or indirectly established, financed, maintained, or controlled by such a national party committee. Nothing in this section shall be construed to prohibit a State, district, or local committee of a political party from jointly raising, under 11 CFR 102.17, Federal funds not to be used for Federal election activity with a national committee of a political party, or its agent, or any entity directly or indirectly established, financed, maintained, or controlled by such a national party committee.

(2) A Federal candidate, or an individual holding Federal office, or an

§ 300.32

agent of a Federal candidate or officeholder, or an entity directly or indirectly established, financed, maintained, or controlled by, or acting on behalf of, one or more Federal candidates or individuals holding Federal office. Notwithstanding 11 CFR 102.17, a State, district, or local committee of a political party must not raise Levin funds by means of joint fundraising with a Federal candidate, an individual holding Federal office, or an entity directly or indirectly established, financed, maintained, or controlled by, or acting on behalf of, one or more candidates or individuals holding Federal office. A Federal candidate or individual holding Federal office may attend, speak, or be a featured guest at a fundraising event for a State, district, or local committee of a political party at which Levin funds are raised. *See* 11 CFR 300.64.

(f) *Certain joint fundraising prohibited.* Notwithstanding 11 CFR 102.17, a State, district, or local committee of a political party must not raise Levin funds by means of any joint fundraising activity with any other State, district, or local committee of any political party, the agent of such a committee, or an entity directly or indirectly established, financed, maintained, or controlled by such a committee. This prohibition includes State, district, and local committees of a political party organized in another State. Nothing in this section shall be construed to prohibit two or more State, district, or local committees of a political party from jointly raising, under 11 CFR 102.17, Federal funds not to be used for Federal election activity.

(g) *Safe Harbor.* The use of a common vendor for fundraising by more than one State, district, or local committee or a political party, or the agent of such a committee does not constitute joint fundraising within the meaning of this section.

§ 300.32 **Expenditures and disbursements.**

(a) *Federal funds.* (1) An association or similar group of candidates for State or local office, or an association or similar group of individuals holding State or local office, must make any expenditures or disbursements for Federal election activity solely with Federal funds.

(2) Except as provided in this part, a State, district, or local committee of a political party that makes expenditures or disbursements for Federal election activity must use Federal funds for that purposes, subject to the provisions of this chapter.

(3) State, district, and local party committees that raise Federal funds to be used, in whole or in part, for Federal election activities must pay the direct costs of such fundraising only with Federal funds. The direct costs of a fundraising program or event include expenses for the solicitation of funds and for the planning and administration of actual fundraising programs and events.

(4) State, district, and local party committees that raise Levin funds to be used, in whole or in part, for Federal election activity must pay the direct costs of such fundraising with either Federal or Levin funds. The direct costs of a fundraising program or event include expenses for the solicitation of funds and for the planning and administration of actual fundraising programs and events.

(b) *Levin funds.* A State, district, or local committee of a political party may spend Levin funds in accordance with this part on the following types of activity:

(1) Subject to the conditions set out in paragraph (c) of this section, only the following types of Federal election activity:

(i) Voter registration activity during the period that begins on the date that is 120 days before the date a regularly scheduled Federal election is held and ends on the date of the election; and

(ii) Voter identification, get-out-the-vote activity, or generic campaign activity conducted in connection with an election in which a candidate for Federal office appears on the ballot (regardless of whether a candidate for State or local office also appears on the ballot).

(2) Any use that is lawful under the laws of the State in which the committee is organized, other than the Federal election activities defined in 11 CFR 100.24(b)(3) and (4). A disbursement of Levin funds under this paragraph

need not comply with paragraphs (c)(1) and (c)(2) of this section, except as required by State law.

(c) *Conditions and restrictions on spending Levin funds.* (1) The Federal election activity for which the disbursement is made must not refer to a clearly identified candidate for Federal office.

(2) The disbursement must not pay for any part of the costs of any broadcasting, cable, or satellite communication, other than a communication that refers solely to a clearly identified candidate for State or local office.

(3) The disbursement must be made from funds raised in accordance with 11 CFR 300.31.

(4) The disbursements for allocable Federal election activity that exceed in the aggregate $5,000 in a calendar year may be paid for entirely with Federal funds or may be allocated between Federal funds and Levin funds according to 11 CFR 300.33. Disbursements for Federal election activity that may be allocated and that aggregate $5,000 or less in a calendar year may be paid for entirely with Federal funds, entirely with Levin funds, or may be allocated between Federal funds and Levin funds according to 11 CFR 300.33.

(d) *Non-Federal activities.* A State, district, or local committee of a political party that makes disbursements for non-Federal activity may make those disbursements from its Federal, Levin, or non-Federal funds, subject to the laws of the State in which it is organized. A State, district, or local party committee that engages in fundraising for solely non-Federal funds may pay the costs related to such fundraising from any account, subject to State law, including a Federal account.

§ 300.33 Allocation of costs of Federal election activity.

(a) *Costs of Federal election activity allocable by State, district, and local party committees and organizations.*

(1) *Costs of voter registration.* Subject to the conditions of 11 CFR 300.32(c), State, district, and local party committees and organizations may allocate disbursements or expenditures, except salaries and wages for employees, between Federal funds and Levin funds for voter registration activity, as de-

fined in 11 CFR 100.24(a)(2), that takes place during the period that begins on the date that is 120 days before the date of a regularly scheduled Federal election and that ends on the date of the election, provided that the activity does not refer to a clearly identified Federal candidate.

(2) *Costs of voter identification, get-out-the-vote activity, or generic campaign activities within certain time periods.* Subject to the conditions of 11 CFR 300.32(c), State, district, and local party committees and organizations may allocate disbursements or expenditures, except salaries and wages for employees, between Federal funds and Levin funds for voter identification, get-out-the-vote activity, or generic campaign activities, as defined in 11 CFR 100.24(a)(3) and (4) and 11 CFR 100.25, that are conducted in connection with an election in which a candidate for Federal office is on the ballot and within the time periods set forth in 11 CFR 100.24(a)(1), provided that the activity does not refer to a clearly identified Federal candidate.

(b) *Allocation percentages.* State, district, and local party committees and organizations that choose to allocate between Federal funds and Levin funds their expenditures and disbursements, except for salaries and wages, in connection with activities described in paragraph (a) of this section that take place within the time periods set forth in 11 CFR 100.24(a)(1) or paragraph (a) of this section must allocate the following minimum percentages to their Federal funds:

(1) *Presidential election years.* If a Presidential candidate, but no Senate candidate appears on the ballot, State, district, and local party committees and organizations must allocate at least 28% of expenses for activities described in paragraph (a) of this section to their Federal funds.

(2) *Presidential and Senate election year.* If a Presidential candidate and a Senate candidate appear on the ballot, State, district, and local party committees and organizations must allocate at least 36% of expenses for activities described in paragraph (a) of this section to their Federal funds.

(3) *Senate election year.* If a Senate candidate, but no Presidential candidate, appears on the ballot, State, district, and local party committees and organizations must allocate at least 21% of expenses for activities described in paragraph (a) of this section to their Federal funds.

(4) *Non-Presidential and non-Senate year.* If neither a Presidential nor a Senate candidate appears on the ballot, State, district, and local party committees and organizations must allocate at least 15% of expenses for activities described in paragraph (a) of this section to their Federal funds.

(c) *Costs of Federal election activity not allocable by State, district, and local party committees.* The following costs incurred by State, district, and local party committees and organizations must be paid only with Federal funds:

(1) *Public communications.* Expenditures for public communications as defined in 11 CFR 100.26 by State, district, and local party committees and organizations that refer to a clearly identified candidate for Federal office and that promote, support, attack, or oppose any such candidate for Federal office must not be allocated between or among Federal, non-Federal, and Levin accounts. Only Federal funds may be used.

(2) *Salaries and wages.* Salaries and wages for employees who spend more than 25% of their compensated time in a given month on Federal election activity or activities in connection with a Federal election must not be allocated between or among Federal, non-Federal, and Levin accounts. Only Federal funds may be used. Salaries and wages for employees who spend 25% or less of their compensated time in a given month on Federal election activity or activities in connection with a Federal election shall be paid from funds that comply with State law.

(3) *Fundraising costs.* Disbursements for direct fundraising costs incurred by State, district, and local party committees and organizations for funds to be used, in whole or in part, for Federal election activity, including the activities described in paragraph (a) of this section, must not be allocated between or among Federal, non-Federal and Levin funds. Only Federal or Levin funds may be used.

(d) *Transfers between accounts to cover allocable expenses.* State, district, and local party committees and organizations may transfer Levin funds from their Levin or non-Federal accounts to their Federal accounts or to allocation accounts solely to meet expenses allocable pursuant to paragraphs (a)(1) and (2) of this section and only pursuant to the following methods:

(1) *Payments from Federal accounts or from allocation accounts.* (i) If Federal accounts are used to make payments for allocable activities, State, district, and local party committees and organizations must pay the entire amount of allocable expenses from their Federal accounts and transfer Levin funds from their Levin or non-Federal accounts to their Federal accounts solely to cover the portions of the expenses for which Levin funds may be used; or

(ii) State, district, and local party committees and organizations may establish separate allocation accounts into which Federal funds and Levin funds may be deposited solely for the purpose of paying allocable expenses.

(2) *Timing.* (i) If Federal or allocation accounts are used to make allocable expenditures and disbursements, State, district, and local party committees and organizations must transfer Levin funds to their Federal or allocation accounts to meet allocable expenses no more than 10 days before and no more than 60 days after the payments for which they are designated are made from a Federal or allocation account, except that transfers may be made more than 10 days before a payment is made from the Federal or allocation account if advance payment is required by the vendor(s) and if such payment is based on a reasonable estimate of the activity's final costs as determined by the committee and the vendor(s) involved.

(ii) Any portion of a transfer of Levin funds to a party committee or organization's Federal or allocation account that does not meet the requirement of paragraph (d)(2)(i) of this section shall be presumed to be a loan or contribution from the Levin or non-Federal account to the Federal or allocation account, in violation of the Act.

§ 300.34 Transfers.

(a) *Federal funds.* (1) Notwithstanding 11 CFR 102.6(a)(1)(ii), a State, district, or local committee of a political party must not use any Federal funds transferred to it from, or otherwise accepted by it from, any of the persons enumerated in paragraphs (b)(1) and (b)(2) of this section as the Federal component of an expenditure or disbursement for Federal election activity under 11 CFR 300.32. A State, district, or local committee of a political party must itself raise the Federal component of an expenditure or disbursement allocated between Federal funds and Levin funds under 11 CFR 300.32 and 300.33.

(2) A State, district, or local committee of a political party that makes an expenditure or disbursement of Federal funds for Federal election activities must demonstrate through a reasonable accounting method approved by the Commission (including any method embedded in software provided or approved by the Commission) that the Federal funds used to make the expenditure or disbursement do not include Federal funds transferred to the committee in violation of this section. Alternatively, a State, district, or local committee of a political party may establish a separate Federal account into which the committee deposits only Federal funds raised by the committee itself, and from which all expenditures or disbursement of Federal funds for Federal election activities are made.

(b) *Levin funds.* Levin funds must be raised solely by the State, district, or local committee of a political party that expends or disburses the funds. A State, district, or local committee of a political party must not use as Levin funds any funds transferred or otherwise provided to the committee by:

(1) Any other State, district, or local committee of any political party, any officer or agent acting on behalf of such a committee, or any entity directly or indirectly established, financed, maintained or controlled by such a committee; or,

(2) The national committee of any political party (including a national congressional campaign committee of a political party), any officer or agent acting on behalf of such a committee,

or any entity directly or indirectly established, financed, maintained, or controlled by such a committee.

(c) *Allocation transfers.* Transfers of Levin funds between the accounts of a State, district, or local committee of a political party for allocation purposes must comply with 11 CFR 300.30 and 11 CFR 300.33.

§ 300.35 Office buildings.

(a) *General provision.* For the purchase or construction of its office building, a State or local party committee may spend Federal funds or non-Federal funds that are not subject to the limitations, prohibitions, and disclosure provisions of the Act, so long as such funds are not contributed or donated by a foreign national. *See* 2 U.S.C. 441e. If non-Federal funds are used, they are subject to State law. An office building must not be purchased or constructed for the purpose of influencing the election of any candidate in any particular election for Federal office. For purposes of this section, the term *local party committee* shall include a *district party committee.*

(b) *Application of State law.* Non-Federal funds received by a State or local party committee that are spent for the purchase or construction of its office building are subject to State law as set forth in paragraphs (b)(1) and (2) of this section.

(1) *Non-Federal account.* If a State or local party committee uses non-Federal funds, Federal law does not preempt or supersede State law as to the source of funds used, the permissibility of the disbursements, or the reporting of the receipt and disbursement of such funds, except as provided in paragraph (a) of this section.

(2) *Levin funds.* Levin funds may be used for the purchase or construction of a State or local party committee office building, if permitted by State law.

(c) *Leasing a portion of the party office building.* A State or local party committee may lease a portion of its office building to others to generate income at the usual and normal charge. If the building is purchased or constructed in whole or in part with non-Federal funds, all rental income shall be deposited in the committee's non-Federal account and used only for non-Federal purposes. Such rental income and its use must also comply with State law. If the building is purchased or constructed solely with Federal funds, the rental income may be deposited in the Federal account. The receipt of such funds shall be reported in compliance with 11 CFR 104.3(a)(4)(vi).

(d) *Transitional Provisions for State Party Building or Facility Account.* Up to and including November 5, 2002, the State committee of a political party may accept funds into its party office building or facility account, established pursuant to repealed 2 U.S.C. 431(8)(B)(viii), designated for the purchase or construction of an office building. Starting on November 6, 2002, the funds in the account may not be used for Federal account or Levin account purposes, but may be used for any non-Federal purposes, as permitted under State law.

§ 300.36   Reporting Federal election activity; recordkeeping.

(a) *Requirements for a State, district, or local committee of a political party, or an association or similar group of candidates for State or local office or of individuals holding State or local office, that is not a political committee.*

(1) A State, district, or local committee of a political party, or an association or similar group of candidates for State or local office or of individuals holding State or local office, that is not a political committee (*see* 11 CFR 100.5) must demonstrate through a reasonable accounting method that whenever it makes a payment of Federal funds or Levin funds (if it is permitted to spend Levin funds) for Federal election activity (*see* 11 CFR 300.32 and 300.33) it has received sufficient funds subject to the limitations and prohibitions of the Act to make the payment. Such an organization must keep records of amounts received or expended under this paragraph and, upon request, shall make such records available for examination by the Commission.

(2) Notwithstanding the foregoing, a payment of Federal funds or Levin funds for Federal election activity shall not constitute an expenditure for purposes of determining whether a

State, district, or local committee of a political party, or an association or similar group of candidates for State or local office or of individuals holding State or local office, qualifies as a political committee under 11 CFR 100.5, unless the payment otherwise qualifies as an expenditure under 2 U.S.C. 431(9). A payment of Federal funds for Federal election activity that refers to a clearly identified Federal candidate and that meets the criteria of 11 CFR 100.140, 100.147, or 100.149 *(exempt activities)* shall be treated as a payment for exempt activity in accordance with all applicable provisions of this chapter, including, but not limited to, 11 CFR 100.5(c).

(b) *Requirements for a State, district, or local committee of a political party, or an association or similar group of candidates for State or local office or of individuals holding State or local office, that is a political committee.*

(1) *Requirements for a State, district, or local committee of a political party that has less than $5,000 of aggregate receipts and disbursements for Federal election activity in a calendar year, and for an association or similar group of candidates for State or local office or of individuals holding State or local office at all times.* This paragraph applies to a State, district, or local committee of a political party that is a political committee, and that has less than $5,000 of aggregate receipts and disbursements for Federal election activity in a calendar year; and, at all times, to an association or similar group of candidates for State or local office or of individuals holding State or local office that is a political committee (*see* 11 CFR 100.5). Such a party committee or association of candidates or officeholders must report all receipts and disbursements of Federal funds for Federal election activity, including the Federally allocated portion of a payment for Federal election activity. A disbursement of Federal funds or Levin funds for Federal election activity (*see* 11 CFR 300.32 and 300.33) by either such party committee or association of candidates or officeholders shall not be deemed an expenditure and reported as such pursuant to 11 CFR part 104, unless the disbursement otherwise qualifies as an expenditure under 2 U.S.C. 431(9).

(2) *Requirements for a State, district, or local committee of a political party that has $5,000 or more of aggregate receipts and disbursements for Federal election activity in a calendar year.* A State, district, or local committee of a political party that is a political committee (*see* 11 CFR 100.5) must report all receipts and disbursements made for Federal election activity if the aggregate amount of such receipts and disbursements is $5,000 or more during the calendar year. The disclosure required by this paragraph must include receipts and disbursements of Federal funds and of Levin funds used for Federal election activity.

(i) *Reporting of allocation of expenses between Federal funds and Levin funds.* A State, district, or local committee of a political party that makes a disbursement for Federal election activity that is allocated between Federal funds and Levin funds (*see* 11 CFR 300.33) must report for each such disbursement:

(A) In the first report of a calendar year disclosing an allocated disbursement for Federal election activity, the committee must state the allocation percentages to be applied for allocable Federal election activity pursuant to 11 CFR 300.33(b).

(B) In each subsequent report in the calendar year itemizing an allocated disbursement for Federal election activity, the committee must state the category of Federal election activity (*see* 11 CFR 100.24(b)) for which each allocated disbursement was made, and must disclose the total amounts disbursed from Federal funds and Levin funds for that year to date for each such category.

(ii) *Reporting of allocation transfers.* A committee that makes allocated disbursements for Federal election activities in accordance with 11 CFR 300.33(d) shall report each transfer of Levin funds from its Levin or non-Federal account, to its Federal account, and each transfer from its Federal account and its Levin or non-Federal account into an allocation account, for the purpose of making such disbursements. In the report covering the period in which each transfer occurred, the committee must explain in a memo entry the allocated disbursement to which the trans-

fer relates and the date on which the transfer was made. If the transfer includes funds for the allocable costs of more than one category of Federal election activity, the committee must itemize the transfer, showing the amounts designated for each category.

(iii) *Reporting of allocated disbursements.* For each disbursement allocated between Federal funds and Levin funds, the committee must report the full name and address of each person to whom the disbursement was made, the date of the disbursement, amount, and purpose of the disbursement. If the disbursement is for the allocable costs of more than one category of Federal election activity, the committee must itemize the disbursement, showing the amounts designated for each category. The committee must also disclose the total amount disbursed from Federal funds and Levin funds for Federal election activity that calendar year, to date, for each category of Federal election activity.

(iv) *Itemization.* The disclosure required by paragraph (b)(2) of this section must include, in addition to any other applicable reporting requirement of this chapter, the itemized disclosure of receipts and disbursements of $200 or more to or from any person for Federal election activities.

(3) *Reporting of disbursements allocated between Federal funds and non-Federal funds, other than Levin funds.* A State, district, or local committee of a political party that makes a disbursement for costs allocable between Federal and non-Federal funds, other than the costs of Federal election activity that is allocated between Federal funds and Levin funds under 11 CFR 300.33, must comply with 11 CFR 104.17.

(c) *Filing.* (1) *Schedule.* A State, district, or local committee of a political party, or an association or similar group of candidates for State or local office or of individuals holding State or local office, that must file reports under paragraph (b) of this section must comply with the monthly filing schedule in 11 CFR 104.5(c)(3).

(2) *Electronic filing.* Receipts of Federal funds for Federal election activity that constitute contributions under 11 CFR part 100, subpart B, and disbursements of Federal funds for Federal

election activity that constitute expenditures under 11 CFR part 100, subpart D, apply when determining whether a political committee must file reports in an electronic format under 11 CFR 104.18.

(d) *Recordkeeping.* A State, district, or local committee of a political party, or an association or similar group of candidates for State or local office or of individuals holding State or local office, that must file reports under paragraph (b) of this section must comply with the requirements of 11 CFR 104.14.

[67 FR 49120, July 29, 2002, as amended at 67 FR 78682, Dec. 26, 2002]

§ 300.37 **Prohibitions on fundraising for and donating to certain tax-exempt organizations (2 U.S.C. 441i(d)).**

(a) *Prohibitions.* A State, district, or local committee of a political party must not solicit any funds for, or make or direct any donations to:

(1) An organization that is described in 26 U.S.C. 501(c) and exempt from taxation under section 26 U.S.C. 501(a) and that makes expenditures or disbursements in connection with an election for Federal office, including expenditures or disbursements for Federal election activity;

(2) An organization that has submitted an application for tax-exempt status under 26 U.S.C. 501(c) and that makes expenditures or disbursements in connection with an election for Federal office, including expenditures or disbursements for Federal election activity; or

(3) An organization described in 26 U.S.C. 527, unless the organization is:

(i) A political committee under 11 CFR 100.5;

(ii) A State, district, or local committee of a political party;

(iii) The authorized campaign committee of a State or local candidate; or

(iv) A political committee under State law, that supports only State or local candidates and that does not make expenditures or disbursements in connection with an election for Federal office, including expenditures or disbursements for Federal election activity.

(b) *Application.* This section also applies to:

(1) An officer or agent acting on behalf of a State, district, or local committee of a political party;

(2) An entity that is directly or indirectly established, financed, maintained, or controlled by a State, district, or local committee or a political party or an officer or agent acting on behalf of such an entity; or

(3) An entity that is directly or indirectly established, financed, maintained, or controlled by an agent of a State, district, or local committee of a political party.

(c) *Determining whether an organization makes expenditures or disbursements in connection with a Federal election.* (1) In determining whether a section 501(c) organization is one that makes expenditures or disbursements in connection with a Federal election, including expenditures or disbursements for Federal election activity, pursuant to paragraphs (a)(1) and (2) of this section, a State, district, or local committee of a political party or any other person described in paragraph (b) of this section, may obtain and rely upon a certification from the organization that satisfies the criteria described in paragraph (d) of this section.

(2) In determining whether a section 527 organization is a State-registered political committee that supports only State or local candidates and does not make expenditures or disbursements in connection with an Federal election, including expenditures or disbursements for Federal election activity, pursuant to paragraph (a)(3)(iv) of this section, a State, district, or local committee of a political party or any other person described in paragraph (b) of this section, may obtain and rely upon a certification from the organization that satisfies the criteria described in paragraph (d) of this section.

(d) *Certification.* A State, district, or local committee of a political party or any person described in paragraph (b) of this section may rely upon a certification that meets all of the following criteria:

(1) The certification is a signed written statement by an officer or other authorized representative of the organization with knowledge of the organization's activities or by the treasurer

Federal Election Commission

of the State-registered political committee described in paragraph (a)(3)(iv) of this section;

(2) The certification states that within the current election cycle, the organization or political committee has not made, and does not intend to make, expenditures or disbursements in connection with an election for Federal office (including for Federal election activity); and

(3) The certification states that the organization or political committee does not intend to pay debts incurred from the making of expenditures or disbursements in connection with an election for Federal office (including for Federal election activity) in a prior election cycle.

(e) If a State, district, or local committee of a political party or any person described in paragraph (b) of this section has actual knowledge that the certification is false, the certification may not be relied upon.

(f) It is not prohibited for a State, district, or local committee of a political party or its agents to respond to a request for information about a tax-exempt group that shares the party's political or philosophical goals.

Subpart C—Tax-Exempt Organizations

§ 300.50 Prohibited fundraising by national party committees (2 U.S.C. 441i(d)).

(a) *Prohibitions on fundraising and donations.* A national committee of a political party, including a national congressional campaign committee, must not solicit any funds for, or make or direct any donations to the following organizations:

(1) An organization that is described in 26 U.S.C. 501(c) and exempt from taxation under section 26 U.S.C. 501(a) and that makes expenditures or disbursements in connection with an election for Federal office, including expenditures or disbursements for Federal election activity;

(2) An organization that has submitted an application for tax-exempt status under 26 U.S.C. 501(c) and that makes expenditures or disbursements in connection with an election for Federal office, including expenditures or

disbursements for Federal election activity; or

(3) An organization described in 26 U.S.C. 527, unless the organization is:

(i) A political committee under 11 CFR 100.5;

(ii) A State, district, or local committee of a political party; or

(iii) The authorized campaign committee of a State or local candidate;

(b) *Application.* This section also applies to:

(1) An officer or agent acting on behalf of a national party committee, including a national congressional campaign committee;

(2) An entity that is directly or indirectly established, financed, maintained, or controlled by a national party committee, including a national congressional campaign committee, or an officer or agent acting on behalf of such an entity; or

(3) An entity that is directly or indirectly established, financed, maintained, or controlled by an agent of a national, State, district, or local committee of a political party, including a national congressional campaign committee.

(c) *Determining whether a section 501(c) organization makes expenditures or disbursements in connection with Federal elections.* In determining whether a section 501(c) organization is one that makes expenditures or disbursements in connection with a Federal election, including expenditures or disbursements for Federal election activity, pursuant to paragraphs (a)(1) and (2) of this section, a national committee of a political party, including a national congressional campaign committee, or any other person described in paragraph (b) of this section, may obtain and rely upon a certification from the organization that satisfies the criteria described in paragraph (d) of this section.

(d) *Certification.* A national committee of a political party, including a national congressional campaign committee, or any person described in paragraph (b) of this section, may rely upon a certification that meets all of the following criteria:

(1) The certification is a signed written statement by an officer or other

authorized representative of the organization with knowledge of the organization's activities;

(2) The certification states that within the current election cycle, the organization has not made, and does not intend to make, expenditures or disbursements in connection with an election for Federal office (including for Federal election activity); and

(3) The certification states that the organization or political committee does not intend to pay debts incurred from the making of expenditures or disbursements in connection with an election for Federal office (including for Federal election activity) in a prior election cycle.

(e) *Reliance on false certification.* If a national committee of a political party or any person described in paragraph (b) of this section has actual knowledge that the certification is false, the certification may not be relied upon.

(f) *Requests for information.* It is not prohibited for a national party or its agent to respond to a request for information about a tax-exempt group that shares the party's political or philosophical goals.

§ 300.51 Prohibited fundraising by State, district, or local party committees (2 U.S.C. 441i(d)).

(a) *Prohibitions.* A State, district, or local committee of a political party must not solicit any funds for, or make or direct any donations to:

(1) An organization that is described in 26 U.S.C. 501(c) and exempt from taxation under section 26 U.S.C. 501(a) and that makes expenditures or disbursements in connection with an election for Federal office, including expenditures or disbursements for Federal election activity;

(2) An organization that has submitted an application for tax-exempt status under 26 U.S.C. 501(c) and that makes expenditures or disbursements in connection with an election for Federal office, including expenditures or disbursements for Federal election activity; or

(3) An organization described in 26 U.S.C. 527, unless the organization is:

(i) A political committee under 11 CFR 100.5;

(ii) A State, district, or local committee of a political party;

(iii) The authorized campaign committee of a State or local candidate; or

(iv) A political committee under State law, that supports only State or local candidates and that does not make expenditures or disbursements in connection with an election for Federal office, including expenditures or disbursements for Federal election activity.

(b) *Application.* This section also applies to:

(1) An officer or agent acting on behalf of a State, district, or local committee of a political party;

(2) An entity that is directly or indirectly established, financed, maintained, or controlled by a State, district, or local committee or a political party or an officer or agent acting on behalf of such an entity; or

(3) An entity that is directly or indirectly established, financed, maintained, or controlled by an agent of a State, district, or local committee of a political party.

(c) *Determining whether an organization makes expenditures or disbursements in connection with a Federal election.*

(1) In determining whether a section 501(c) organization is one that makes expenditures or disbursements in connection with a Federal election, including expenditures or disbursements for Federal election activity, pursuant to paragraphs (a)(1) and (2) of this section, a State, district, or local committee of a political party or any other person described in paragraph (b) of this section, may obtain and rely upon a certification from the organization that satisfies the criteria described in paragraph (d) of this section.

(2) In determining whether a section 527 organization is a State-registered political committee that supports only State or local candidates and does not make expenditures or disbursements in connection with a Federal election, including expenditures or disbursements for Federal election activity, pursuant to paragraph (a)(3)(iv) of this section, a State, district, or local committee of a political party or any other person described in paragraph (b) of this section,

may obtain and rely upon a certification from the organization that satisfies the criteria described in paragraph (d) of this section.

(d) *Certification.* A State, district, or local committee of a political party or any person described in paragraph (b) of this section may rely upon a certification that meets all of the following criteria:

(1) The certification is a signed written statement by an officer or other authorized representative of the organization with knowledge of the organization's activities or by the treasurer of the State-registered political committee described in paragraph (a)(3)(iv) of this section;

(2) The certification states that within the current election cycle, the organization or political committee has not made, and does not intend to make, expenditures or disbursements in connection with an election for Federal office (including for Federal election activity); and

(3) The certification states that the organization does not intend to pay debts incurred from the making of expenditures or disbursements in connection with an election for Federal office (including for Federal election activity) in a prior election cycle.

(e) If a State, district, or local committee of a political party or any person described in paragraph (b) of this section has actual knowledge that the certification is false, the certification may not be relied upon.

(f) It is not prohibited for a State, district, or local committee of a political party or its agents to respond to a request for information about a tax-exempt group that shares the party's political or philosophical goals.

§300.52 Fundraising by Federal candidates and Federal officeholders (2 U.S.C. 441i(e)(1)&(4)).

A Federal candidate, an individual holding Federal office, and an individual agent acting on behalf of either may make the following solicitations of funds on behalf of any organization described in 26 U.S.C. 501(c) and exempt from taxation under 26 U.S.C. 501(a), or an organization that has submitted an application for determination of tax-exempt status under 26 U.S.C. 501(c):

(a) *General solicitations.* A Federal candidate, an individual holding Federal office, or an individual agent acting on behalf of either, may make a general solicitation of funds, without regard to source or amount limitation, if:

(1) The organization does not engage in activities in connection with an election, including any activity described in paragraph (c) of this section; or

(2)(i) The organization conducts activities in connection with an election, but the organization's principal purpose is not to conduct election activities or any activity described in paragraph (c) of this section; and

(ii) The solicitation is not to obtain funds for activities in connection with an election or any activity described in paragraph (c) of this section.

(b) *Specific solicitations.* A Federal candidate, an individual holding Federal office, or an individual agent acting on behalf of either, may make a solicitation explicitly to obtain funds for any activity described in paragraph (c) of this section or for an organization whose principal purpose is to conduct that activity, if:

(1) The solicitation is made only to individuals; and

(2) The amount solicited from any individual does not exceed $20,000 during any calendar year.

(c) *Voter registration, voter identification, get-out-the-vote activity and generic campaign activity.* This section applies to only the following types of Federal election activity:

(1) Voter registration activity, as described in 11 CFR 100.24(a)(2), during the period that begins on the date that is 120 days before the date a regularly scheduled Federal election is held and ends on the date of the election; or

(2) The following activities conducted in connection with an election in which one or more Federal candidates appear on the ballot (*see* 11 CFR 100.24(a)(1)), regardless of whether one or more State candidates also appears on the ballot:

(i) Voter identification as described in 11 CFR 100.24(a)(4);

(ii) Get-out-the-vote activity as described in 11 CFR 100.24(a)(3); or

§ 300.60

(iii) Generic campaign activity as defined in 11 CFR 100.25.

(d) *Prohibited solicitations.* A Federal candidate, an individual holding Federal office, and an individual who is an agent acting on behalf of either, must not make any solicitation on behalf of any organization described in 26 U.S.C. 501(c) and exempt from taxation under 26 U.S.C. 501(a), or an organization that has submitted an application for determination of tax-exempt status under 26 U.S.C. 501(c) for any election activity other than a Federal election activity as described in paragraph (c) of this section.

(e) *Safe Harbor.* In determining whether a 501(c) organization is one whose principal purpose is to conduct election activities, including activity described in paragraph (c) of this section, a Federal candidate, an individual holding Federal office, or an individual agent acting on behalf of either, may obtain and rely upon a certification from the organization that satisfies the following criteria:

(1) The certification is a signed written statement by an officer or other authorized representative of the organization with knowledge of the organization's activities;

(2) The certification states that the organization's principal purpose is not to conduct election activities, including election activity described in paragraph (c) of this section; and

(3) The certification states that the organization does not intend to pay debts incurred from the making of expenditures or disbursements in connection with an election for Federal office (including for Federal election activity) in a prior election cycle.

(f) If a Federal candidate, an individual holding Federal office, or an individual agent acting on behalf of either has actual knowledge that the certification is false, the certification may not be relied upon.

Subpart D—Federal Candidates and Officeholders

§ 300.60 Scope (2 U.S.C. 441i(e)(1)).

This subpart applies to:

(a) Federal candidates;

(b) Individuals holding Federal office (*see* 11 CFR 300.2(o));

(c) Agents acting on behalf of a Federal candidate or individual holding Federal office; and

(d) Entities that are directly or indirectly established, financed, maintained, or controlled by, or acting on behalf of, one or more Federal candidates or individuals holding Federal office.

§ 300.61 Federal elections (2 U.S.C. 441i(e)(1)(A)).

No person described in 11 CFR 300.60 shall solicit, receive, direct, transfer, spend, or disburse funds in connection with an election for Federal office, including funds for any Federal election activity as defined in 11 CFR 100.24, unless the amounts consist of Federal funds that are subject to the limitations, prohibitions, and reporting requirements of the Act.

§ 300.62 Non-Federal elections (2 U.S.C. 441i(e)(1)(B)).

A person described in 11 CFR 300.60 may solicit, receive, direct, transfer, spend, or disburse funds in connection with any non-Federal election, only in amounts and from sources that are consistent with State law, and that do not exceed the Act's contribution limits or come from prohibited sources under the Act.

§ 300.63 Exception for State party candidates (2 U.S.C. 441i(e)(2)).

Section 300.62 shall not apply to a Federal candidate or individual holding Federal office who is a candidate for State or local office, if the solicitation, receipt or spending of funds is permitted under State law; and refers only to that State or local candidate, to any other candidate for that same State or local office, or both. If an individual is simultaneously running for both Federal and State or local office, the individual must raise, accept, and spend only Federal funds for the Federal election.

§ 300.64 Exemption for attending, speaking, or appearing as a featured guest at fundraising events (2 U.S.C. 441i(e)(3)).

Notwithstanding the provisions of 11 CFR 100.24, 300.61 and 300.62, a Federal candidate or individual holding Federal office may attend, speak, or be a featured guest at a fundraising event for a State, district, or local committee of a political party, including but not limited to a fundraising event at which Levin funds are raised, or at which non-Federal funds are raised. In light of the foregoing:

(a) State, district, or local committees of a political party may advertise, announce or otherwise publicize that a Federal candidate or individual holding Federal office will attend, speak, or be a featured guest at a fundraising event, including, but not limited to, publicizing such appearance in pre-event invitation materials and in other party committee communications; and

(b) Candidates and individuals holding Federal office may speak at such events without restriction or regulation.

§ 300.65 Exceptions for certain tax-exempt organizations (2 U.S.C. 441i(e)(1) and (4)).

A Federal candidate, an individual holding Federal office, and an individual agent acting on behalf of either may make the following solicitations of funds on behalf of any organization described in 26 U.S.C. 501(c) and exempt from taxation under 26 U.S.C. 501(a), or an organization that has submitted an application for determination of tax-exempt status under 26 U.S.C. 501(c):

(a) *General solicitations.* A Federal candidate, an individual holding Federal office or an individual agent acting on behalf of either, may make a general solicitation of funds, without regard to source or amount limitation, if:

(1) The organization does not engage in activities in connection with an election, including any activity described in paragraph (c) of this section; or

(2)(i) The organization conducts activities in connection with an election, but the organization's principal purpose is not to conduct election activities or any activity described in paragraph (c) of this section; and

(ii) The solicitation is not to obtain funds for activities in connection with an election or any activity described in paragraph (c) of this section.

(b) *Specific solicitations.* A Federal candidate, an individual holding Federal office, or an individual agent acting on behalf of either, may make a solicitation explicitly to obtain funds for any activity described in paragraph (c) of this section or for an organization whose principal purpose is to conduct that activity, if:

(1) The solicitation is made only to individuals; and

(2) The amount solicited from any individual does not exceed $20,000 during any calendar year.

(c) *Voter registration, voter identification, get-out-the-vote activity and generic campaign activity.* This section applies to only the following types of Federal election activity:

(1) Voter registration activity, as described in 11 CFR 100.24(a)(2), during the period that begins on the date that is 120 days before the date a regularly scheduled Federal election is held and ends on the date of the election; or

(2) The following activities conducted in connection with an election in which one or more Federal candidates appear on the ballot (see 11 CFR 100.24(a)(1)), regardless of whether one or more State candidates also appears on the ballot:

(i) Voter identification as described in 11 CFR 100.24(a)(4);

(ii) Get-out-the-vote activity as described in 11 CFR 100.24(a)(3); or

(iii) Generic campaign activity as defined in 11 CFR 100.25.

(d) *Prohibited solicitations.* A Federal candidate, an individual holding Federal office, and an individual who is an agent acting on behalf of either, must not make any solicitation on behalf of any organization described in 26 U.S.C. 501(c) and exempt from taxation under 26 U.S.C. 501(a), or an organization that has submitted an application for determination of tax-exempt status under 26 U.S.C. 501(c) for any election activity other than a Federal election activity as described in paragraph (c) of this section.

(e) *Safe Harbor.* In determining whether a 501(c) organization is one whose principal purpose is to conduct election activities, including activity described in paragraph (c) of this section, a Federal candidate, an individual holding Federal office, or an individual agent acting on behalf of either may obtain and rely upon a certification from the organization that satisfies the following criteria:

(1) The certification is a signed written statement by an officer or other authorized representative of the organization with knowledge of the organization's activities;

(2) The certification states that the organization's principal purpose is not to conduct election activities, including election activities described in paragraphs (c) of this section.

(3) The certification states that the organization does not intend to pay debts incurred from the making of expenditures or disbursements in connection with an election for Federal office (including for Federal election activity) in a prior election cycle.

(f) If a Federal candidate, an individual holding Federal office, or an individual agent acting on behalf of either has actual knowledge that the certification is false, the certification may not be relied upon.

Subpart E—State and Local Candidates

§ 300.70 Scope (2 U.S.C. 441i(f)(1)).

This subpart applies to any candidate for State or local office, individual holding State or local office, or an agent acting on behalf of any such candidate or individual. For example, this subpart applies to an individual holding Federal office who is a candidate for State or local office. This subpart does not apply to an association or similar group of candidates for State or local office or of individuals holding State or local office.

§ 300.71 Federal funds required for certain public communications (2 U.S.C. 441i(f)(1)).

No individual described in 11 CFR 300.70 shall spend any funds for a public communication that refers to a clearly identified candidate for Federal office (regardless of whether a candidate for State or local office is also mentioned or identified), and that promotes or supports any candidate for that Federal office, or attacks or opposes any candidate for that Federal office (regardless of whether the communication

expressly advocates a vote for or against a candidate) unless the funds consist of Federal funds that are subject to the limitations, prohibitions, and reporting requirements of the Act. *See* definition of *public communication* at 11 CFR 100.26

§ 300.72 Federal funds not required for certain communications (2 U.S.C. 441i(f)(2)).

The requirements of section 11 CFR 300.71 shall not apply if the public communication is in connection with an election for State or local office, and refers to one or more candidates for State or local office or to a State or local officeholder but does not promote, support, attack, or oppose any candidate for Federal office.

PART 400—INCREASED LIMITS FOR CANDIDATES OPPOSING SELF-FINANCED CANDIDATES

Subpart A—Scope and Definitions

Federal Election Commission **§ 400.4**

400.31 Preventing disproportionate advantage resulting from increased contribution and coordinated party expenditure limits.
400.32 Effect of the withdrawal of an opposing candidate.

Subpart D—Calculation of Increased Limits for Senate and House of Representatives Candidates

400.40 Calculating the increased limits for Senate elections.
400.41 Calculating the increased limits for House of Representatives elections.
400.42 Effect of increased limits on the aggregate contribution limitations for individuals.

Subpart E—Disposal of Excess Contributions

400.50 Definition of Excess contributions.
400.51 Relation of excess contributions to the election in which they are made.
400.52 Prohibition against redesignation of excess contributions.
400.53 Disposal of excess contributions.
400.54 Notification of disposal of excess contributions.

AUTHORITY: 2 U.S.C. 431, 434(a)(6), 438(a)(8), 441a(i), 441a(j), 441a–1.

SOURCE: 68 FR 3997, Jan. 27, 2003, unless otherwise noted.

EFFECTIVE DATE NOTE: At 68 FR 3997, Jan. 27, 2003, part 400 was added, effective Feb. 26, 2003.

Subpart A—Scope and Definitions

§ 400.1 Scope and effective date.

(a) *Introduction.* This part applies to elections to the office of United States Senator, or Representative in, or Delegate or Resident Commissioner to, the Congress, in which a candidate is permitted increased limits to allow response to certain expenditures from personal funds by an opposing candidate. This part does not apply to elections to the Office of President or Vice President of United States.

(b) *Effective dates.* Except as otherwise specifically provided in this part, this part shall take effect on February 26, 2003.

§ 400.2 Election cycle.

(a) For purposes of this part, *election cycle* means the period beginning on the day after the date of the most recent election for the specific office or seat that a candidate is seeking and ending on the date of the next election for that office or seat.

(b) For purposes of paragraph (a) of this section, a primary election and a general election are considered to be separate election cycles.

(c) For purposes of this part, a run-off election is considered to be part of the election cycle of the election necessitating the run-off election.

§ 400.3 Opposing candidate.

(a) For purposes of a primary election, *opposing candidate* means another candidate seeking the nomination of the same political party for election to the office of Senator, or Representative in, or Delegate or Resident Commissioner to, the Congress, that the candidate is seeking. A candidate in a primary election may have more than one opposing candidate.

(b) For purposes of a general election, *opposing candidate* means another candidate seeking election to the same office of Senator, or Representative in, or Delegate or Resident Commissioner to, the Congress, that the candidate is seeking. A candidate in a general election may have more than one opposing candidate.

§ 400.4 Expenditure from personal funds.

(a) *Expenditure from personal funds* means the aggregation of all the following:

(1) An expenditure made by a candidate, using the candidate's personal funds, for the purpose of influencing the election in which he or she is a candidate;

(2) A contribution or loan made by a candidate to the candidate's authorized committee, using the candidate's personal funds (*see* 11 CFR 100.33 for definition of *personal funds*);

(3) A loan by any person to the candidate's authorized committee that is secured using the candidate's personal funds. (*see* 11 CFR 100.33 for definition of *personal funds*); and

(4) Any obligation to make an expenditure from personal funds that is legally enforceable against the candidate.

(b) An expenditure from personal funds shall be considered to be made on

§ 400.5

the date the funds are deposited into the account designated by the candidate's authorized committee as the campaign depository, under 11 CFR 103.1 and 11 CFR 103.2, on the date the instrument transferring the funds is signed, or on the date the contract obligating the personal funds is executed, whichever is earlier.

§ 400.5 Applicable limit.

Applicable limit means the contribution amount limitation set forth in 11 CFR 110.1(b)(1).

§ 400.6 Increased limit.

Increased limit means a contribution amount limitation that applies to a person other than a multicandidate political committee that, pursuant to this part, exceeds the applicable limit specified in 11 CFR 110.1 in order to allow response to expenditures from an opposing candidate's personal funds. *Increased limit* also means, where applicable, a suspension, pursuant to this part, of the limitations on expenditures by a national or State political party committee in connection with the general election campaign of a candidate for the Senate or the House of Representatives under 11 CFR 109.32(b).

§ 400.7 Contribution that exceeds the applicable limit.

Amount of contribution above the applicable limit means the difference between the amount of a contribution accepted under this part and the applicable limit.

§ 400.8 Gross receipts.

Gross receipts means the sum of all receipts of the candidate's authorized committee described in 11 CFR 104.3(a)(3) (i) through (x).

§ 400.9 Threshold amount.

(a) *Senate.* For an election to the office of United States Senator, *threshold amount* means the sum of $150,000 plus an amount equal to the voting age population of the State multiplied by $0.04. As used in this paragraph, voting age population means the voting age population of the State of the candidate as certified under 11 CFR 110.18.

(b) *House of Representatives.* For an election to the office of Representative

in, or Delegate or Resident Commission to, the Congress, *threshold amount* means $350,000.

§ 400.10 Opposition personal funds amount.

(a) To compute the *opposition personal funds amount,* one of the following formulas must be used, depending on the date of the computation. The variables used in the formulas are defined in paragraph (b) of this section.

(1) To compute the opposition personal funds amount prior to July 16 of the year preceding the year in which the general election is held, the following formula must be used:

opposition personal funds amount = $a - b$.

(2) To compute the opposition personal funds amount from July 16 of the year preceding the year in which the general election is held to January 31 of the year in which the general election is held, one of the following formulas must be used:

(i) If $c > d$, opposition personal funds amount = $a - b - ((c - d) \div 2)$.

(ii) If $c \leq d$, opposition personal funds amount = $a - b$.

(3) To compute the opposition personal funds amount from February 1 of the year in which the general election is held to the day of the general election, one of the following formulas must be used:

(i) If $e > f$, opposition personal funds amount = $a - b - ((e - f) \div 2)$.

(ii) If $e \leq f$, opposition personal funds amount = $a - b$.

(b) *Variables.* The variables used in the formulas set out in paragraph (a) of this section are defined as follows:

a = Greatest aggregate amount of expenditures from personal funds made by the opposing candidate in the same election.

b = Greatest aggregate amount of expenditures from personal funds made by the candidate in the same election.

c = Aggregate amount of the gross receipts of the candidate's authorized committee minus any contributions by the candidate from personal funds as reported under 11 CFR 104.19(b)(1)(v) or (vi), during any election cycle that may be expended in connection with the election for the nomination for election, or election, to Federal office sought, as determined on June 30 of the year preceding the year in which the general election is held.

Federal Election Commission §400.21

d = Aggregate amount of the gross receipts of the opposing candidate's authorized committee minus any contributions by that opposing candidate from personal funds as reported under 11 CFR 104.19(b)(1)(v) or (vi), during any election cycle that may be expended in connection with the election for the nomination for election, or election, to Federal office sought, as determined on June 30 of the year preceding the year in which the general election is held.

e = Aggregate amount of the gross receipts of the candidate's authorized committee minus any contributions by the candidate from personal funds as reported under 11 CFR 104.19(b)(2)(v) or (vi), during any election cycle that may be expended in connection with the election for the nomination for election, or election, to Federal office sought, as determined on December 31 of the year preceding the year in which the general election is held.

f = Aggregate amount of the gross receipts of the opposing candidate's authorized committee minus any contributions by that opposing candidate from personal funds as reported under 11 CFR 104.19(b)(2)(v) or (vi), during any election cycle that may be expended in connection with the election for the nomination for election, or election, to Federal office sought, as determined on December 31 of the year preceding the year in which the general election is held.

Subpart B—Notification and Reporting Requirements

§400.20 Declaration of intent.

(a) *Senate and House of Representatives*—(1) *When and where filed.* Within 15 days of becoming candidate, the candidate must file a Declaration of Intent with the Commission and with each opposing candidate.

(2) *Contents of declaration.* The Declaration of Intent must state the total amount of expenditures from personal funds that the candidate intends to make with respect to the election that will exceed the threshold amount as defined in 11 CFR 400.9. A candidate who does not intend to make expenditures from personal funds that will exceed the threshold amount as defined in 11 CFR 400.9 may state the amount as $0.

(b) *Methods of filing*—(1) *Senate.* Declarations of Intent must be noted on the candidate's Statement of Candidacy, FEC Form 2. (*See* 11 CFR 101.1.) The candidate must send a copy of his or her Statement of Candidacy to the Commission using a facsimile machine

or electronic mail in addition to filing his or her official copy of the Statement of Candidacy on paper with the Secretary of the Senate. The candidate must send by facsimile machine or electronically mail his or her FEC Form 2 or the information required therein by 11 CFR 101.1, including the amount by which the candidate intends to exceed the threshold amount, to each opposing candidate.

(2) *House of Representatives.* Declarations of Intent must be noted on the candidate's Statement of Candidacy, FEC Form 2. (*See* 11 CFR 101.1.) FEC Form 2 must be filed electronically in accordance with 11 CFR 104.18 if the candidate intends to exceed the threshold amount defined in 11 CFR 400.9(b). Candidates must send by facsimile machine or electronically mail his or her FEC Form 2 or the information required therein by 11 CFR 101.1, including the amount by which he or she intends to exceed the threshold amount, to each opposing candidate.

§400.21 Initial notification of expenditures from personal funds.

(a) *Senate.* A candidate's principal campaign committee must notify the Secretary of the Senate, the Commission, and each opposing candidate when the candidate makes an expenditure from personal funds with respect to the election that causes the candidate's aggregate expenditures from personal funds to exceed two times the threshold amount as defined in 11 CFR 400.9. Such notification must be received by the Secretary of the Senate, the Commission, and each opposing candidate within 24 hours of the time such expenditure is made.

(b) *House of Representatives.* A candidate's principal campaign committee must notify the Commission, each opposing candidate, and the national party of each opposing candidate when the candidate makes an expenditure from personal funds with respect to the election that causes the candidate's aggregate expenditures from personal funds to exceed the $350,000 threshold amount (*see* 11 CFR 400.9). Such notification must be received by the Commission, each opposing candidate, and the national party of each opposing

§ 400.22

candidate within 24 hours of the time such expenditure is made.

§ 400.22 Additional notification of expenditures from personal funds.

(a) *Senate.* After filing the initial notification of expenditures from personal funds under 11 CFR 400.21, a candidate's principal campaign committee must notify the Secretary of the Senate, the Commission, and each opposing candidate when the candidate makes expenditures from personal funds in connection with the election exceeding $10,000. Such notification must be received by the Secretary of the Senate, the Commission, and each opposing candidate within 24 hours of the time such expenditures are made.

(b) *House of Representatives.* After filing the initial notification of expenditures from personal funds under 11 CFR 400.21, a candidate's principal campaign committee must notify the Commission, each opposing candidate, and the national party of each opposing candidate when the candidate makes expenditures from personal funds in connection with the election exceeding $10,000. Such notification must be received by the Commission, each opposing candidate, and the national party of each opposing candidate within 24 hours of the time such expenditures are made.

§ 400.23 Contents of notifications of expenditures from personal funds.

Each notification filed under 11 CFR 400.21 and 400.22 must contain the following information:

(a) The name of the candidate making the expenditures from personal funds.

(b) The office sought by the candidate making the expenditures from personal funds, including the State and, for candidates for the House of Representatives, the District.

(c) The date and amount of each expenditure from personal funds made since the last notification filed pursuant to 11 CFR 400.21 or 400.22.

(d) The total amount of expenditures from personal funds the candidate has made (as defined in 11 CFR 400.4(e)) in connection with the election from the beginning of the election cycle to the date of the expenditure that is the reason for the notification.

§ 400.24 Methods of filing notifications.

(a) *Senate.* Each notification required to be filed by the candidate's principal campaign committee under 11 CFR 400.21(a) and 400.22 must be filed with the Secretary of the Senate on FEC Form 10. The candidate's principal campaign committee must send a copy of its FEC Form 10 by facsimile machine, as an attachment to an electronic mail, or as an electronic mail containing the information required in 11 CFR 400.23 to the Commission and to each opposing candidate.

(b) *House of Representatives.* Each notification required to be filed by the candidate's principal campaign committee under 11 CFR 400.21(b) and 400.22 must be filed with the Commission electronically on FEC Form 10. The candidate's principal campaign committee must send a copy of its FEC Form 10 to each opposing candidate and to the national party committee of each opposing candidate by facsimile machine, as an attachment to an electronic mail, or as an electronic mail containing the information required by 11 CFR 400.23.

§ 400.25 Reporting obligations of candidates and candidates' principal campaign committees.

Candidates must ensure that their principal campaign committees file all reports required under this part in a timely manner.

Subpart C—Determining When the Increased Limits Apply

§ 400.30 Receipt of notification of opposing candidate's expenditures from personal funds.

(a) *Applicable to Senate and to House of Representatives elections.* This section applies to elections to the office of United States Senator, and to the office of Representative in, or Delegate or Resident Commission to, the Congress.

(b) *Candidates and authorized committees.* (1) The candidate and the candidate's authorized committee must not accept, pursuant to this part, any contribution that exceeds the applicable limit, as defined in 11 CFR 400.7, until the candidate has received actual or constructive notification of an opposing candidate's expenditures from personal funds under subpart B of this part. The candidate and the candidate's authorized committee must calculate the opposition personal funds amount each time they receive an opposing candidate's notification of expenditures from personal funds under 11 CFR 400.21 or 400.22.

(2) Upon calculating the opposition personal funds amount, if the candidate or the candidate's authorized committee determines that such amount exceeds the appropriate threshold under 11 CFR 400.40 or 400.41 that permits national and State committees of political parties to make coordinated party expenditures that exceed the limitations set forth in 11 CFR 109.32, the candidate or the candidate's authorized committee must inform the Commission and the national and State committee of their political party of such opposition personal funds amount by facsimile machine or electronic mail within 24 hours of receipt of an opposing candidate's initial or additional notification of expenditure from personal funds.

(c) *Political party committees.* (1) A national or State committee of a political party (including a national Congressional campaign committee) must not make, pursuant to this part, coordinated party expenditures in connection with the general election campaign of a candidate in excess of the limits set forth in 11 CFR 109.32(b) until the political party committee has received actual or constructive notification under subpart B of this part and the opposition personal funds amount under paragraph (b) of this section indicating that the opposing candidate's expenditures from personal funds exceeds the applicable threshold amount set forth in 11 CFR 400.40 or 400.41.

(2) If the national or State committee of a political party makes coordinated party expenditures in excess of the limitations set forth in 11 CFR 109.32 pursuant to this part, the national or State committee of a political party must inform the Commission and the candidate on whose behalf such

expenditure is made, or the candidate's authorized committee, of the amount of such expenditures by facsimile machine or electronic mail within 24 hours of making such expenditures.

(d) *Constructive notification.* For purposes of this section, *constructive notification* means that the candidate, the candidate's authorized committee, or the national or State committee of the political party obtains a copy of the FEC Form 10 received by the Commission.

§ 400.31 **Preventing disproportionate advantage resulting from increased contribution and coordinated party expenditure limits.**

(a) *Applicability.* This section applies to elections to the office of United States Senator, and to the office of Representative in, or Delegate or Resident Commission to, the Congress.

(b) *Persons with responsibilities under this section.* A candidate and the candidate's authorized committee that accepts contributions under the increased limits pursuant to this part, and any national or State political party committee (including a national Congressional campaign committee) that makes coordinated party expenditures on behalf of the candidate under the increased expenditure limits pursuant to this part, must comply with this section.

(c) *Information to be monitored.* Any person described in paragraph (b) of this section must monitor all of the following amounts while accepting contributions, or making coordinated party expenditures, respectively, under the increased limits:

(1) The aggregate amount of contributions previously accepted by the candidate and the candidate's authorized committee under the increased limits.

(2) The aggregate amount of coordinated party expenditures in connection with the general election campaign of the candidate previously made by any political party committee under the increased limits.

(3) The opposition personal funds amount related to each opposing candidate.

(d) *Senate elections*—(1) *Responsibilities of candidates and their authorized committees*. (i) A candidate and the candidate's authorized committee must not accept that amount of any contribution above the applicable limit if the sum of that amount of the contribution above the applicable limit plus the aggregate amounts described in paragraphs (c)(1) of this section and the aggregate amounts described in paragraph (c)(2) of this section is greater than 110% of the opposition personal funds amount.

(ii) When the aggregate amounts described in paragraph (c)(1) of this section plus the aggregate amounts described in paragraph (c)(2) of this section exceed 110% of the opposition personal funds amount, the candidate or the candidate's authorized committee must inform the national and State committees of their political party and the Commission, by facsimile or electronic mail, of this information within 24 hours of reaching 110% of the opposition personal funds amount.

(2) *Responsibilities of the national and State committees of the political party.* A national or State political party committee must not make, pursuant to this part, a coordinated party expenditure in connection with a candidate's general election campaign in excess of the expenditure limitations under 11 CFR 109.32(b) if the sum of the amount of that expenditure plus the aggregate amounts described in paragraph (c)(1) of this section and the aggregate amounts described in paragraph (c)(2) of this section with regard to that candidate is greater than 110% of the opposition personal funds amount.

(e) *House of Representatives elections*—(1) *Responsibilities of candidates and their authorized committees.* (i) A candidate and the candidate's authorized committee must not accept that amount of any contribution above the applicable limit if the sum of that amount of the contribution above the applicable limit plus the aggregate amounts described in paragraphs (c)(1) of this section and the aggregate amounts described in paragraph (c)(2) of this section is greater than 100% of the opposition personal funds amount.

(ii) When the aggregate amounts described in paragraph (c)(1) of this sec-

tion plus the aggregate amounts described in paragraph (c)(2) of this section exceed 100% of the opposition personal funds amount, the candidate or the candidate's authorized committee must inform the national and State committees of their political party and the Commission, by facsimile machine or electronic mail, of this information within 24 hours of reaching 100% of the opposition personal funds amount.

(2) *Responsibilities of the national and State committees of the political party.* A national or State political party committee must not make, pursuant to this part, a coordinated party expenditure in connection with a candidate's general election campaign in excess of the expenditure limitations under 11 CFR 109.32(b) if the sum of the amount of that expenditure plus the aggregate amounts described in paragraph (c)(1) of this section and the aggregate amounts described in paragraph (c)(2) of this section with regard to that candidate is greater than 100% of the opposition personal funds amount.

§ 400.32   **Effect of the withdrawal of an opposing candidate.**

(a) *Applicability.* (1) This section applies to all elections covered by this part.

(2) This section applies when an opposing candidate, whose expenditures from personal funds allowed another candidate the benefit of increased limits pursuant to this part, ceases to be a candidate. For purposes of this section, an opposing candidate ceases to be a candidate as of the earlier of the following dates:

(i) The date on which the opposing candidate publicly announces that he or she will no longer be a candidate in that election for that office and ceases to conduct campaign activities with respect to that election; or,

(ii) The date on which the opposing candidate is, or becomes, ineligible for nomination or election to that office by operation of law.

(b) *Candidates.* A candidate and a candidate's authorized committee must not accept any contribution under the increased limits, pursuant to this part, to the extent that such increased limit is attributable to the opposing candidate who has ceased to be a candidate.

(c) *Party committees.* The national and State political party committees must not make any coordinated party expenditure in excess of the limits in 11 CFR 109.32(b), pursuant to this part, to the extent that such increased limit is attributable to an opposing candidate who has ceased to be a candidate.

Subpart D—Calculation of Increased Limits for Senate and House of Representatives Candidates

§ 400.40 **Calculating the increased limits for Senate elections.**

(a) *Applicability.* This section applies to candidates for election to the office of United States Senator.

(b) *Procedure.* To calculate the increased limits:

(1) Determine the opposition personal funds amount, as defined in 11 CFR 400.10.

(2) Determine the voting age population (VAP) of the State of the candidate, as defined in 11 CFR 110.18.

(3) Based on the opposition personal funds amount and the VAP, use the following table to determine the increased limits:

If the opposition personal funds amount is more than—	But less than or equal to—	The increased limit for contributions by individuals is—	The amount limitation on co-ordinated party committee expenditures is—
(i)($0.08 × VAP) + $300,000	($0.16 × VAP) + $600,000	3 × applicable limit	The limitation set forth in 11 CFR 109.32(b).
(ii)($0.16 × VAP) + $600,000	($0.40 × VAP) + $1,500,000	6 × applicable limit	The limitation set forth in 11 CFR 109.32(b).
(iii)($0.40 × VAP) + $1,500,000		6 × applicable limit	The limitation set forth in 11 CFR 109.32 (b) does not apply subject to the provisions of 11 CFR 400.31(d).

§ 400.41 **Calculating the increased limits for House of Representatives elections.**

(a) *Applicability.* This section applies to candidates for election to the office of Representative in, or Delegate or Resident Commissioner to, the Congress.

(b) *Increased limits.* Subject to subpart C of this part, if the opposition personal funds amount exceeds the threshold amount, $350,000, the following will apply:

(1) The increased limit for contributions by individuals is three times the applicable limit.

(2) The national and State party committee expenditure limitation under 11 CFR 109.32(b) on behalf of the candidate will not apply subject to the provisions of 11 CFR 400.31(e).

§ 400.42 **Effect of increased limits on the aggregate contribution limitations for individuals.**

(a) This section shall apply to all elections covered by this part.

(b) The portions of contributions made under the increased limits pursuant to this part that, when aggregated with previous contributions made by the same individual to the candidate or the candidate's authorized committee in the same election cycle, exceed the contribution limits in 11 CFR 110.1 shall not be aggregated with other contributions made by that same individual for purposes of applying the aggregate contribution limitations for individuals under 11 CFR 110.5. This paragraph (b) applies only to such contributions that are accepted during the period in which the candidate may accept contributions under the increased limits.

(c) Individual contributors who have reached their aggregate bi-annual contribution limitations to candidates and authorized committees of candidates under 11 CFR 110.5(b)(1)(i) may make contributions under this part if:

(1) The candidate who accepts the contribution may accept contributions that exceed the applicable limit under this part; and

(2) The amount of the contribution, when aggregated with other contributions made under this paragraph (c), does not exceed the amount that the candidate described in paragraph (c)(1) of this section may accept under this part *minus* the applicable limit.

Subpart E—Disposal of Excess Contributions

§ 400.50 Definition of excess contributions.

For purposes of this subpart, excess contributions mean contributions that are made under the increased limit, as defined in 11 CFR 400.6 in subpart B of this part, but not expended in connection with the election to which they relate.

§ 400.51 Relation of excess contributions to the election in which they are made.

(a) *Primary elections.* If the excess contributions were received during the primary election cycle, the candidate's authorized committee must refund the excess contributions within 50 days of the primary election in accordance with 11 CFR 400.53.

(b) *General elections.* If the excess contributions were received during the general election cycle, the candidate's authorized committee must refund the excess contributions within 50 days of the general election in accordance with 11 CFR 400.53.

(c) *Run-off elections.* For purposes of this section only, when a primary or general election results in a run-off election, the run-off election is considered part of the respective primary or general election. Notwithstanding paragraphs (a) and (b) of this section, the candidate's authorized committee must refund the excess contributions within 50 days of the run-off election in accordance with 11 CFR 400.53.

§ 400.52 Prohibition against redesignation of excess contributions.

(a) The candidate's authorized committee shall not redesignate or seek redesignation of excess contributions under 11 CFR 110.1(b)(5).

(b) Once an individual has made a contribution under the increased limits, the individual must not redesignate the contribution for another election.

§ 400.53 Disposal of excess contributions.

(a) The candidate's authorized committee must refund the excess contributions to individuals who made contributions to the candidate or the candidate's authorized committee under this part. The refund to each individual must not exceed that individual's aggregate contributions to the candidate or the candidate's authorized committee for the relevant election cycle.

(b) The amount of any refund checks, made under paragraph (a) of this section that are not cashed, deposited, or otherwise negotiated within 6 months of the date of the refund check must be disgorged to the United States Treasury. The candidate's authorized committee must disgorge this amount to the United States Treasury within nine months of the election.

§ 400.54 Notification of disposal of excess contributions.

The candidate's principal campaign committee shall submit to the Commission information indicating the source and amount of any excess contributions (*see* 11 CFR 400.50) and the manner in which the candidate, the candidate's principal campaign committee, or the candidate's authorized committee refunded such funds. This information shall be included in the first report that the principal campaign committee is required to file, under 11 CFR 104.5, the date of which falls more than 50 days after the election for which a candidate seeks nomination for election to, or election to, Federal office. Such report must be submitted with the candidate's FEC Form 3.

The Millionaire's Amendment: A Hypothetical Offered by the FEC

Millionaires' Amendment Hypothetical

In an effort to provide a better understanding of the manner in which the various provisions of the Millionaires' Amendment would operate in the context of a primary and general election, the Commission presents the following hypothetical example. All candidates in the following example are fictional and any similarities to past or present candidates or elections for Federal office are purely coincidental. The contribution and coordinated party expenditure limits in the example will probably be different in subsequent years due to indexing for inflation.

Statement of Candidacy

For months, local newspapers had been speculating about the possibility that Frank Rogers, an independently wealthy investment banker from New Franklin, was planning to enter the race for the Democratic Party's nomination for the U.S. Senate. Some of Rogers's most ardent supporters had already formed a committee, called the "Draft Frank Rogers Committee" and had been soliciting contributions on behalf of his potential candidacy. By February 1, 2003, the Draft Frank Rogers Committee ("Committee") had received contributions aggregating in excess of $5,000. On February 15, 2003, Rogers received a letter from the Federal Election Commission ("FEC" or "Commission") notifying him of the Committee's efforts on his behalf and informing Rogers that, unless he disavowed the Committee's activities within 30 days of receiving the Commission's notification, the Commission would consider Frank Rogers to be a candidate, under 11 CFR 100.3(a).

On March 3, 2003, Frank Rogers filed a Statement of Candidacy on FEC Form 2 and designated a principal campaign committee by filing a Statement of Organization on FEC Form 1, pursuant to 11 CFR 102.12 and 102.2, respectively. Because Rogers was running for the Senate, he was required to file the original FEC Form 2 and FEC Form 1 with the Secretary of the United States Senate, under 11 CFR 105.2. Rogers noticed that he was also required to send a copy of FEC Form 2 (but not FEC Form 1) to the Commission and to each opposing candidate in the same election, under 11 CFR 400.20.

When he began to fill out the forms, Rogers noticed that they had changed since the last time he had seen them, a year earlier, when he considered but decided against a race for Federal office. In addition to the information Form 2 used to require (name, address, party affiliation, office sought, etc.), he was now also required to state a dollar figure representing the amount of his personal funds that he intended to spend on behalf of his campaign in excess of a certain "threshold amount," as defined in 11 CFR 400.9. In addition, the new Form 1 required Rogers' principal campaign committee to provide either its electronic mail address or its facsimile number. Rogers completed Form 1 first and then turned his attention to FEC Form 2.

Rogers retrieved his copy of the Code of Federal Regulations and determined that, for Senate candidates like him, the threshold amount was equal to the sum of $150,000 plus the product of the voting age population of his State (as certified under 11 CFR 110.18) multiplied by $0.04. After looking at 11 CFR 110.18, Rogers realized that, in order to determine the voting age population of New Franklin, he needed to search the **Federal Register** for the most recent voting age population estimate published annually by the Department of Commerce. Considering that the voting age population of New Franklin was listed as 24,800,000, he calculated the threshold amount, as follows:

$150,000 + (24,800,000 × $0.04) = $1,142,000.

Rogers's personal fortune was estimated to be at least $500 million. Frank Rogers had determined that his campaign would need an initial infusion of $7.5 million of his personal funds. Rogers sincerely hoped he would not have to spend any more of his personal funds, but he was willing to spend more if necessary. Thus, on FEC Form 2, Rogers stated his intention to exceed the threshold amount by $6,358,000 ($7,500,000 − $1,142,000 threshold amount). In addition to filing the original FEC Form 2 and FEC Form 1 with the Secretary of the Senate, Rogers faxed a copy of FEC Form 2 to the Commission as required by 11 CFR 400.20. Considering that Rogers was the only candidate in the race at that point, he was not required to fax or e-mail a copy of FEC Form 2 to any opposing candidates.

On March 31, 2003, Arlene Miller announced her intention to oppose Frank Rogers for the Democratic Party's nomination for the U.S. Senate. Although Miller was not nearly as wealthy as Frank Rogers, she stated on her FEC Form 2 that she intended to exceed the threshold amount ($1,142,000) by $1,858,000. This meant that Miller intended to make expenditures from personal funds totaling $3,000,000 ($1,858,000 + $1,142,000 threshold amount). Miller also designated a principal campaign committee on FEC Form 1. Miller filed her original FEC Form 2 and FEC Form 1 with the Secretary of the Senate, faxed a copy of FEC Form 2 to the Commission, and sent an electronic copy of FEC Form 2 to opposing candidate Frank Rogers as an attachment to an e-mail message.

On April 3, 2003, Jim Hyer entered the Democratic primary race. Given his position as Chairman of the New Franklin Democratic Party, Hyer had high name recognition among party activists but almost no money. He was counting on his popularity with the state's Democratic Party activists to carry him to victory in the June 1, 2004, primary election. Within 15 days of becoming a candidate, Hyer filed his original FEC Form 2 and FEC Form 1 with the Secretary of the Senate, and faxed copies of FEC Form 2 to the Commission and to the Rogers and Miller campaigns. On FEC Form 2, Hyer indicated that he did not intend to spend any of his personal funds on the race.

On April 15, 2003, James Rockford, a venture capitalist, announced his intention to seek the Republican Party's nomination for the U.S. Senate. Rockford had made a fortune in the technology boom of the late 1990s (he was worth an estimated $20 billion) and was extremely well known throughout the state for his support of a popular statewide referendum, Proposition 895. At the time that Rockford announced his candidacy, he was the only candidate seeking the Republican Party's nomination. Within 15 days of becoming a candidate, Rockford filed his original FEC Form 2 and FEC Form 1 with the Secretary of the Senate. On FEC Form 2, Rockford stated that he intended to exceed the threshold amount ($1,142,000) by $148,858,000. This meant that Rockford intended to spend $150 million of his personal funds on the race ($148,858,000 = $150,000,000 − $1,142,000 threshold amount). The same day, Rockford

deposited $50 million in his authorized committee's account and filed an initial notification of expenditures from personal funds on FEC Form 10 with the Secretary of the Senate. Given that there were no opposing candidates vying for the Republican nomination, Rockford satisfied his remaining reporting obligations by faxing copies of his FEC Form 2 and FEC Form 10 to the Commission.

Initial Notification of Expenditure From Personal Funds

On April 4, 2003, the day after Hyer entered the race, Rogers immediately pumped $7.5 million of his personal funds into his authorized committee's account. Because $7.5 million was more than two times the threshold amount of $1,142,000, within 24 hours of depositing the funds, Rogers filed an initial notification of expenditures from personal funds on FEC Form 10 with the Secretary of the Senate and faxed a copy of the form to the FEC and to the Miller and Hyer campaigns, as required by 11 CFR 400.21, 400.23, and 400.24.

Miller's campaign received Rogers's notification on April 5, 2003. Miller responded by contributing to her authorized committee $3,000,000. Because a contribution from a candidate to the candidate's authorized committee was considered an expenditure of personal funds under 11 CFR 400.4 and because the total contribution amount ($3,000,000) exceeded two times the threshold amount (2 × $1,142,000 = $2,284,000), within 24 hours of making the loan, Miller was required to file a notification of expenditures from personal funds on FEC Form 10. On April 6, 2003, Miller filed her original FEC Form 10 with the Secretary of the Senate and faxed copies of the form to the Commission and to the Rogers and Hyer campaigns.

Miller was aware that once she received Rogers's initial notification, it was possible for her authorized committee to begin receiving contributions from individuals in excess of the usual $2,000 limit. She scrambled to do the necessary calculations to determine the increased limit. According to the procedure outlined in 11 CFR 400.40, Miller first needed to determine the "opposition personal funds amount," the computation of which is explained at 11 CFR 400.10.

Calculating the Opposition Personal Funds Amount for the Miller Campaign

Miller quickly noticed that there were three different formulas for calculating the opposition personal funds amount and that the appropriate formula depended on the date of calculation.

Because the date was April 7, 2003, she determined that the first formula was the correct one to use because April 7, 2003, was prior to July 16 of the year preceding the year in which the general election was to be held. (The general election was scheduled to be held on November 8, 2004.) According to the formula, the opposition personal funds amount on April 6, 2003 was equal to the greatest aggregate amount of expenditures from personal funds made by her opposing candidate (Rogers) minus the greatest aggregate amount of expenditures from personal funds made by her. Thus, as of April 7, 2003, the opposition personal funds amount was $7,500,000 minus $3,000,000, or $4,500,000. Miller notified her national and State party committees and the Commission of this calculation, as required by 11 CFR 400.30(b).

Calculating the Increased Contribution and Coordinated Party Expenditure Limits for the Miller Campaign

Miller returned to the table in 11 CFR 400.10 to continue calculating the increased limit. According to the table, if the opposition personal funds amount ($4,500,000) was greater than the sum of the product of $0.08 times the voting age population of New Franklin (24,800,000) plus $300,000 but less than or equal to the sum of the product of $0.16 times the voting age population of New Franklin (24,800,000) plus $600,000, then her authorized committee may accept three times the ordinary contribution limit of $2,000, or $6,000.

Miller made the following calculations:

($0.08 × 24,800,000) + $300,000 = $2,284,000
($0.16 × 24,800,000) + $600,000 = $4,568,000.

Because the opposition personal funds amount ($4,500,000) was between $2,284,000 and $4,568,000, the increased limit for individual contributions to Miller's authorized committee was $6,000 (three times the ordinary limit). According to the table, Miller's national party committee was also able to make coordinated expenditures on behalf of her campaign in connection with the general election. Miller located a copy of the March 2002 FEC Record, which contained a table showing the coordinated party expenditure limits for 2002 Senate nominees. Miller found the amount for New Franklin, $1,781,136, which represented $0.02 times the voting age population of New Franklin (24,800,000), indexed for inflation. Given that her national and State party

committees have a policy of not making coordinated expenditures before the primary election when there are multiple candidates vying for the Democratic Party's nomination, Miller knew that she could not count on any assistance from either committee until the general election.

Calculating the Proportionality Provision Amount for the Miller Campaign

Miller was all set to call her closest supporters to begin soliciting $6,000 checks when she suddenly realized that she and her authorized committee were required, under 11 CFR 400.31 to constantly monitor a certain proportion to make sure that the aggregate amount of contributions made under the increased limit never exceeded 110 percent of the opposition personal funds amount ($4,500,000). Miller made the calculation as follows: 1.10 × $4,500,000 = $4,950,000. She immediately started making calls, realizing that she could accept contributions under the increased limits only until the aggregate amount of such contributions to her campaign equaled $4,950,000.

Calculating the Opposition Personal Funds Amount for the Hyer Campaign

Having received Rogers's initial notification of expenditure from personal funds on April 5, 2003, and Miller's initial notification on April 6, 2003, Hyer set out to determine the increased contribution and coordinated party expenditure limits applicable to his campaign. In order to perform the necessary calculations, Hyer first needed to determine the opposition personal funds amount as of April 5, 2003.

Under 11 CFR 400.10, the opposition personal funds amount prior to June 30 of the year preceding the year in which the general election is held is the difference between the greatest aggregate amount of expenditures from personal funds made by the opposing candidate and the candidate himself in the same election. Hyer considered for a minute which of the three announced Senate candidates, Rogers, Miller, or Rockford, was his "opposing candidate," for purposes of the formula. He quickly ruled out Rockford because he realized that in the primary election cycle, he and Rockford were not seeking the nomination of the same political party.

Of the two remaining candidates, Hyer concluded that the contribution and coordinated expenditure limits would be much higher if Rogers were the opposing candidate. As of April 6, 2003, the aggregate amount of Rogers's expenditures from personal funds was $7.5 million while the aggregate amount of Miller's expenditures from personal funds was $3 million. Unlike Arlene Miller, Hyer had not yet made any expenditures from personal funds, so the aggregate amount of his expenditures was $0.00. Plugging these numbers into the formula, Hyer calculated the possible opposition personal funds amounts as follows:

Opposing candidate Rogers: $7,500,000 − $0.00 = $7,500,000

Opposing candidate Miller: $3,000,000 − $0.00 = $3,000,000

Thus, Hyer concluded that it would be to his advantage to consider Rogers to be his "opposing candidate" for purposes of determining the opposition personal funds amount. According to his calculations, the applicable opposition personal funds amount as of April 6, 2003, was $7.5 million. Hyer notified his national and State party committees and the Commission of this calculation, as required by 11 CFR 400.30(b).

Calculating the Increased Contribution and Coordinated Party Expenditure Limits for the Hyer Campaign

Hyer proceeded to calculate the increased contribution and coordinated party expenditure limits pursuant to the formulas in 11 CFR 400.40. Doing the necessary calculations according to the formulas in the table (illustrated below), Hyer determined that because the opposition personal funds amount ($7,500,000) was between $4,568,000 and $11,420,000, the increased limit for individual contributions to his campaign was $12,000 (six times the applicable limit ($2,000)).

($0.16 × 24,800,000 (VAP of New Franklin)) + $600,000 = $4,568,000

($0.40 × 24,800,000 (VAP of New Franklin)) + $1,500,000 = $11,420,000

Hyer also determined that the increased coordinated party expenditure limit applicable to his campaign was $1,781,136 (the greater of $20,000 or $0.02 times the voting age population of the State of New Franklin (24,800,000), as adjusted for inflation). Like Miller, Hyer was well aware of his party committees' policy of not making coordinated expenditures prior to the date of nomination when there was a contested primary.

Calculating the Proportionality Provision Amount for the Hyer Campaign

Before soliciting $12,000 checks, however, Hyer decided it would be wise to figure out the aggregate amount of contributions his committee could accept under the increased limit before it would become necessary, under 11 CFR 400.31, to refuse that portion of contributions made under the increased limit that exceeded the ordinary limit of $2,000. Given that the opposition personal funds amount as of April 6, 2003, was $7,500,000, Hyer made the following calculation: 1.10 × $7,500,000 = $8,250,000. Hyer began fundraising at once, knowing that he could accept contributions under the increased limits only until the aggregate amount all such contributions received by his campaign equaled $8,250,000.

Additional Notification of Expenditure from Personal Funds

Meanwhile, Frank Rogers was starting to flounder. His campaign had already spent the $7.5 million he had deposited on April 4th plus an additional $1,000,000 in contributions his authorized committee had received to date. He decided that, in order to remain competitive with Miller and Hyer, he had no choice but to commit more of his personal funds to the race. So, on June 30, 2003, Rogers deposited an additional $2,500,000 into his authorized committee's account. Because this expenditure from personal funds exceeded $10,000, within 24 hours of depositing the funds, Rogers was required to file an additional notification of expenditure from personal funds on FEC Form 10, under 11 CFR 400.22. As he did with the initial notification, Rogers filed the original form with the Secretary of the Senate, and faxed copies of the form to the FEC and the Miller and Hyer campaigns. Although this amount was in excess of the amount stated on Roger's FEC Form 2, he was *not* required to amend that form.

Calculating the New Opposition Personal Funds Amount for the Miller and Hyer Campaigns

The Miller and Hyer campaigns received Rogers's additional notification of expenditures from personal funds on July 1, 2003. The Miller and Hyer campaigns endeavored to determine how Rogers's increase in spending from personal funds might affect their increased contribution limits. Before figuring out their new limits, however, each campaign first had to recalculate the opposition personal funds amount.

Turning to the formulas in 11 CFR 400.10, each candidate realized that as soon as July 16 the applicable formula would no longer be the one that applied prior to July 16, 2003. With vacations taking many staffers and potential contributors away, both committees elected to wait until the new formulas were in effect before accepting any contributions. Once it was July 16, 2003, which was between July 16 of the year preceding the year in which the general election would be held and February 1 of the year in which the general election would be held, the formula required that the gross receipts advantage be taken into account.

Opposition Personal Funds Amount— Miller Campaign

To calculate the opposition personal funds amounts for the Miller campaign as of July 16, 2003, the following formula had to be used: $a - b - ((c - d) + 2)$, where:

(a) Represented the greatest amount of expenditures from personal funds made by the opposing candidate (Rogers) in the same election;

(b) Represented the greatest amount of expenditures from personal funds made by Miller in the same election;

(c) Represented the aggregate amount of the gross receipts of Miller's authorized committee, minus any contributions by Miller from personal funds, during any election cycle that may be expended in connection with the primary election, as determined on June 30 of the year (2003) preceding the year in which the general election was to be held (2004); and

(d) Represented the aggregate amount of the gross receipts of Rogers's authorized committee, minus any contributions by Rogers from personal funds, during any election cycle that may be expended in connection with the primary election, as determined on June 30, 2003.

Variable (a)—Miller Campaign

Considering each variable in turn, as of June 30, 2003, Rogers had made aggregate expenditures from personal funds in the amount of $10 million. So, as of that date, variable (a) in the formula for the Miller campaign equaled $10,000,000.

Variable (b)—Miller Campaign

As of June 30, 2003, Miller had made aggregate expenditures from personal funds in the amount of $3,000,000. Thus, as of that date, variable (b) in the formula for Miller's campaign equaled $3,000,000.

Variable (c)—Miller Campaign

As of June 30, 2003, Miller's authorized committee had received contributions in connection with the primary election totaling $4,000,000 and Miller's aggregate contributions from personal funds totaled $3,000,000. Accordingly, as of June 30, 2003, variable (c) in the formula for the Miller

campaign equaled $4,000,000 - $3,000,000, or $1,000,000.

Variable (d)—Miller Campaign

As of June 30, 2003, Rogers's authorized committee had received contributions in connection with the primary election totaling $11,000,000 and Rogers's aggregate contributions from personal funds totaled $10,000,000. Accordingly, as of June 30, 2003, variable (d) in the formula for the Miller campaign equaled $11,000,000 - $10,000,000, or $1,000,000.

Plugging the above numbers into the applicable formula $(a - b - ((c - d) + 2))$, the opposition personal funds amount for the Miller campaign as of June 30, 2003, was $7,000,000, calculated as follows:

$10,000,000 - $3,000,000 - (($1,000,000 - $1,000,000)/2) = $7,000,000.

Opposition Personal Funds Amount— Hyer Campaign

To calculate the opposition personal funds amounts for the Hyer campaign as of July 16, 2003, the following formula had to be used: $a - b - ((c - d) + 2)$, where:

(a) Represented the greatest amount of expenditures from personal funds made by the opposing candidate (Rogers) in the same election;

(b) Represented the greatest amount of expenditures from personal funds made by Hyer in the same election;

(c) Represented the aggregate amount of the gross receipts of Hyer's authorized committee, minus any contributions by Hyer from personal funds, during any election cycle that may be expended in connection with the primary election, as determined on June 30 of the year (2003) preceding the year in which the general election was to be held (2004); and

(d) Represented the aggregate amount of the gross receipts of Rogers's authorized committee, minus any contributions by Rogers from personal funds, during any election cycle that may be expended in connection with the primary election, as determined on June 30, 2003.

Variable (a)—Hyer Campaign

Considering each variable in turn, as of June 30, 2003, Rogers had made aggregate expenditures from personal funds in the amount of $10 million. So, as of that date, variable (a) in the formula for the Hyer campaign equaled $10,000,000.

Variable (b)—Hyer Campaign

As of June 30, 2003, Hyer had not made any expenditures from personal funds. Accordingly, as of that date, variable (b) in the formula for Hyer's campaign equaled $0.

Variable (c)—Hyer Campaign

As of June 30, 2003, Hyer's authorized committee had received contributions in connection with the primary election totaling $1,000,000 and Hyer's aggregate contributions from personal funds totaled $0. Accordingly, as of June 30, 2003, variable (c) in the formula for the Hyer campaign equaled $1,000,000 − $0, or $1,000,000.

Variable (d)—Hyer Campaign

As of June 30, 2003, Rogers's authorized committee had received contributions in connection with the primary election totaling $11,000,000 and Rogers's aggregate contributions from personal funds totaled $10,000,000. Accordingly, as of June 30, 2002, variable (d) in the formula for the Hyer campaign equaled $11,000,000 − $10,000,000, or $1,000,000.

Plugging the above numbers into the applicable formula $(a − b − ((c − d) + 2))$, the opposition personal funds amount for the Hyer campaign as of June 30, 2003, was $10,000,000, calculated as follows:

$10,000,000 − $0 − (($1,000,000 − $1,000,000 + 2) = $10,000,000.

Both Miller and Hyer notified their national and state party committees and the Commission of their calculations, as required by 11 CFR 400.30(b).

Calculating the New Contribution Limits for the Miller and Hyer Campaigns

After calculating the new opposition personal funds amount, the Miller and Hyer campaigns recalculated the new individual contribution limits as follows:

Contribution Limit—Miller Campaign

Because the opposition personal funds amount of $7,000,000 was greater than:

$4,568,000 = ($0.16 × 24,800,000 (VAP of New Franklin)) + $600,000

But less than or equal to:

$11,420,000 = ($0.40 × 24,800,000 (VAP of New Franklin)) + $1,500,000

Miller determined that the new increased contribution limit for the Miller campaign was:

$12,000 = 6 × $2,000 (the applicable limit).

Contribution Limit—Hyer Campaign

Because the opposition personal funds amount of $10,000,000 was greater than:

$4,568,000 = ($0.16 × 24,800,000 (VAP of New Franklin)) + $600,000

But less than or equal to:

$11,420,000 = ($0.40 × 24,800,000 (VAP of New Franklin)) + $1,500,000

Hyer determined that the new increased contribution limit for the Hyer campaign was the same as the old increased contribution limit:

$12,000 = 6 × $2,000 (the applicable limit).

Calculating the New Proportionality Provision Amount for the Miller and Hyer Campaigns

Before calling to solicit contributions under the new increased limits, however, both the Miller and Hyer campaigns sought to determine the maximum amount they could accept before being in danger of exceeding 110 percent of the new opposition personal funds amount in violation of the proportionality provision (11 CFR 400.31).

Proportionality Provision Amount—Miller Campaign

Taking into account the new opposition personal funds amount ($7,000,000), the Miller campaign determined that the new proportionality provision amount was $7,700,000, calculated as follows:

1.10 × $7,000,000 = $7,700,000

As of July 16, 2003, the Miller campaign had received $4,500,000 in contributions, $1,500,000 from contributors plus the $3,000,000 contribution from Miller's personal funds. Of the $1,500,000, the Miller Committee received $500,000 under the increased limits. Only this $500,000 of her committee's gross receipts counted towards the proportionality provision limit. Accordingly, the Miller campaign determined that it could receive another $7,200,000 ($7,700,000 limit − $500,000 already received) in contributions under the increased limit without violating the proportionality provision.

Proportionality Provision Amount—Hyer Campaign

As of July 16, 2003, the Hyer campaign had received $1,000,000 in contributions, $400,000 of which was received under the increased limits, well short of the old $5,500,000 maximum proportionality provision amount. Taking into account the new opposition personal funds amount

($10,000,000), the Hyer campaign determined that the new proportionality provision amount was $11,000,000, calculated as follows:

$1.10 \times \$10,000,000 = \$11,000,000$

Accordingly, the Hyer campaign determined that it could receive another $10,600,000 ($11,000,000 limit − $400,000 already received) in contributions under the increased limit without violating the proportionality provision.

Withdrawal of Opposing Candidate

As summer turned into fall and fall faded into winter, the polls consistently showed Miller with a double-digit lead over Rogers. The Hyer campaign polled in the single digits.

Rogers had already spent $10 million of his personal funds and, although willing to spend more, he did not want to do so unless there was a real chance that he might make some headway against Miller. Rogers figured that he could not gain ground against Miller. So, on December 20, 2003, Rogers held a press conference and announced his decision to quit the race.

Once the initial shock of Rogers's withdrawal from the race wore off, both Miller and Hyer realized that his departure might have a significant impact on their ability to raise funds for the last seven months of the primary campaign. Under 11 CFR 400.32, Rogers ceased to be a candidate on December 20, 2003, the date he publicly announced his withdrawal from the race. From that day forward, Miller was prohibited from accepting that portion of contributions made under the increased limits that exceeded the applicable limit ($2,000 per person) because it was Rogers's expenditures from personal funds that allowed her to receive contributions above the applicable limit in the first place. While her campaign was permitted to continue accepting contributions up to the applicable limit ($2,000 per individual), it would have to refuse any portion of any contribution above the applicable limit. Any amount above the applicable limit would have to be refunded to the contributor.

Calculating the New Opposition Personal Funds Amount for the Hyer Campaign

Rogers's withdrawal from the race affected the Hyer campaign differently than the Miller campaign. With Rogers out of the race, Hyer must now consider Miller to be his "opposing candidate" for purposes of calculating the opposition personal funds amount and the increased contribution limits. To determine the new opposition personal funds amount as of December 20, 2003, Hyer used the same formula he had used on July 16, 2003 $(a - b - ((c - d) \div 2))$, substituting Miller for Rogers, where:

(a) Represented the greatest amount of expenditures from personal funds made by the opposing candidate (Miller) in the same election;

(b) Represented the greatest amount of expenditures from personal funds made by Hyer in the same election;

(c) Represented the aggregate amount of the gross receipts of Hyer's authorized committee, minus any contributions by Hyer from personal funds, during any election cycle that may be expended in connection with the primary election, as determined on June 30 of the year (2003) preceding the year in which the general election was to be held (2004); and

(d) Represented the aggregate amount of the gross receipts of Miller's authorized committee, minus any contributions by Miller from personal funds, during any election cycle that may be expended in connection with the primary election, as determined on June 30, 2003.

Variable (a)—Hyer Campaign

Considering each variable in turn, as of June 30, 2003, Miller had made aggregate expenditures from personal funds in the amount of $3,000,000. So, as of that date, variable (a) in the formula for the Hyer campaign equaled $3,000,000.

Variable (b)—Hyer Campaign

As of June 30, 2003, Hyer had not made any expenditures from personal funds. Accordingly, as of that date, variable (b) in the formula for Hyer's campaign equaled $0.

Variable (c)—Hyer Campaign

As of June 30, 2003, Hyer's authorized committee had received contributions in connection with the primary election totaling $1,000,000 and Hyer's aggregate contributions from personal funds totaled $0. Accordingly, as of June 30, 2003, variable (c) in the formula for the Hyer campaign equaled $1,000,000 − $0, or $1,000,000.

Variable (d)—Hyer Campaign

As of June 30, 2003, Miller's authorized committee had received contributions in connection with the primary election totaling $4,000,000 and Miller's aggregate contributions from personal funds totaled $3,000,000. Accordingly, as of June 30, 2003, variable (d) in the formula for the Hyer

campaign equaled
$4,000,000 − $3,000,000, or $1,000,000.

Inserting the above numbers into the applicable formula $(a − b − ((c − d) ÷ 2))$, the opposition personal funds amount for the Hyer campaign as of December 20, 2003, was $3,000,000, calculated as follows:

$3,000,000 − $0 − (($1,000,000 − $1,000,000) ÷ 2) = $3,000,000

Hyer notified his national and State party committees and the Commission of this calculation, as required by 11 CFR 400.30(b).

Calculating the New Increased Contribution Limit for the Hyer Campaign

Hyer was optimistic that he would still be able to receive contributions above the applicable limit. Hyer performed the following calculations and determined that with the new opposition personal funds amount of $3,000,000, the new contribution limit applicable to his campaign was three times the applicable limit, or $6,000:

Opposition personal funds amount of $3,000,000 was more than * * *

$2,284,000 = ($0.08 × 24,800,000 (VAP of New Franklin)) + $300,000

But less than or equal to * * *

$4,568,000 = ($0.16 × 24,800,000 (VAP of New Franklin)) + $600,000

Calculating the New Proportionality Provision Amount for the Hyer Campaign

Before calling to solicit contributions under the new increased limit, however, the Hyer campaign sought to determine the maximum amount he could accept before being in danger of exceeding 110 percent of the new opposition personal funds amount in violation of the proportionality provision (11 CFR 400.31).

As of December 20, 2003, the Hyer campaign had received $1,200,000 in contributions, $750,000 of which was received under the increased limits. Taking into account the new opposition personal funds amount ($3,000,000), the Hyer campaign determined that the new proportionality provision amount was $3,300,000, calculated as follows:

1.10 × $3,000,000 = $3,300,000

Accordingly, the Hyer campaign determined that it could receive $2,550,000 ($3,300,000 limit − $750,000 already received) in contributions under the increased limit without violating the proportionality provision.

Reporting of Gross Receipts as of December 31, 2003

On January 31, 2004, the principal campaign committees of Arlene Miller, Jim Hyer, and James Rockford filed the reports required under 11 CFR 104.19(b)(2) disclosing gross receipts as of December 31, 2003. Frank Rogers's principal campaign committee did not have to file a report because he had withdrawn from the election.

Arlene Miller's principal campaign committee reported that it had received $6 million in gross receipts in connection with the primary. That $6 million included her $3 million contribution from personal funds. The committee also reported that it had $2 million in gross receipts that could be spent on the general election. This amount came from contributions it had received under the applicable limit that had been designated for the general election. Miller did not make any contribution from personal funds for the general election.

Jim Hyer's principal campaign committee disclosed that it had $1.2 million in gross receipts that could be spent for the primary. He did not make any contribution from personal funds. Additionally, the committee reported that it had no gross receipts for the general election.

James Rockford was a candidate for the Republican nomination for the Senate. His principal campaign committee was also required to file this report. It disclosed that it had received $50.3 million in gross receipts in connection with the primary including a $50 million contribution from Rockford's personal funds. The committee also reported that, as of December 31, 2003, it had $1.1 million in gross receipts for the general election, $1 million of which was a contribution from Rockford's personal funds made on December 15, 2003. The remaining $100,000 of the committee's gross receipts represented contributions from contributors other than Rockford.

The remaining months of the primary campaign were brutal. As the primary election day neared, polls showed Miller and Hyer in a statistical dead heat. On June 1, 2004, Miller received 47% of the vote, Hyer received 43% of the vote, and, despite the fact that he withdrew from the race more than five months before the primary election, 10% of New Franklin's Democratic primary voters wrote in Frank Rogers name. Because neither Miller nor Hyer received 50% or more of the vote, New Franklin law required that a run-off election be held.

The run-off election was scheduled for July 1, 2004. Neither campaign had much money left at this point because both had spent nearly every available dollar on a last-minute advertising blitz. The Miller campaign, however, was in a better position than the Hyer campaign. Whereas Hyer's authorized committee had only $25,000 cash on hand, Miller's authorized committee had $2,075,000 total cash on hand, but only $75,000 was available for the primary run-off. Both candidates wondered whether they were permitted to use any of these funds for the run-off election, though, considering that they were raised in the primary election cycle under the increased contribution limits. They turned to the definition of "election cycle" at 11 CFR 400.2, however, and determined that a run-off election was considered to be an extension of the election cycle containing the election that necessitated the run-off election. Thus, the Miller and Hyer campaigns were permitted to use the funds remaining from the primary election for the July 1, 2004, run-off election because the July 1, 2004, run-off was considered to be part of the June 1, 2004, primary election cycle.

On July 1, 2004, Arlene Miller won the run-off election and prepared to face off against James Rockford in the general election. Rockford ran unopposed in the Republican primary and managed to secure the Republican Party's nomination without spending more than $1 million of his personal funds. After winning the Republican endorsement, Rockford's authorized committee refunded the remaining $49 million to the candidate. (His contribution on December 15th of $1 million was for the general election.) Miller's authorized committee was completely out of primary cash by the time the run-off election ended.

General Election Campaign

The general election cycle got off to a raucous start. On July 2, 2004, Rockford used his own funds to purchase $20 million in air time, locking up key commercial slots in every major media market in the state through Labor Day. As required by 11 CFR 400.21, within 24 hours of executing the air time contract, Rockford filed an initial notification of expenditures from personal funds on FEC Form 10. He filed the original form with the Secretary of the Senate and faxed copies to the Commission and the Miller campaign.

When Miller received Rockford's initial notification on July 3, 2004, she scrambled to determine the opposition personal funds amount, under 11 CFR 400.10, and the increased contribution and party expenditure limits under 11 CFR 400.40.

Calculating the Opposition Personal Funds Amount for the Miller Campaign

Given that the date of computation was on or after December 31 of the year preceding the year in which the general election was to be held, the applicable formula was the one outlined in 11 CFR 400.10(a)(3) $(a - b - ((e - f) + (2))$, where:

(a) Represented the greatest aggregate amount of expenditures from personal funds made by Rockford in the general election ($21 million);

(b) Represented the greatest amount of expenditures from personal funds made by Miller in the general election ($0);

(e) Represented the aggregate amount of gross receipts of Miller's authorized committee ($2 million), minus any contributions by Miller from personal funds (Note: This amount is $0, because the $3 million Miller contributed to her authorized committee on April 5, 2003 was made in connection with the primary and entirely spent), during any election cycle that may be expended in connection with the general election, as determined on December 31, 2003; and

(f) Represented the aggregate amount of gross receipts of Rockford's authorized committee ($1.1 million), minus any contributions by Rockford from personal funds ($1 million), during any election cycle that may be expended in connection with the general election, as determined on December 31, 2003, so the July 2, 2004, $20 million expenditure is *not* included.

Miller determined the value of each variable as follows:

(a) = $21,000,000
(b) = $0.00
(e) = $2,000,000 ($2,000,000 − $0)
(f) = $100,000 ($1,100,000 − $100,000)

Inserting these above values into the applicable formula $(a - b - ((e - f) + (2))$, Miller determined that the opposition personal funds amount was $20,050,000, calculated as follows:

$21,000,000 − $0 − (($2,000,000 − $100,000) + (2) = $20,050,000

Miller notified her national and State party committees and the Commission of this calculation, as required by 11 CFR 400.30(b).

Calculating the Increased Contribution and Coordinated Party Expenditure Limits for the Miller campaign

Having determined that the opposition personal funds amount was $20,050,000, Miller determined that, because the opposition personal funds amount was more than $11,420,000 ($0.40 × 24,800,000 (VAP of New Franklin) + $1,500,000), the following increased contribution and coordinated party expenditure limits applied to her campaign, under 11 CFR 400.40:

Increased contribution limit
$12,000 (6 × $2,000 (applicable limit))
Coordinated party expenditure limit
Unlimited

Calculating the Proportionality Provision Amount for the Miller Campaign

Miller next calculated the aggregate amount of contributions her authorized committee would be able to receive before being in danger of exceeding 110 percent of the opposition personal funds amount ($20,050,000), under 11 CFR 400.31:

1.10 × $20,050,000 = $22,055,000

Miller started raising money in earnest. By the end of July, her campaign had managed to raise $4,500,000, $2,300,000 of which was received under the increased limits. In addition, sometime in the middle of the month, someone from the DSCC called to say they had not made any independent expenditures on her behalf, and wanted to make coordinated party expenditures to help her out. The DSCC official wanted to know what sort of help Miller needed most. Miller told the DSCC official that her campaign desperately needed air time in all of New Franklin's major media markets in order to compete with Rockford. The DSCC immediately purchased as much air time as was available between July 15, 2004, and Labor Day. The DSCC notified Miller that the total cost of the air time that the DSCC purchased on Miller's behalf was $19,753,000 above the coordinated party expenditure limit. Although the New Franklin State Democratic Committee could also spend above the ordinarily-applicable $1,781,136 coordinated party spending limit, Miller was told they planned to make no coordinated party expenditures on her behalf.

On August 1, 2004, Arlene Miller received a telephone call from Rex Duncan, an old college friend. Duncan said that he knew Miller was running against a self-financed candidate and he wanted to send her a contribution but he wasn't sure how much he was allowed to give. Duncan explained that, since Election Day 2002, he had made a number of contributions to other Federal candidates. As of August 1, 2004, the aggregate amount of Duncan's contributions was $35,500, just $2,000 shy of the aggregate 2-year limit of $37,500 for individual contributions to

Federal candidate committees under 2 U.S.C. 441a(a)(3)(A). He asked Miller how much he would be allowed to contribute to her campaign. Miller informed Duncan that only the first $2,000 of his contribution to any one Federal candidate counted against his 2-year aggregate limit, pursuant to 11 CFR 400.42. Any amount above the applicable limit given to candidates running against self-financing candidates was excluded from the calculation.

Nevertheless, Miller suspected that Duncan could not send her $12,000, however, because she knew that her campaign was getting close to a crucial limit of its own under the proportionality provision. Miller told Duncan that she would have to call him back after she figured out how much of his money her campaign could legally accept. Miller calculated the aggregate amount of contributions already received and coordinated party expenditures already made under the increased limits, as follows: $2,300,000 (contributions) + $19,753,000 (coordinated expenditures) = $22,053,000.

After performing these calculations, Miller realized that she could only accept $2,000 from Duncan above the applicable limit of $2,000. This meant that her campaign could accept a check from Duncan in the amount of $4,000 because, although the first $2,000 of his contribution would count against his 2-year aggregate limit of $37,500, it would not count against the Miller campaign's proportionality provision limit of $22,055,000. Miller called Duncan back and asked him to send her a check for $4,000.

Realizing that, under 11 CFR 400.31(d)(1)(ii), Miller or her authorized committee was required to notify the national and State committees of her political party and the Commission within 24 hours of the time her campaign reached the proportionality provision limit, Miller immediately sent electronic mail messages to the DSCC, the New Franklin Democratic Federal Campaign Committee, and the Commission. Both committees were now on notice that they could no longer make coordinated expenditures on behalf of Miller's general election campaign in excess of the coordinated expenditure limitation in 11 CFR 109.32(b).

Miller realized that, unless Rockford spent more of his personal funds on behalf of his campaign, from that point forward, her campaign could only accept contributions up to the applicable limit ($2,000 per individual). In addition, the national party committee would be prohibited from making any more coordinated expenditures on behalf of the Miller campaign, although it could still contribute up to $35,000 directly to her principal campaign committee.

On August 3, 2004, Rockford reluctantly used his personal funds to purchase $30 million worth of air time between Labor Day and Election Day. Disappointed that he was again using personal funds, Rockford deemed $20 million a contribution and $10 million a personal loan. As required, Rockford filed his original FEC Form 10 with the Secretary of the Senate and faxed copies of the form to the Commission and the Miller campaign. Miller scrambled to recalculate the new opposition personal funds amount and increased contribution and coordinated party expenditure limits.

Calculating the New Opposition Personal Funds Amount for the Miller Campaign

Given that the date of computation (August 4, 2004) was on or after February 1 of the year in which the general election was to be held, the applicable formula was the one outlined in 11 CFR 400.10(a)(3) $(a - b - ((e - f) \div 2))$, where:

(a) Represented the greatest aggregate amount of expenditures from personal funds made by Rockford in the general election ($51 million);

(b) Represented the greatest amount of expenditures from personal funds made by Miller in the general election ($0);

(e) Represented the aggregate amount of gross receipts of Miller's authorized committee ($2 million), minus any contributions by Miller from personal funds ($0), during any election cycle that may be expended in connection with the general election, as determined on December 31, 2003; and

(f) Represented the aggregate amount of gross receipts of Rockford's authorized committee ($1.1 million), minus any contributions by Rockford from personal funds ($1 million), during any election cycle that may be expended in connection with the general election, as determined on December 31, 2003.

Miller determined the value of each variable as follows:

(a) = $51,000,000
(b) = $0
(e) = $2,000,000 ($2,000,000 − $0)
(f) = $100,000 ($1,100,000 − $1,000,000)

Plugging these values into the applicable formula, Miller determined that the opposition personal funds amount was $45,750,000, calculated as follows:

$51,000,000 − $0 −
(($2,000,000 − $100,000) ÷ 2) =
$50,050,000
Miller notified her national and State party committees and the Commission of this calculation, as required by 11 CFR 400.30(b).

Calculating the New Increased Contribution and Coordinated Party Expenditure Limits for the Miller Campaign

Having determined that the opposition personal funds amount was $50,050,000, Miller determined that, because the opposition personal funds amount was more than $11,420,000 ($0.40 × 24,800,000 (VAP of New Franklin) + $1,500,000), the following increased contribution and coordinated party expenditure limits applied to her campaign, under 11 CFR 400.40:

Increased contribution limit—Miller campaign
$12,000 (6 × $2,000 (applicable limit))
Coordinated party expenditure limit—Miller campaign
Unlimited

Calculating the New Proportionality Provision Amount for the Miller Campaign

Miller next calculated the aggregate amount of contributions her authorized committee would be able to receive before being in danger of exceeding 110 percent of the opposition personal funds amount ($45,750,000), under 11 CFR 400.31:

1.10 × $50,050,000 = $55,055,000

As of August 4, 2004, the aggregate amount of contributions received under the increased limits (including Duncan's $2,000) and coordinated party expenditures made under the increased limits equaled $22,055,000. Accordingly, Miller's campaign could now receive an additional $33,000,000 ($55,055,000 − $22,055,000) in contributions and/or coordinated party expenditures. Miller immediately called her old friend Rex Duncan and told him that he could now send her campaign an additional $8,000 if he still wished to support her. Miller then received a call from a multicandidate political committee (PAC) wanting to know how much it could contribute to her campaign. She told the PAC's treasurer that she could accept up to $5,000, as the PAC's contribution limits had not been raised.

Prohibition on Redesignation of Contributions Received Above the Applicable Limit to Another Election Cycle

When the election was over, Miller's authorized committee had $50,000 in contributions accepted under the increased limit left in its campaign account. Looking ahead to the 2010 primary and general elections, Miller wondered whether it would be possible to redesignate the $50,000 to a future race, in the manner prescribed under 11 CFR 110.1(b)(5). Miller quickly determined, however, that redesignation of contributions received under the increased limits was strictly prohibited, under 11 CFR 400.52.

Disposal of Excess Contributions Received Above the Applicable Limit

Miller was puzzled about what her authorized committee was supposed to do with the extra $50,000 in contributions her committee had received during the general election cycle. Under 11 CFR 400.51, Miller's authorized committee was required to refund the excess contributions within 50 days of the general election. Miller's committee refunded the $50,000 in excess contributions to those individuals who had made increased contributions during the general election cycle, being careful to make sure that no individual contributor received a refund that exceeded the aggregate amount of their contributions to the Miller campaign, pursuant to 11 CFR 400.53.

Miller's committee was required to notify the Commission about the disposition of these excess contributions under 11 CFR 400.54. Information about the source and amount of these excess contributions and the manner in which the committee used the funds had to be included in the first report that was due more than 50 days after the general election. According to the regulation, the report had to be submitted with Miller's FEC Form 3. Miller noted that the first report due more than 50 days after the November 8, 2004, general election was not the post-general report, which was due on December 8, 2004, but the year-end report, due on January 31, 2005.

Repayment of Rockford's Personal Loan

Rockford's authorized committee spent every available dollar on the general election campaign and, after the election was over, had no funds remaining to repay Rockford's $10 million personal loan. Rockford wondered whether his authorized committee could use funds raised after the date of the election to repay the loan. He quickly realized, however, that BCRA set a limit on the amount of personal loans that may be repaid with funds raised after the end of an election cycle. The Commission's regulation at 11 CFR 116.11, implementing the new

statutory limit, prohibited Rockford from using more than $250,000 in contributions received after the date of the election to pay off his $10 million personal loan. *See* 2 U.S.C. 441a(j). This meant, of course, that Rockford would never be able to recover the remaining $9,750,000 ($10,000,000 personal loan − $250,000 limit) he lent his authorized committee during the general election cycle.

Excerpts from McConnell v. FEC

Cite as: 540 U. S. ____ (2003)

Opinion of the Court

SUPREME COURT OF THE UNITED STATES

Nos. 02–1674, 02–1675, 02–1676, 02–1702, 02–1727, 02–1733, 02–1734; 02–1740, 02–1747, 02–1753, 02–1755, AND 02–1756

MITCH McCONNELL, UNITED STATES SENATOR, ET AL., APPELLANTS

02–1674   v.

FEDERAL ELECTION COMMISSION, ET AL.;

ON APPEALS FROM THE UNITED STATES DISTRICT COURT FOR THE DISTRICT OF COLUMBIA

[December 10, 2003]

JUSTICE STEVENS and JUSTICE O'CONNOR delivered the opinion of the Court with respect to BCRA Titles I and II.*

...Many contributions of soft money were dramatically larger than the contributions of hard money permitted by FECA. For example, in 1996 the top five corporate soft-money donors gave, in total, more than $9 million in nonfederal funds to the two national party committees.[10] In the most recent election cycle the political parties raised almost $300 million—60% of their total soft-money fundraising—from just 800 donors, each of which contributed a minimum of $120,000.[11] Moreover, the largest corporate donors often made substantial contributions to both parties.[12] Such practices corroborate evidence indicating that many corporate contributions were motivated by a desire for access to candidates and a fear of being placed at a

---

[10] Id., at 494 (Kollar-Kotelly, J.).

[11] Mann Expert Report 24.

[12] In the 2000 election cycle, 35 of the 50 largest soft-money donors gave to both parties; 28 of the 50 gave more than $100,000 to both parties. Mann Expert Report Tbl. 6; see also 251 F. Supp. 2d, at 509 (Kollar-Kotelly, J.); id., at 785, n. 77 (Leon, J.).

McCONNELL *v.* FEDERAL ELECTION COMM'N

Opinion of the Court

disadvantage in the legislative process relative to other contributors, rather than by ideological support for the candidates and parties.[13]

Not only were such soft-money contributions often designed to gain access to federal candidates, but they were in many cases solicited by the candidates themselves. Candidates often directed potential donors to party committees and tax-exempt organizations that could legally accept soft money. For example, a federal legislator running for reelection solicited soft money from a supporter by advising him that even though he had already "contributed the legal maximum" to the campaign committee, he could still make an additional contribution to a joint program supporting federal, state, and local candidates of his party.[14] Such solicitations were not uncommon.[15]

---

[13]A former chief executive officer of a large corporation explained:

"Business and labor leaders believe, based on their experience, that disappointed Members, and their party colleagues, may shun or disfavor them because they have not contributed. Equally, these leaders fear that if they refuse to contribute (enough), competing interests who do contribute generously will have an advantage in gaining access to and influencing key Congressional leaders on matters of importance to the company or union." App. 283, ¶9 (declaration of Gerald Greenwald, United Airlines (hereinafter Greenwald Decl.)).

Amici Curiae Committee for Economic Development and various business leaders attest that corporate soft-money contributions are "coerced and, at bottom, wholly commercial" in nature, and that "[b]usiness leaders increasingly wish to be freed from the grip of a system in which they fear the adverse consequences of refusing to fill the coffers of the major parties." Brief for Committee for Economic Development et al. as *Amici Curiae* 28.

[14]See 251 F. Supp. 2d, at 480 (Kollar-Kotelly, J.); *id.*, at 842 (Leon, J.).

[15]See *id.*, at 479–480 (Kollar-Kotelly, J.); *id.*, at 842–843 (Leon, J.). One former party official explained to the District Court:

"'Once you've helped a federal candidate by contributing hard money to his or her campaign, you are sometimes asked to do more for the candidate by making donations of hard and/or soft money to the na-

The solicitation, transfer, and use of soft money thus enabled parties and candidates to circumvent FECA's limitations on the source and amount of contributions in connection with federal elections. ...

... While the distinction between "issue" and express advocacy seemed neat in theory, the two categories of advertisements proved functionally identical in important respects. Both were used to advocate the election or defeat of clearly identified federal candidates, even though the so-called issue ads eschewed the use of magic words.[16]

---

tional party committees, the relevant state party (assuming it can accept corporate contributions), or an outside group that is planning on doing an independent expenditure or issue advertisement to help the candidate's campaign.'" *Id.*, at 479 (Kollar-Kotelly, J.).

[16] *Id.*, at 532–537 (Kollar-Kotelly, J.); *id.*, at 875–879 (Leon, J.). As

McCONNELL *v.* FEDERAL ELECTION COMM'N

Opinion of the Court

Little difference existed, for example, between an ad that urged viewers to "vote against Jane Doe" and one that condemned Jane Doe's record on a particular issue before exhorting viewers to "call Jane Doe and tell her what you think."[17] Indeed, campaign professionals testified that the most effective campaign ads, like the most effective commercials for products such as Coca-Cola, should, and did, avoid the use of the magic words.[18] Moreover, the conclusion that such ads were specifically intended to affect election results was confirmed by the fact that almost all of them aired in the 60 days immediately preceding a federal election.[19] Corporations and unions spent hundreds of millions of dollars of their general funds to pay for these ads,[20] and those expenditures, like soft-money dona-

---

the former chair of one major advocacy organization's PAC put it, "'[i]t is foolish to believe there is any practical difference between issue advocacy and advocacy of a political candidate. What separates issue advocacy and political advocacy is a line in the sand drawn on a windy day.'" *Id.*, at 536–537 (Kollar-Kotelly, J.) (quoting Tanya K. Metaksa, Opening Remarks at the American Assn. of Political Consultants Fifth General Session on "Issue Advocacy," Jan. 17, 1997, p. 2); 251 F. Supp. 2d, at 878–879 (Leon, J.) (same).

[17]*Id.*, at 304 (Henderson, J., concurring in judgment in part and dissenting in part); *id.*, at 534 (Kollar-Kotelly, J.); *id.*, at 875–879 (Leon, J.).

[18]It is undisputed that very few ads—whether run by candidates, parties, or interest groups—used words of express advocacy. *Id.*, at 303 (Henderson, J.); *id.*, at 529 (Kollar-Kotelly, J.); *id.*, at 874 (Leon, J.). In the 1998 election cycle, just 4% of candidate advertisements used magic words; in 2000, that number was a mere 5%. App. 1334 (report of Jonathan S. Krasno, Yale University, & Frank J. Sorauf, University of Minnesota, pp. 53–54 (hereinafter Krasno & Sorauf Expert Report); see 1 Defs. Exhs., Tab 2, pp. 53–54).

[19]251 F. Supp. 2d, at 564, and n. 6 (Kollar-Kotelly, J.) (citing report of Kenneth M. Goldstein, University of Wisconsin-Madison, App. A, Tbl. 16; see 3-R Defs. Exhs., Tab 7); Tr. of Oral Arg. 202–203; see also 251 F. Supp. 2d, at 305 (Henderson, J.).

[20]The spending on electioneering communications climbed dramati-

Opinion of the Court

tions to the political parties, were unregulated under
FECA. Indeed, the ads were attractive to organizations
and candidates precisely because they were beyond
FECA's reach, enabling candidates and their parties to
work closely with friendly interest groups to sponsor so-
called issue ads when the candidates themselves were
running out of money.[21] ...

---

cally during the last decade. In the 1996 election cycle, $135 to $150
million was spent on multiple broadcasts of about 100 ads. In the next
cycle (1997-1998), 77 organizations aired 423 ads at a total cost between $270 and $340 million. By the 2000 election, 130 groups spent
over an estimated $500 million on more than 1,100 different ads. Two
out of every three dollars spent on issue ads in the 2000 cycle were
attributable to the two major parties and six major interest groups. *Id.,*
at 303–304 (Henderson, J.) (citing Annenberg Public Policy Center,
Issue Advertising in the 1999–2000 Election Cycle 1–15 (2001) (hereinafter Annenberg Report); see 38 Defs. Exhs., Tab 22); 251 F. Supp. 2d,
at 527 (Kollar-Kotelly, J.) (same); *id.,* at 879 (Leon, J.) (same).

[21]*Id.,* at 540 (Kollar-Kotelly, J.) (quoting internal AFL-CIO Memo-
randum from Brian Weeks to Mike Klein, "Electronic Buy for Illinois
Senator," (Oct. 9, 1996), AFL-CIO 005244); 251 F. Supp. 2d, at 886
(Leon, J.) (same).

McCONNELL v. FEDERAL ELECTION COMM'N

Opinion of the Court

... As one expert noted, "'[t]here is no meaningful distinction between the national party committees and the public officials who control them.'" 251 F. Supp. 2d, at 468–469 (Kollar-Kotelly, J.) (quoting Mann Expert Report 29). The national committees of the two major parties are both run by, and largely composed of, federal officeholders and candidates. Indeed, of the six national committees of the two major parties, four are composed entirely of federal officeholders. *Ibid.* The nexus between national parties and federal officeholders prompted one of Title I's framers to conclude:

> "Because the national parties operate at the national level, and are inextricably intertwined with federal officeholders and candidates, who raise the money for the national party committees, there is a close connection between the funding of the national parties and the corrupting dangers of soft money on the federal political process. The only effective way to address this [soft-money] problem of corruption is to ban entirely all raising and spending of soft money by the national parties." 148 Cong. Rec. H409 (Feb. 13, 2002) (statement of Rep. Shays).

Given this close connection and alignment of interests, large soft-money contributions to national parties are likely to create actual or apparent indebtedness on the part of federal officeholders, regardless of how those funds are ultimately used.

This close affiliation has also placed national parties in a position to sell access to federal officeholders in exchange for soft-money contributions that the party can then use for its own purposes. Access to federal officeholders is the most valuable favor the national party committees are able to give in exchange for large donations. The fact that officeholders comply by donating their valuable time indicates either that officeholders place

Opinion of the Court

substantial value on the soft-money contribution themselves, without regard to their end use, or that national
committees are able to exert considerable control over
federal officeholders. See, *e.g.*, App. 1196–1198 (Expert
Report of Donald P. Green, Yale University) ("Once elected
to legislative office, public officials enter an environment
in which political parties-in-government control the resources crucial to subsequent electoral success and legislative power. Political parties organize the legislative caucuses that make committee assignments"); App. 1298
(Krasno & Sorauf Expert Report) (indicating that officeholders' re-election prospects are significantly influenced
by attitudes of party leadership). Either way, large soft-
money donations to national party committees are likely
to buy donors preferential access to federal officeholders
no matter the ends to which their contributions are eventually put. As discussed above, Congress had sufficient
grounds to regulate the appearance of undue influence
associated with this practice. The Government's strong
interests in preventing corruption, and in particular the
appearance of corruption, are thus sufficient to justify
subjecting all donations to national parties to the source,
amount, and disclosure limitations of FECA.[51] ...

---

[51] The close relationship of federal officeholders and candidates to
their parties answers not only THE CHIEF JUSTICE's concerns about
§323(a), but also his fear that our analysis of §323's remaining provisions bespeaks no limiting principle. *Post*, at 6–7 (dissenting opinion).
As set forth in our discussion of those provisions, the record demonstrates close ties between federal officeholders and the state and local
committees of their parties. That close relationship makes state and
local parties effective conduits for donors desiring to corrupt federal
candidates and officeholders. Thus, in upholding §§323(b), (d), and (f),
we rely not only on the fact that they regulate contributions used to
fund activities influencing federal elections, but also that they regulate
contributions to or at the behest of entities uniquely positioned to serve
as conduits for corruption. We agree with THE CHIEF JUSTICE that

... Finally, plaintiffs assert that §323(a) is unconstitutional because it impermissibly interferes with the ability of national committees to associate with state and local committees. By way of example, plaintiffs point to the Republican Victory Plans, whereby the RNC acts in concert with the state and local committees of a given State to plan and implement joint, full-ticket fundraising and electioneering programs. See App. 693, 694–697 (declaration of John Peschong, RNC Western Reg. Political Dir. (describing the Republican Victory Plans)). The political parties assert that §323(a) outlaws *any* participation in Victory Plans by RNC officers, including merely sitting down at a table and engaging in collective decisionmaking about how soft money will be solicited, received, and spent. Such associational burdens, they argue, are too great for the First Amendment to bear.

We are not persuaded by this argument because it hinges on an unnaturally broad reading of the terms "spend," "receive," "direct," and "solicit." 2 U. S. C. A. §441i(a) (Supp. 2003). Nothing on the face of §323(a) prohibits national party officers, whether acting in their official or individual capacities, from sitting down with state and local party committees or candidates to plan and advise how to raise and spend soft money. As long as the national party officer does not personally spend, receive, direct, or solicit soft money, §323(a) permits a wide range of joint planning and electioneering activity. Intervenor-defendants, the principal drafters and proponents of the legislation, concede as much. Brief for Intervenor-Defendants Sen. John McCain et al. in No. 02–1674 et al., p. 22 ("BCRA leaves parties and candidates free to coordinate campaign plans and activities, political messages, and fundraising goals with one another"). The FEC's current definitions of §323(a)'s terms are consistent with that view. See, *e.g.*, 11 CFR §300.2(m) (2002) (defin-

McCONNELL *v.* FEDERAL ELECTION COMM'N

Opinion of the Court

ing "solicit" as "to *ask* . . . another person" (emphasis added)); §300.2(n) (defining "direct" as "to *ask* a person who has expressed an intent to make a contribution . . . to make that contribution . . . including through a conduit or intermediary" (emphasis added)); §300.2(c) (laying out the factors that determine whether an entity will be considered to be controlled by a national committee).

Given the straightforward meaning of this provision, JUSTICE KENNEDY is incorrect that "[a] national party's mere involvement in the strategic planning of fundraising for a state ballot initiative" or its assistance in developing a state party's Levin-money fundraising efforts risks a finding that the officers are in "'indirect control'" of the state party and subject to criminal penalties. *Post,* at 5–6. Moreover, §323(a) leaves national party committee officers entirely free to participate, in their official capacities, with state and local parties and candidates in soliciting and spending hard money; party officials may also solicit soft money in their unofficial capacities. **. . .**

McCONNELL *v.* FEDERAL ELECTION COMM'N

Opinion of the Court

... The record also makes quite clear that federal office-holders are grateful for contributions to state and local parties that can be converted into GOTV-type efforts. See *id.*, at 459 (quoting a letter thanking a California Democratic Party donor and noting that CDP's voter registration and GOTV efforts would help "'increase the number of Californian Democrats in the United States Congress'" and "'deliver California's 54 electoral votes'" to the Democratic presidential candidate).

Because voter registration, voter identification, GOTV, and generic campaign activity all confer substantial benefits on federal candidates, the funding of such activities creates a significant risk of actual and apparent corruption. Section 323(b) is a reasonable response to that risk. Its contribution limitations are focused on the subset of voter registration activity that is most likely to affect the election prospects of federal candidates: activity that occurs within 120 days before a federal election. And if the voter registration drive does not specifically mention a federal candidate, state committees can take advantage of the Levin Amendment's higher contribution limits and relaxed source restrictions. 2 U. S. C. A. §§441i(b)(2)(B)(i)–(ii) (Supp. 2003). Similarly, the contribution limits applicable to §301(20)(A)(ii) activities target only those voter identification, GOTV, and generic campaign efforts that occur "in connection with an election in which a candidate for a Federal office appears on the ballot." 2 U. S. C. A. §431(20)(A)(ii). Appropriately, in implementing this subsection, the FEC has categorically excluded all activity that takes place during the run-up to elections when no federal office is at stake.[63] Furthermore, state committees can take advantage of the Levin Amendment's higher contribution limits to fund any §301(A)(20)(i) and §301(A)(20)(ii) activities that do not specifically mention a federal candidate. 2 U. S. C. A. §§441i(b)(2)(B)(i)–(ii). The prohibition on the use of soft money in connection with these activities is therefore closely drawn to meet the sufficiently important governmental interests of avoiding corruption and its appearance.

"Public communications" that promote or attack a candidate for federal office—the third category of "Federal election activity," §301(20)(A)(iii)—also undoubtedly have a dramatic effect on federal elections. Such ads were a prime motivating force behind BCRA's passage. See 3 1998 Senate Report 4535 (additional views of Sen. Collins) ("[T]he hearings provided overwhelming evidence that the twin loopholes of soft money and bogus issue advertising have virtually destroyed our campaign finance laws, leaving us with little more than a pile of legal rubble"). As explained below, any public communication that promotes or attacks a clearly identified federal candidate directly affects the election in which he is participating. The record on this score could scarcely be more abundant.

---

[63] With respect to GOTV, voter identification, and other generic campaign activity, the FEC has interpreted §323(b) to apply only to those activities conducted after the earliest filing deadline for access to the federal election ballot or, in States that do not conduct primaries, after January 1 of even-numbered years. 11 CFR §100.24(a)(1) (2002). Any activities conducted outside of those periods are completely exempt from regulation under §323(b). Of course, this facial challenge does not present the question of the FEC regulations' constitutionality. But the fact that the statute provides this basis for the FEC reasonably to narrow §301(20)(A)(ii) further calls into question plaintiffs' claims of facial overbreadth. See *Broadrick* v. *Oklahoma*, 413 U. S. 601, 613 (1973).

McCONNELL *v.* FEDERAL ELECTION COMM'N

Opinion of the Court

Given the overwhelming tendency of public communications, as carefully defined in §301(20)(A)(iii), to benefit directly federal candidates, we hold that application of §323(b)'s contribution caps to such communications is also closely drawn to the anticorruption interest it is intended to address.[64]

As for the final category of "Federal election activity," §301(20)(A)(iv), we find that Congress' interest in preventing circumvention of §323(b)'s other restrictions justifies the requirement that state and local parties spend federal funds to pay the salary of any employee spending more than 25% of his or her compensated time on activities in connection with a federal election. In the absence of this provision, a party might use soft money to pay for the equivalent of a full-time employee engaged in federal electioneering, by the simple expedient of dividing the federal workload among multiple employees. Plaintiffs have suggested no reason for us to strike down this provi-

---

[64] We likewise reject the argument that §301(20)(A)(iii) is unconstitutionally vague. The words "promote," "oppose," "attack," and "support" clearly set forth the confines within which potential party speakers must act in order to avoid triggering the provision. These words "provide explicit standards for those who apply them" and "give the person of ordinary intelligence a reasonable opportunity to know what is prohibited." *Grayned* v. *City of Rockford*, 408 U. S. 104, 108–109 (1972). This is particularly the case here, since actions taken by political parties are presumed to be in connection with election campaigns. See *Buckley*, 424 U. S., at 79 (noting that a general requirement that political committees disclose their expenditures raised no vagueness problems because the term "political committee" "need only encompass organizations that are under the control of a candidate or the major purpose of which is the nomination or election of a candidate" and thus a political committee's expenditures "are, by definition, campaign related"). Furthermore, should plaintiffs feel that they need further guidance, they are able to seek advisory opinions for clarification, see 2 U. S. C. §437f(a)(1), and thereby "remove any doubt there may be as to the meaning of the law," *Civil Service Comm'n* v. *Letter Carriers*, 413 U. S. 548, 580 (1973).

sion. Accordingly, we give "deference to [the] congressional determination of the need for [this] prophylactic rule." *National Conservative Political Action Comm.*, 470 U. S., at 500. ...

... That justification is entirely reasonable. The history of Congress' efforts at campaign finance reform well demonstrates that "candidates, donors, and parties test the limits of the current law." *Colorado II*, 533 U. S., at 457. Absent the solicitation provision, national, state, and local party committees would have significant incentives to mobilize their formidable fundraising apparatuses, including the peddling of access to federal officeholders, into the service of like-minded tax-exempt organizations that conduct activities benefiting their candidates.[68] All of the corruption and appearance of corruption attendant on the operation of those fundraising apparatuses would follow. Donations made at the behest of party committees would almost certainly be regarded by party officials, donors, and federal officeholders alike as benefiting the party as well as its candidates. Yet, by soliciting the

---

[68] The record shows that many of the targeted tax-exempt organizations engage in sophisticated and effective electioneering activities for the purpose of influencing federal elections, including waging broadcast campaigns promoting or attacking particular candidates and conducting large-scale voter registration and GOTV drives. For instance, during the final weeks of the 2000 presidential campaign, the NAACP's National Voter Fund registered more than 200,000 people, promoted a GOTV hotline, ran three newspaper print ads, and made several direct mailings. 251 F. Supp. 2d, at 348–349 (Henderson, J.). The NAACP reports that the program turned out one million additional African-American voters and increased turnout over 1996 among targeted groups by 22% in New York, 50% in Florida, and 140% in Missouri. *Ibid.* The effort, which cost $10 million, was funded primarily by a $7 million contribution from an anonymous donor. *Id.*, at 349 (citing cross-examination of Donald P. Green, Yale University 15–20, Exh. 3; see I Defs. Refiling Trs. on Pub. Record); 251 F. Supp. 2d, at 522 (Kollar-Kotelly, J.) (same); *id.*, at 851 (Leon, J.) (same); see also *id.*, at 349 (Henderson, J.) (stating that in 2000 the National Abortion and Reproductive Rights Action League (NARAL) spent $7.5 million and mobilized 2.1 million pro-choice voters (citing declaration of Mary Jane Gallagher, Exec. V. P., NARAL, 8, App. 271–272, ¶24)); 251 F. Supp. 2d, at 522 (Kollar-Kotelly, J.) (same).

McCONNELL *v.* FEDERAL ELECTION COMM'N

Opinion of the Court

donations to third-party organizations, the parties would avoid FECA's source-and-amount limitations, as well as its disclosure restrictions. See 251 F. Supp. 2d, at 348 (Henderson, J.) (citing various declarations demonstrating that, prior to BCRA, most tax-exempt organizations did not disclose the source or amount of contributions); *id.*, at 521 (Kollar-Kotelly, J.) (same). **...**

... These observations do not, however, require us to sustain plaintiffs' facial challenge to §323(d)'s donation restriction. "When the validity of an act of the Congress is drawn in question, and . . . a serious doubt of constitutionality is raised, it is a cardinal principle that this Court will first ascertain whether a construction of the statute is fairly possible by which the question may be avoided." *Crowell* v. *Benson,* 285 U. S. 22, 62 (1932); see also *Boos* v. *Barry,* 485 U. S. 312, 331 (1988); *New York* v. *Ferber,* 458 U. S. 747, 769, n. 24 (1982). Given our obligation to avoid constitutional problems, we narrowly construe §323(d)'s ban to apply only to donations of funds not raised in compliance with FECA. This construction is consistent with the concerns animating Title I, whose purpose is to plug the soft-money loophole. Though there is little legislative history regarding BCRA generally, and almost nothing on §323(d) specifically, the abuses identified in the 1998 Senate report regarding campaign finance practices involve the use of nonprofit organizations as conduits for large *soft-money* donations. See, *e.g.,* 3 1998 Senate Report 4565 ("The evidence indicates that the soft-money loophole is fueling many of the campaign abuses investigated by the Committee. . . . Soft money also supplied the funds parties used to make contributions to tax-exempt groups, which in turn used the funds to pay for election-related activities"); *id.*, at 4568–4569 (describing as an "egregious exampl[e]" of misuse a $4.6 million donation of nonfederal funds by the RNC to Americans for Tax Reform, which the organization spent on "direct mail and phone bank operations to counter anti-Republican advertising"). We have found no evidence that Congress was concerned about, much less that it intended to prohibit, donations of money already fully regulated by FECA. Given Title I's exclusive focus on abuses related to soft money, we would expect that if Congress meant §323(d)'s restriction to have this dramatic and constitutionally questionable effect, it would say so explicitly. Because there is nothing that compels us to conclude that Congress intended "donations" to include transfers of federal money, and because of the constitutional infirmities such an interpretation would raise, we decline to read §323(d) in that way. Thus, political parties remain free to make or direct donations of money to any tax-exempt organization that has otherwise been raised in compliance with FECA. ...

... No party seriously questions the constitutionality of §323(e)'s general ban on donations of soft money made directly to federal candidates and officeholders, their agents, or entities established or controlled by them. Even on the narrowest reading of *Buckley*, a regulation restricting donations to a federal candidate, regardless of the ends to which those funds are ultimately put, qualifies

---

analogous hard-money contribution limits or come from prohibited sources. In effect, §323(e)(1)(B) doubles the limits on what individuals can contribute to or at the behest of federal candidates and officeholders, while restricting the use of the additional funds to activities not related to federal elections. If the federal candidate or officeholder is also a candidate for state or local office, he or she may solicit, receive, and spend an unlimited amount of nonfederal money in connection with that election, subject only to state regulation and the requirement that such solicitation or expenditures refer only to the relevant state or local office. 2 U. S. C. A. §441i(e)(2).

as a contribution limit subject to less rigorous scrutiny. Such donations have only marginal speech and associational value, but at the same time pose a substantial threat of corruption. By severing the most direct link between the soft-money donor and the federal candidate, §323(e)'s ban on donations of soft money is closely drawn to prevent the corruption or the appearance of corruption of federal candidates and officeholders.

Section 323(e)'s restrictions on solicitations are justified as valid anticircumvention measures. Large soft-money donations at a candidate's or officeholder's behest give rise to all of the same corruption concerns posed by contributions made directly to the candidate or officeholder. Though the candidate may not ultimately control how the funds are spent, the value of the donation to the candidate or officeholder is evident from the fact of the solicitation itself. Without some restriction on solicitations, federal candidates and officeholders could easily avoid FECA's contribution limits by soliciting funds from large donors and restricted sources to like-minded organizations engaging in federal election activities. As the record demonstrates, even before the passage of BCRA, federal candidates and officeholders had already begun soliciting donations to state and local parties, as well as tax-exempt organizations, in order to help their own, as well as their party's, electoral cause. See *Colorado II*, 533 U. S., at 458 (quoting fundraising letter from a Congressman explaining to contributor that "'you are at the limit of what you can directly contribute to my campaign,' but 'you can further help my campaign by assisting the Colorado Republican Party'"); 251 F. Supp. 2d, at 479–480 (Kollar-Kotelly, J.) (surveying evidence of federal officeholders' soliciting funds to state and local parties); *id.*, at 848 (Leon, J.) (same); *id.*, at 518 (Kollar-Kotelly, J.) (surveying evidence of federal officeholders' soliciting funds for non-profits for electioneering purposes); *id.*, at 849 (Leon, J.)

McCONNELL v. FEDERAL ELECTION COMM'N

Opinion of the Court

(same). The incentives to do so, at least with respect to solicitations to tax-exempt organizations, will only increase with Title I's restrictions on the raising and spending of soft money by national, state, and local parties.

Section 323(e) addresses these concerns while accommodating the individual speech and associational rights of federal candidates and officeholders. Rather than place an outright ban on solicitations to tax-exempt organizations, §323(e)(4) permits limited solicitations of soft money. 2 U. S. C. A. §441i(e)(4). This allowance accommodates individuals who have long served as active members of nonprofit organizations in both their official and individual capacities. Similarly, §§323(e)(1)(B) and 323(e)(3) preserve the traditional fundraising role of federal officeholders by providing limited opportunities for federal candidates and officeholders to associate with their state and local colleagues through joint fundraising activities. 2 U. S. C. A. §§441i(e)(1)(B), 441i(e)(3). Given these many exceptions, as well as the substantial threat of corruption or its appearance posed by donations to or at the behest of federal candidates and officeholders, §323(e) is clearly constitutional. We accordingly uphold §323(e) against plaintiffs' First Amendment challenge. ...

... Finally, plaintiffs argue that Title I violates the equal protection component of the Due Process Clause of the Fifth Amendment because it discriminates against political parties in favor of special interest groups such as the National Rifle Association (NRA), American Civil Liberties Union (ACLU), and Sierra Club. As explained earlier, BCRA imposes numerous restrictions on the fundraising abilities of political parties, of which the soft-money ban is only the most prominent. Interest groups, however, remain free to raise soft money to fund voter registration, GOTV activities, mailings, and broadcast advertising (other than electioneering communications). We conclude that this disparate treatment does not offend the Constitution. ...

... The major premise of plaintiffs' challenge to BCRA's use of the term "electioneering communication" is that *Buckley* drew a constitutionally mandated line between express advocacy and so-called issue advocacy, and that speakers possess an inviolable First Amendment right to engage in the latter category of speech. Thus, plaintiffs maintain, Congress cannot constitutionally require disclosure of, or regulate expenditures for, "electioneering communications" without making an exception for those "communications" that do not meet *Buckley*'s definition of express advocacy.

That position misapprehends our prior decisions, for the express advocacy restriction was an endpoint of statutory interpretation, not a first principle of constitutional law. In *Buckley* we began by examining then-18 U. S. C. §608(e)(1) (1970 ed., Supp. IV), which restricted expenditures "'relative to a clearly identified candidate,'" and we found that the phrase "'relative to'" was impermissibly vague. 424 U. S., at 40–42. We concluded that the vagueness deficiencies could "be avoided only by reading §608(e)(1) as limited to communications that include explicit words of advocacy of election or defeat of a candi-

McCONNELL *v.* FEDERAL ELECTION COMM'N

Opinion of the Court

date."[74] *Id.*, at 43. We provided examples of words of express advocacy, such as "'vote for,' 'elect,' 'support,' . . . 'defeat,' [and] 'reject,'" *id.*, at 44, n. 52, and those examples eventually gave rise to what is now known as the "magic words" requirement.

We then considered FECA's disclosure provisions, including 2 U. S. C. §431(f) (1970 ed., Supp. IV), which defined "'expenditur[e]'" to include the use of money or other assets "'for the purpose of . . . influencing'" a federal election. *Buckley*, 424 U. S., at 77. Finding that the "ambiguity of this phrase" posed "constitutional problems," *ibid.*, we noted our "obligation to construe the statute, if that can be done consistent with the legislature's purpose, to avoid the shoals of vagueness," *id.*, at 77–78 (citations omitted). "To insure that the reach" of the disclosure requirement was "not impermissibly broad, we construe[d] 'expenditure' for purposes of that section in the same way we construed the terms of §608(e)—to reach only funds used for communications that expressly advocate the election or defeat of a clearly identified candidate." *Id.*, at 80 (footnote omitted).

Thus, a plain reading of *Buckley* makes clear that the express advocacy limitation, in both the expenditure and the disclosure contexts, was the product of statutory interpretation rather than a constitutional command.[75] In narrowly reading the FECA provisions in *Buckley* to avoid

---

[74]We then held that, so construed, the expenditure restriction did not advance a substantial government interest, because independent express advocacy did not pose a danger of real or apparent corruption, and the line between express advocacy and other electioneering activities was easily circumvented. Concluding that §608(e)(1)'s heavy First Amendment burden was not justified, we invalidated the provision. *Buckley*, 424 U. S., at 45–48.

[75]Our adoption of a narrowing construction was consistent with our vagueness and overbreadth doctrines. See *Broadrick*, 413 U. S., at 613; *Grayned*, 408 U. S., at 108–114.

Cite as: 540 U. S. ___ (2003)

Opinion of the Court

problems of vagueness and overbreadth, we nowhere suggested that a statute that was neither vague nor overbroad would be required to toe the same express advocacy line. Nor did we suggest as much in *MCFL*, 479 U. S. 238 (1986), in which we addressed the scope of another FECA expenditure limitation and confirmed the understanding that *Buckley*'s express advocacy category was a product of statutory construction.[76]

In short, the concept of express advocacy and the concomitant class of magic words were born of an effort to avoid constitutional infirmities. See *NLRB* v. *Catholic Bishop of Chicago*, 440 U. S. 490, 500 (1979) (citing *Murray* v. *Schooner Charming Betsy*, 2 Cranch 64, 118 (1804)). We have long "rigidly adhered" to the tenet "'never to formulate a rule of constitutional law broader than is required by the precise facts to which it is to be applied,'" *United States* v. *Raines*, 362 U. S. 17, 21 (1960) (citation omitted), for "[t]he nature of judicial review constrains us to consider the case that is actually before us," *James B. Beam Distilling Co.* v. *Georgia*, 501 U. S. 529, 547 (1991) (Blackmun, J., dissenting). Consistent with that principle, our decisions in *Buckley* and *MCFL* were specific to the statutory language before us; they in no way drew a constitutional boundary that forever fixed the permissible scope of provisions regulating campaign-related speech.

Nor are we persuaded, independent of our precedents, that the First Amendment erects a rigid barrier between

---

[76]The provision at issue in *MCFL*—2 U. S. C. §441b (1982 ed.)—required corporations and unions to use separate segregated funds, rather than general treasury moneys, on expenditures made "'in connection with'" a federal election. *MCFL*, 479 U. S., at 241. We noted that *Buckley* had limited the statutory term "'expenditure'" to words of express advocacy "in order to avoid problems of overbreadth." 479 U. S., at 248. We held that "a similar *construction*" must apply to the expenditure limitation before us in *MCFL* and that the reach of 2 U. S. C. §441b was therefore constrained to express advocacy. 479 U. S., at 249 (emphasis added).

McCONNELL *v.* FEDERAL ELECTION COMM'N

Opinion of the Court

express advocacy and so-called issue advocacy. That notion cannot be squared with our longstanding recognition that the presence or absence of magic words cannot meaningfully distinguish electioneering speech from a true issue ad. See *Buckley, supra,* at 45. Indeed, the unmistakable lesson from the record in this litigation, as all three judges on the District Court agreed, is that *Buckley's* magic-words requirement is functionally meaningless. 251 F. Supp. 2d, at 303–304 (Henderson, J.); *id.,* at 534 (Kollar-Kotelly, J.); *id.,* at 875–879 (Leon, J.). Not only can advertisers easily evade the line by eschewing the use of magic words, but they would seldom choose to use such words even if permitted.[77] And although the resulting advertisements do not urge the viewer to vote for or against a candidate in so many words, they are no less clearly intended to influence the election.[78] *Buckley's*

---

[77] As one major-party political consultant testified, "'it is rarely advisable to use such clumsy words as "vote for" or "vote against."'" 251 F. Supp. 2d, at 305 (Henderson, J.) (quoting declaration of Douglas L. Bailey, founder, Bailey, Deardourff & Assoc., 1–2, App. 24, ¶3). He explained: "'All advertising professionals understand that the most effective advertising leads the viewer to his or her own conclusion without forcing it down their throat.'" 251 F. Supp. 2d, at 305 (Henderson, J.). Other political professionals and academics confirm that the use of magic words has become an anachronism. See *id.,* at 531 (Kollar-Kotelly, J.) (quoting declaration of Raymond D. Strother, Pres., Strother/Duffy/Strother ¶4, 9 Defs. Exhs., Tab 40); see Unsealed Pp. Vol., Tab 7); App. 1334–1335 (Krasno & Sorauf Expert Report)); see also 251 F. Supp. 2d, at 305 (Henderson, J.); *id.,* at 532 (Kollar-Kotelly, J.); *id.,* at 875–76 (Leon, J.).

[78] One striking example is an ad that a group called "Citizens for Reform" sponsored during the 1996 Montana congressional race, in which Bill Yellowtail was a candidate. The ad stated:
"Who is Bill Yellowtail? He preaches family values but took a swing at his wife. And Yellowtail's response? He only slapped her. But 'her nose was not broken.' He talks law and order . . . but is himself a convicted felon. And though he talks about protecting children, Yellowtail failed to make his own child support payments—then voted against

Cite as: 540 U. S. ____ (2003)

Opinion of the Court

express advocacy line, in short, has not aided the legislative effort to combat real or apparent corruption, and Congress enacted BCRA to correct the flaws it found in the existing system.

Finally we observe that new FECA §304(f)(3)'s definition of "electioneering communication" raises none of the vagueness concerns that drove our analysis in *Buckley.* The term "electioneering communication" applies only (1) to a broadcast (2) clearly identifying a candidate for federal office, (3) aired within a specific time period, and (4) targeted to an identified audience of at least 50,000 viewers or listeners. These components are both easily understood and objectively determinable. See *Grayned* v. *City of Rockford,* 408 U. S. 104, 108–114 (1972). Thus, the constitutional objection that persuaded the Court in *Buckley* to limit FECA's reach to express advocacy is simply inapposite here. ...

---

child support enforcement. Call Bill Yellowtail. Tell him to support family values." 5 1998 Senate Report 6305 (minority views).

The notion that this advertisement was designed purely to discuss the issue of family values strains credulity.

... In light of our precedents, plaintiffs do not contest that the Government has a compelling interest in regulating advertisements that expressly advocate the election or defeat of a candidate for federal office. Nor do they contend that the speech involved in so-called issue advocacy is any more core political speech than are words of express advocacy. After all, "the constitutional guarantee has its fullest and most urgent application precisely to the conduct of campaigns for political office," *Monitor Patriot Co.* v. *Roy,* 401 U. S. 265, 272 (1971), and "[a]dvocacy of the election or defeat of candidates for federal office is no less entitled to protection under the First Amendment than the discussion of political policy generally or advocacy of the passage or defeat of legislation." *Buckley,* 424 U. S., at 48. Rather, plaintiffs argue that the justifications that adequately support the regulation of express advocacy do not apply to significant quantities of speech encompassed by the definition of electioneering communications.

This argument fails to the extent that the issue ads broadcast during the 30- and 60-day periods preceding federal primary and general elections are the functional equivalent of express advocacy. The justifications for the regulation of express advocacy apply equally to ads aired during those periods if the ads are intended to influence

100   McCONNELL *v.* FEDERAL ELECTION COMM'N

Opinion of the Court

the voters' decisions and have that effect. The precise percentage of issue ads that clearly identified a candidate and were aired during those relatively brief preelection time spans but had no electioneering purpose is a matter of dispute between the parties and among the judges on the District Court. See 251 F. Supp. 2d, at 307–312 (Henderson, J.); *id.*, at 583–587 (Kollar-Kotelly, J.); *id.*, at 796–798 (Leon, J.). Nevertheless, the vast majority of ads clearly had such a purpose. Annenberg Report 13–14; App. 1330–1348 (Krasno & Sorauf Expert Report); 251 F. Supp. 2d, at 573–578 (Kollar-Kotelly, J.); *id.*, at 826–827 (Leon, J.). Moreover, whatever the precise percentage may have been in the past, in the future corporations and unions may finance genuine issue ads during those time frames by simply avoiding any specific reference to federal candidates, or in doubtful cases by paying for the ad from a segregated fund.[88]

We are therefore not persuaded that plaintiffs have

---

[88] As JUSTICE KENNEDY emphasizes in dissent, *post*, at 44–45, we assume that the interests that justify the regulation of campaign speech might not apply to the regulation of genuine issue ads. The premise that apparently underlies JUSTICE KENNEDY's principal submission is a conclusion that the two categories of speech are nevertheless entitled to the same constitutional protection. If that is correct, JUSTICE KENNEDY must take issue with the basic holding in *Buckley* and, indeed, with our recognition in *First Nat. Bank of Boston* v. *Bellotti*, 435 U. S. 765 (1978), that unusually important interests underlie the regulation of corporations' campaign-related speech. In *Bellotti* we cited *Buckley*, among other cases, for the proposition that "[p]reserving the integrity of the electoral process, preventing corruption, and 'sustain[ing] the active, alert responsibility of the individual citizen in a democracy for the wise conduct of the government' are interests of the highest importance." 435 U. S., at 788–789 (citations and footnote omitted). "Preservation of the individual citizen's confidence in government," we added, "is equally important." *Id.*, at 789. BCRA's fidelity to those imperatives sets it apart from the statute in *Bellotti*—and, for that matter, from the Ohio statute banning the distribution of anonymous campaign literature, struck down in *McIntyre* v. *Ohio Elections Comm'n*, 514 U. S. 334 (1995).

carried their heavy burden of proving that amended FECA §316(b)(2) is overbroad. See *Broadrick* v. *Oklahoma,* 413 U. S. 601, 613 (1973). Even if we assumed that BCRA will inhibit some constitutionally protected corporate and union speech, that assumption would not "justify prohibiting all enforcement" of the law unless its application to protected speech is substantial, "not only in an absolute sense, but also relative to the scope of the law's plainly legitimate applications." *Virginia* v. *Hicks,* 539 U. S. ___, ___ (2003) (slip op., at 5–6). Far from establishing that BCRA's application to pure issue ads is substantial, either in an absolute sense or relative to its application to election-related advertising, the record strongly supports the contrary conclusion. ...

... The Government argues that §315(d)(4) nevertheless is constitutional because it is not an outright ban (or cap) on independent expenditures, but rather offers parties a voluntary choice between a constitutional right and a statutory benefit. Whatever merit that argument might have in the abstract, it fails to account for new §315(d)(4)(B), which provides:

> "For purposes of this paragraph, all political committees established and maintained by a national political party (including all congressional campaign committees) and all political committees established and maintained by a State political party (including any subordinate committee of a State committee) shall be considered to be a single political committee." 2 U. S. C. A. §441a(d)(4)(B) (Supp. 2003).

Given that provision, it simply is not the case that each party committee can make a voluntary and independent choice between exercising its right to engage in independent advocacy and taking advantage of the increased limits on coordinated spending under §§315(d)(1)–(3). Instead, the decision resides solely in the hands of the first mover, such that a local party committee can bind both the state and national parties to its chosen spending option.[96] It is one thing to say that Congress may require a party committee to give up its right to make independent expenditures if it believes that it can accomplish more with coordinated expenditures. It is quite another thing, however, to say that the RNC must limit itself to $5,000 in coordinated expenditures in support of its presidential nominee if any state or local committee first makes an independent expenditure for an ad that uses magic words. That odd result undermines any claim that new §315(d)(4) can withstand constitutional scrutiny simply because it is cast as a voluntary choice rather than an outright prohibition on independent expenditures.

The portion of the judgment of the District Court invalidating BCRA §213 is affirmed. ...

---

[96] Although the District Court and all the parties to this litigation endorse the interpretation set forth in the text, it is not clear that subparagraph (B) should be read so broadly: The reference to "a State" instead of "the States" suggests that Congress meant to distinguish between committees associated with the party for each State (which would be grouped together by State, with each grouping treated as a single committee for purposes of the choice) and committees associated with a national party (which would likewise be grouped together and treated as a separate political committee). We need not resolve the interpretive puzzle, however, because even under the more limited reading a local party committee would be able to tie the hands of a state committee or other local committees in the same State.

Cite as: 540 U. S. ___ (2003)

Opinion of the Court

... Plaintiffs do not dispute that Congress may apply the same coordination rules to parties as to candidates. They argue instead that new FECA §315(a)(7)(B)(ii) and its implementing regulations are overbroad and unconstitutionally vague because they permit a finding of coordination even in the absence of an agreement. Plaintiffs point out that political supporters may be subjected to criminal liability if they exceed the contribution limits with expenditures that ultimately are deemed coordinated. Thus, they stress the importance of a clear definition of "coordination" and argue any definition that does not hinge on the presence of an agreement cannot provide the "precise guidance" that the First Amendment demands. Brief for Chamber of Commerce of the United States et al., Appellant in No. 02–1756, p. 48. As plaintiffs readily admit, that argument reaches beyond BCRA, calling into question FECA's pre-existing provisions governing expenditures coordinated with candidates.

We are not persuaded that the presence of an agreement marks the dividing line between expenditures that are coordinated—and therefore may be regulated as indirect contributions—and expenditures that truly are independent. We repeatedly have struck down limitations on expenditures "made totally independently of the candidate and his campaign," *Buckley*, 424 U. S., at 47, on the ground that such limitations "impose far greater restraints on the freedom of speech and association" than do limits on contributions and coordinated expenditures, *id.*, at 44, while "fail[ing] to serve any substantial governmental interest in stemming the reality or appearance of corruption in the electoral process," *id.*, at 47–48. See also *Colorado I,* 518 U. S., at 613–614 (striking down limit on expenditure made by party officials prior to nomination of

McCONNELL *v.* FEDERAL ELECTION COMM'N

Opinion of the Court

candidates and without any consultation with potential nominees). We explained in *Buckley:*

> "Unlike contributions, . . . independent expenditures may well provide little assistance to the candidate's campaign and indeed may prove counterproductive. The absence of prearrangement and coordination of an expenditure with the candidate or his agent not only undermines the value of the expenditure to the candidate, but also alleviates the danger that expenditures will be given as a *quid pro quo* for improper commitments from the candidate." 424 U. S., at 47.

Thus, the rationale for affording special protection to wholly independent expenditures has nothing to do with the absence of an agreement and everything to do with the functional consequences of different types of expenditures. Independent expenditures "are poor sources of leverage for a spender because they might be duplicative or counterproductive from a candidate's point of view." *Colorado II,* 533 U. S., at 446. By contrast, expenditures made after a "wink or nod" often will be "as useful to the candidate as cash." *Id.,* at 442, 446. For that reason, Congress has always treated expenditures made "at the request or suggestion of" a candidate as coordinated.[99] 2 U. S. C. A. §441a(a)(7)(B)(i) (Supp. 2003). A supporter easily could comply with a candidate's request or suggestion without

---

[99] Contrary to plaintiffs' contention, the statutory framework was not significantly different at the time of our decision in *Buckley.* The relevant provision, 18 U. S. C. §608(e)(1), treated as coordinated any expenditures "authorized *or requested* by the candidate." (Emphasis added.) And the legislative history, on which we relied for "guidance in differentiating individual expenditures that are contributions . . . from those treated as independent expenditures," described as "independent" an expenditure made by a supporter "'completely on his own, and not at the request or suggestion of the candidate or his agen[t].'" 424 U. S., at 46–47, n. 53 (quoting S. Rep. No. 93–689, p. 18 (1974)).

first agreeing to do so, and the resulting expenditure would be "'virtually indistinguishable from [a] simple contributio[n],'" *Colorado II, supra,* at 444–445. Therefore, we cannot agree with the submission that new FECA §315(a)(7)(B)(ii) is overbroad because it permits a finding of coordination or cooperation notwithstanding the absence of a pre-existing agreement. ...

McCONNELL v. FEDERAL ELECTION COMM'N

Opinion of the Court

CHIEF JUSTICE REHNQUIST delivered the opinion of the Court with respect to BCRA Titles III and IV.*

...   Minors enjoy the protection of the First Amendment. See, *e.g.*, *Tinker* v. *Des Moines Independent Community School Dist.*, 393 U. S. 503, 511–513 (1969). Limitations on the amount that an individual may contribute to a candidate or political committee impinge on the protected freedoms of expression and association. See *Buckley, supra,* at 20–22. When the Government burdens the right to contribute, we apply heightened scrutiny. See *ante,* at 25–26 (joint opinion of STEVENS and O'CONNOR, JJ.) ("[A] contribution limit involving even 'significant interference' with associational rights is nevertheless valid if it satisfies the 'lesser demand' of being 'closely drawn' to match a 'sufficiently important interest.'" (quoting *Federal Election Comm'n v. Beaumont,* 539 U. S. ___, ___ (2003) (slip op., at 15)). We ask whether there is a "sufficiently important interest" and whether the statute is "closely drawn" to avoid unnecessary abridgment of First Amendment freedoms. *Ante,* at 25–26; *Buckley,* 424 U. S., at 25. The Government asserts that the provision protects against corruption by conduit; that is, donations by parents through their minor children to circumvent contribution limits applicable to the parents. But the Government offers scant evidence of this form of evasion.[3] Perhaps the Gov-

---

[3] Although some examples were presented to the District Court, 251 F. Supp. 2d 176, 588–590 (2003) (Kollar-Kotelly, J.), none were offered to this Court.

Opinion of the Court

ernment's slim evidence results from sufficient deterrence of such activities by §320 of FECA, which prohibits any person from "mak[ing] a contribution in the name of another person" or "knowingly accept[ing] a contribution made by one person in the name of another," 2 U. S. C. §441f. Absent a more convincing case of the claimed evil, this interest is simply too attenuated for §318 to withstand heightened scrutiny. See *Nixon* v. *Shrink Missouri Government PAC,* 528 U. S. 377, 391 (2000) ("The quantum of empirical evidence needed to satisfy heightened judicial scrutiny of legislative judgments will vary up or down with the novelty and plausibility of the justification raised").

Even assuming, *arguendo,* the Government advances an important interest, the provision is overinclusive. The States have adopted a variety of more tailored approaches—*e.g.,* counting contributions by minors against the total permitted for a parent or family unit, imposing a lower cap on contributions by minors, and prohibiting contributions by very young children. Without deciding whether any of these alternatives is sufficiently tailored, we hold that the provision here sweeps too broadly. We therefore affirm the District Court's decision striking down §318 as unconstitutional. ...